Python Multimedia
Beginner's Guide

Learn how to develop multimedia applications using Python with this practical step-by-step guide

Ninad Sathaye

BIRMINGHAM - MUMBAI

Python Multimedia

Beginner's Guide

First published: August 2010

Production Reference: 1060810

Published by Packt Publishing Ltd.
32 Lincoln Road
Olton
Birmingham, B27 6PA, UK.

ISBN 978-1-849510-16-5

www.packtpub.com

Cover Image by Ed Maclean (edmaclean@gmail.com)

Credits

Author
Ninad Sathaye

Reviewers
Maurice HT Ling

Daniel Waterworth

Sivan Greenberg

Acquisition Editor
Steven Wilding

Development Editor
Eleanor Duffy

Technical Editor
Charumathi Sankaran

Indexers
Hemangini Bari

Tejal Daruwale

Editorial Team Leader
Aanchal Kumar

Project Team Leader
Priya Mukherji

Project Coordinator
Prasad Rai

Proofreader
Lynda Sliwoski

Graphics
Geetanjali Sawant

Production Coordinators
Shantanu Zagade

Aparna Bhagat

Cover Work
Aparna Bhagat

About the Author

Ninad Sathaye (ninad.consult@gmail.com) has more than six years of experience in software design and development. He is currently working at IBM, India. Prior to working for IBM, he was a Systems Programmer at Nanorex Inc. based in Michigan, U.S.A. At Nanorex, he was involved in the development of an open source, interactive 3D CAD software, written in Python and C. This is where he developed passion for the Python programming language. Besides programming, his favorite hobbies are reading and traveling.

Ninad holds a Master of Science degree in Mechanical Engineering from Kansas State University, U.S.A.

I would like to thank everyone at Packt Publishing, especially, Eleanor Duffy, Steven Wilding, Charu Sankaran, and Prasad Rai for their co-operation. This book wouldn't have been possible without your help. I also want to thank all the technical reviewers of the book for their valuable suggestions. I wish to express my sincere thanks and appreciation to Rahul Nayak, my colleague, who provided many professional quality photographs for this book. I owe a special thanks to Mark Sims and Bruce Smith, my former colleagues, for introducing me to the amusing world of Python. Finally, this book wouldn't have been possible without the encouragement and support of my whole family. I owe my loving thanks to my wife, Arati, for providing valuable feedback. She also happens to be the photographer of several of the pictures used throughout this book.

About the Reviewers

Maurice HT Ling completed his Ph.D. in Bioinformatics and B.Sc (Hons) in Molecular and Cell Biology, where he worked on microarray analysis and text mining for protein-protein interactions. He is currently an Honorary Fellow at The University of Melbourne and a Lecturer at Singapore Polytechnic where he lectures on microbiology and computational biology.

Maurice holds several Chief Editorships including *The Python Papers*, *iConcept Journal of Computational and Mathematical Biology*, and *Methods and Cases in Computational*, *Mathematical*, and *Statistical Biology*. In his free time, Maurice likes to train in the gym, read, and enjoy a good cup of coffee. He is also a Senior Fellow of the International Fitness Association, U.S.A.

Daniel Waterworth is a Python fanatic who can often be found behind his keyboard. He is always beavering away on a new project having learned to program from a young age. He is a keen blogger and his ideas can be found at `http://active-thought.com`.

Sivan Greenberg is a Forum Nokia Champion, with almost ten years of multi-disciplinary IT experience and a sharp eye for quality. He started with open source technologies and the Debian project back in 2002. Joining Ubuntu development two years later, Sivan also contributed to various other open source projects, such as Plone and Nokia's Maemo.

He has experience with quality assurance, application and web development, UNIX system administration (including some rather exotic IBM platforms), and GUI programming and documentation. He's been using Python for all of his development needs for the last five years. He is currently involved with Nokia's MeeGo project and works with CouchDB and Python in his day job for a living.

I thank my unique and amazing family, specifically my Dad Eric for igniting the spark of curiosity from day zero.

To my daughter, Anvita

Table of Contents

Preface

Multimedia applications are used in a broad spectrum of fields. Writing applications that work with images, videos, and other sensory effects is great. Not every application gets to make full use of audio/visual effects, but a certain amount of multimedia makes any application very appealing.

This book is all about multimedia processing using Python. This step by step guide gives you a hands-on experience with developing exciting multimedia applications. You will build applications for processing images, creating 2D animations and processing audio and video.

There are numerous multimedia libraries for which Python bindings are available. These libraries enable working with different kinds of media, such as images, audio, video, games, and so on. This book introduces the reader to some of these (open source) libraries through several implausibly exciting projects. Popular multimedia frameworks and libraries, such as GStreamer, Pyglet, QT Phonon, and Python Imaging library are used to develop various multimedia applications.

What this book covers

Chapter 1, *Python and Multimedia* teaches you a few things about popular multimedia frameworks for multimedia processing using Python and shows you how to develop a simple interactive application using PyGame.

Chapter 2, *Working with Images* explains basic image conversion and manipulation techniques using the Python Imaging Library. With the help of several examples and code snippets, we will perform some basic manipulations on the image, such as pasting an image on to another, resizing, rotating/flipping, cropping, and so on. We will write tools to capture a screenshot and convert image files between different formats. The chapter ends with an exciting project where we develop an image processing application with a graphical user interface.

Chapter 3, Enhancing Images describes how to add special effects to an image using Python Imaging Library. You will learn techniques to enhance digital images using image filters, for example, reducing 'noise' from a picture, smoothing and sharpening images, embossing, and so on. The chapter will cover topics such as selectively changing the colors within an image. We will develop some exiting utilities for blending images together, adding transparency effects, and creating watermarks.

Chapter 4, Fun with Animations introduces you to the fundamentals of developing animations using Python and Pyglet multimedia application development frameworks. We will work on some exciting projects such as animating a fun car out for a ride in a thunderstorm, a 'bowling animation' with keyboard controls, and so on.

Chapter 5, Working with Audios teaches you how to get to grips with the primer on GStreamer multimedia framework and use this API for audio and video processing. In this chapter, we will develop some simple audio processing tools for 'everyday use'. We will develop tools such as a command-line audio player, a file format converter, an MP3 cutter and audio recorder.

Chapter 6, Audio Controls and Effects describes how to develop tools for adding audio effects, mixing audio tracks, creating custom music tracks, visualizing an audio track, and so on.

Chapter 7, Working with Videos explains the fundamentals of video processing. This chapter will cover topics such as converting video between different video formats, mixing or separating audio and video tracks, saving one or more video frames as still images, performing basic video manipulations such as cropping, resizing, adjusting brightness, and so on.

Chapter 8, GUI-based Media Players using QT Phonon takes you through the fundamental components of the QT Phonon framework. We will use QT Phonon to develop audio and video players using a graphical user interface.

Who this book is for

Python developers who want to dip their toes into working with images, animations, and audio and video processing using Python.

Conventions

In this book, you will find several headings appearing frequently.

To give clear instructions of how to complete a procedure or task, we use:

Time for action – heading

1. Action 1

2. Action 2

3. Action 3

Instructions often need some extra explanation so that they make sense, so they are followed with:

What just happened?

This heading explains the working of tasks or instructions that you have just completed.

You will also find some other learning aids in the book, including:

Pop quiz – heading

These are short multiple choice questions intended to help you test your own understanding.

Have a go hero – heading

These set practical challenges and give you ideas for experimenting with what you have learned.

You will also find a number of styles of text that distinguish between different kinds of information. Here are some examples of these styles, and an explanation of their meaning.

Code words in text are shown as follows: "The dictionary `self.addedEffects` keeps track of all the audio."

A block of code is set as follows:

```
1 def __init__(self):
2   self.constructPipeline()
3   self.is_playing = False
4   self.connectSignals()
```

When we wish to draw your attention to a particular part of a code block, the relevant lines or items are set in bold:

```
1 def constructPipeline(self):
2    self.pipeline = gst.Pipeline()
3    self.filesrc = gst.element_factory_make(
4                 "gnlfilesource")
```

Any command-line input or output is written as follows:

```
>>>import pygst
```

New terms and **important words** are shown in bold. Words that you see on the screen, in menus or dialog boxes for example, appear in the text like this: "You will need to tweak the **Effects** menu UI and make some other changes in the code to keep track of the added effects."

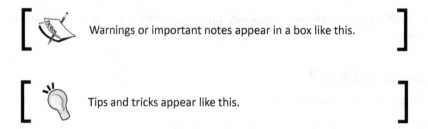

Warnings or important notes appear in a box like this.

Tips and tricks appear like this.

Reader feedback

Feedback from our readers is always welcome. Let us know what you think about this book—what you liked or may have disliked. Reader feedback is important for us to develop titles that you really get the most out of.

To send us general feedback, simply send an e-mail to feedback@packtpub.com, and mention the book title via the subject of your message.

If there is a book that you need and would like to see us publish, please send us a note in the **SUGGEST A TITLE** form on www.packtpub.com or e-mail suggest@packtpub.com.

If there is a topic that you have expertise in and you are interested in either writing or contributing to a book, see our author guide on www.packtpub.com/authors.

Customer support

Now that you are the proud owner of a Packt book, we have a number of things to help you to get the most from your purchase.

Downloading the example code for this book

You can download the example code files for all Packt books you have purchased from your account at http://www.PacktPub.com. If you purchased this book elsewhere, you can visit http://www.PacktPub.com/support and register to have the files e-mailed directly to you.

Errata

Although we have taken every care to ensure the accuracy of our content, mistakes do happen. If you find a mistake in one of our books—maybe a mistake in the text or the code—we would be grateful if you would report this to us. By doing so, you can save other readers from frustration and help us improve subsequent versions of this book. If you find any errata, please report them by visiting http://www.packtpub.com/support, selecting your book, clicking on the **errata submission form** link, and entering the details of your errata. Once your errata are verified, your submission will be accepted and the errata will be uploaded on our website, or added to any list of existing errata, under the Errata section of that title. Any existing errata can be viewed by selecting your title from http://www.packtpub.com/support.

Piracy

Piracy of copyright material on the Internet is an ongoing problem across all media. At Packt, we take the protection of our copyright and licenses very seriously. If you come across any illegal copies of our works, in any form, on the Internet, please provide us with the location address or website name immediately so that we can pursue a remedy.

Please contact us at copyright@packtpub.com with a link to the suspected pirated material.

We appreciate your help in protecting our authors, and our ability to bring you valuable content.

Questions

You can contact us at questions@packtpub.com if you are having a problem with any aspect of the book, and we will do our best to address it.

1

Python and Multimedia

Since its conception in 1989, Python has gained increasing popularity as a general purpose programming language. It is a high-level, object-oriented language with a comprehensive standard library. The language features such as automatic memory management and easy readability have attracted the attention of a wide range of developer communities. Typically, one can develop complex applications in Python very quickly compared to some other languages. It is used in several open source as well as commercial scientific modeling and visualization software packages. It has already gained popularity in industries such as animation and game development studios, where the focus is on multimedia application development. This book is all about multimedia processing using Python.

In this introductory chapter, we shall:

- ◆ Learn about multimedia and multimedia processing
- ◆ Discuss a few popular multimedia frameworks for multimedia processing using Python
- ◆ Develop a simple interactive application using PyGame

So let's get on with it.

Multimedia

We use multimedia applications in our everyday lives. It is multimedia that we deal with while watching a movie or listening to a song or playing a video game. Multimedia applications are used in a broad spectrum of fields. Multimedia has a crucial role to play in the advertising and entertainment industry. One of the most common usages is to add audio and video effects to a movie. Educational software packages such as a flight or a drive simulator use multimedia to teach various topics in an interactive way.

So what really is *multimedia*? In general, any application that makes use of different *sources* of digital media is termed as a **digital multimedia**. A video, for instance, is a combination of different *sources* or *contents*. The *contents* can be an audio track, a video track, and a subtitle track. When such video is played, all these media sources are presented together to accomplish the desired effect.

A multichannel audio can have a background music track and a lyrics track. It may even include various *audio effects*. An animation can be created by using a bunch of digital images that are displayed quickly one after the other. These are different examples of multimedia.

In the case of computer or video games, another dimension is added to the application, the user interaction. It is often termed as an *interactive* type of multimedia. Here, the users determine the way the multimedia contents are presented. With the help of devices such as keyboard, mouse, trackball, joystick, and so on, the users can interactively control the game.

Multimedia processing

We discussed some of the application domains where multimedia is extensively used. The focus of this book will be on *multimedia processing*, using which various multimedia applications will be developed.

Image processing

After taking a snap with a digital camera, we often tweak the original digital image for various reasons. One of the most common reasons is to remove blemishes from the image, such as removing 'red-eye' or increasing the brightness level if the picture was taken in insufficient light, and so on. Another reason for doing so is to add special effects that give a pleasing appearance to the image. For example, making a family picture black and white and digitally adding a frame around the picture gives it a nostalgic effect. The next illustration shows an image before and after the enhancement. Sometimes, the original image is modified just to make you understand important information presented by the image. Suppose the picture represents a complicated assembly of components. One can add special effects to the image so that only edges in the picture are shown as highlighted. This information can then be used to detect, for instance, interference between the components. Thus, we *digitally process* the image further until we get the desired output image.

An example where a border is added around an image to change its appearance is as follows:

Digital image processing can be viewed as an application of various algorithms/filters on the image data. One of the examples is an image smoothing filter. **Image smoothing** means reducing the noise from the image. The random changes in brightness and color levels within the image data are typically referred to as image **noise**. The smoothing algorithms modify the input image data so that this noise is reduced in the resultant image.

Another commonly performed image processing operation is **blending**. As the name suggests, blending means mixing two compatible images to create a new image. Typically, the data of the two input images is interpolated using a constant value of alpha to produce a final image. The next illustration shows the two input images and the resultant image after blending. In the coming chapters we will learn several of such digital image processing techniques.

The pictures of the bridge and the flying birds are taken at different locations. Using image processing techniques these two images can be blended together so that they appear as a single picture:

Audio and video processing

When you are listening to music on your computer, your music player is doing several things in the background. It processes the digital media data so that it can be transformed into a playable format that an output media device, such as an audio speaker, requires. The media data flows through a number of interconnected media handling components, before it reaches a media output device or a media file to which it is written. This is shown in the next illustration.

The following image shows a media data processing pipeline:

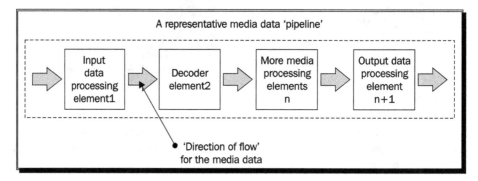

Audio and video processing encompasses a number of things. Some of them are briefly discussed in this section. In this book, we will learn various audio-video processing techniques using Python bindings of the GStreamer multimedia framework.

Compression

If you record footage on your camcorder and then transfer it to your computer, it will take up a lot of space. In order to save those moments on a VCD or a DVD, you almost always have to compress the audio-video data so that it occupies less space. There are two types of audio and video compression; *lossy* and *lossless*. The lossy compression is very common. Here, some data is assumed unnecessary and is not retained in the compressed media. For example, in a *lossy* video compression, even if some of the original data is lost, it has much less impact on the overall quality of the video. On the other hand, in *lossless* compression, the data of a compressed audio or video perfectly matches the original data. The compression ratio, however, is very low. As we go along, we will write audio-video data conversion utilities to compress the media data.

Mixing

Mixing is a way to create composite media using more than one media source. In case of audio mixing, the audio data from different sources is combined into one or more audio channels. For example, it can be used to add audio effect, in order to synchronize separate music and lyrics tracks. In the coming chapters, we will learn more about the media mixing techniques used with Python.

Editing

Media mixing can be viewed as a type of media editing. Media editing can be broadly divided into linear editing and non-linear editing. In **linear editing**, the programmer doesn't control the way media is presented. Whereas in **non-linear editing**, editing is done interactively. This book will cover the basics of media editing. For example, we will learn how to create a new audio track by combining portions of different audio files.

Animations

An **animation** can be viewed as an optical illusion of motion created by displaying a sequence of image frames one after the other. Each of these image frames is slightly different from the previously displayed one. The next illustration shows animation frames of a 'grandfather's clock':

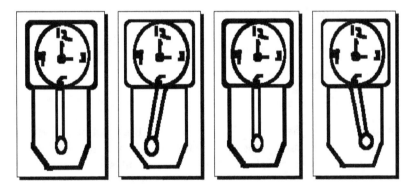

As you can see, there are four image frames in a clock animation. These frames are quickly displayed one after the other to achieve the desired animation effect. Each of these images will be shown for 0.25 seconds. Therefore, it simulates the pendulum oscillation of one second.

Cartoon animation is a classic example of animation. Since its debut in the early twentieth century, animation has become a prominent entertainment industry. Our focus in this book will be on 2D cartoon animations built using Python. In *Chapter 4*, we will learn some techniques to build such animations. Creating a cartoon character and bringing it to 'life' is a laborious job. Until the late 70s, most of the animations and effects were created without the use of computers. In today's age, much of the image creation work is produced digitally. The state-of-the-art technology makes this process much faster. For example, one can apply image transformations to display or move a portion of an image, thereby avoiding the need to create the whole cartoon image for the next frame.

Built-in multimedia support

Python has a few built-in multimedia modules for application development. We will skim through some of these modules.

winsound

The `winsound` module is available on the Windows platform. It provides an interface which can be used to implement fundamental audio-playing elements in the application. A sound can be played by calling `PlaySound(sound, flags)`. Here, the argument sound is used to specify the path of an audio file. If this parameter is specified as `None`, the presently streaming audio (if any) is stopped. The second argument specifies whether the file to be played is a sound file or a system sound. The following code snippet shows how to play a wave formatted audio file using `winsound` module.

```
from winsound import PlaySound, SND_FILENAME

PlaySound("C:/AudioFiles/my_music.wav", SND_FILENAME )
```

This plays the sound file specified by the first argument to the function `PlaySound`. The second argument, `SND_FILENAME`, says that the first argument is an audio file. If the flag is set as `SND_ALIAS`, it means the value for the first argument is a system sound from the registry.

audioop

This module is used for manipulating the raw audio data. One can perform several useful operations on sound fragments. For example, it can find the minimum and maximum values of all the samples within a sound fragment.

wave

The `wave` module provides an interface to read and write audio files with `WAV` file format. The following line of code opens a wav file.

```
import wave
fil = wave.open('horn.wav', 'r')
```

The first argument of method `open` is the location where the path to the wave file is specified. The second argument 'r' returns a `Wave_read` object. This is the mode in which the audio file is opened, 'r' or 'rb' for read-only mode and 'w' or 'wb' for write-only mode.

External multimedia libraries and frameworks

There are several open source multimedia frameworks available for multimedia application development. The Python bindings for most of these are readily available. We will discuss a few of the most popular multimedia frameworks here. In the chapters that follow, we will make use of many of these libraries to create some useful multimedia applications.

Python Imaging Library

Python Imaging Library provides image processing functionality in Python. It supports several image formats. Later in this book, a number of image processing techniques using PIL will be discussed thoroughly. We will learn things such as image format conversion and various image manipulation and enhancement techniques using the Python Imaging Library.

PyMedia

PyMedia is a popular open source media library that supports audio/video manipulation of a wide range of multimedia formats.

GStreamer

This framework enables multimedia manipulation. It is a framework on top of which one can develop multimedia applications. The rich set of libraries it provides makes it easier to develop applications with complex audio/video processing capabilities. GStreamer is written in C programming language and provides bindings for some other programming languages including Python. Several open source projects use GStreamer framework to develop their own multimedia application. Comprehensive documentation is available on the GStreamer project website. GStreamer Application Development Manual is a very good starting point. This framework will be extensively used later in this group to develop audio and video applications.

Pyglet

Interested in animations and gaming applications? Pyglet is here to help. Pyglet provides an API for developing multimedia applications using Python. It is an OpenGL-based library that works on multiple platforms. It is one of the popular multimedia frameworks for development of games and other graphically intense applications. It supports multiple monitor configuration typically needed for gaming application development. Later in this book, we will be extensively using this Pyglet framework for creating animations.

PyGame

PyGame (www.pygame.org) is another very popular open source framework that provides an API for gaming application development needs. It provides a rich set of graphics and sound libraries. We won't be using PyGame in this book. But since it is a prominent multimedia framework, we will briefly discuss some of its most important modules and work out a simple example. The PyGame website provides ample resources on use of this framework for animation and game programming.

Sprite

The Sprite module contains several classes; out of these, Sprite and Group are the most important. Sprite is the super class of all the visible game objects. A Group object is a container for several instances of Sprite.

Display

As the name suggests, the Display module has functionality dealing with the display. It is used to create a Surface instance for displaying the Pygame window. Some of the important methods of this module include flip and update. The former is called to make sure that everything drawn is properly displayed on the screen. Whereas the latter is used if you just want to update a portion of the screen.

Surface

This module is used to display an image. The instance of Surface represents an image. The following line of code creates such an instance.

```
surf = pygame.display.set_mode((800,600))
```

The API method, display.set_mode, is used to create this instance. The width and height of the window are specified as arguments to this method.

Draw

With the Draw module, one can render several basic shapes within the Surface. Examples include circles, rectangles, lines, and so on.

Event

This is another important module of PyGame. An event is said to occur when, for instance, the user clicks a mouse button or presses a key and so on. The event information is used to instruct the program to execute in a certain way.

Image

The `Image` module is used to process images with different file formats. The loaded image is represented by a surface.

Music

`Pygame.mixer.music` provides convenient methods for controlling playback such as play, reverse, stop, and so on.

The following is a simple program that highlights some of the fundamental concepts of animation and game programming. It shows how to display objects in an application window and then interactively modify their positions. We will use PyGame to accomplish this task. Later in this book, we will use a different multimedia framework, Pyglet, for creating animations.

Time for action – a simple application using PyGame

This example will make use of the modules we just discussed. For this application to work, you will need to install PyGame. The binary and source distribution of PyGame is available on Pygame's website.

1. Create a new Python source file and write the following code in it.

```
1   import pygame
2   import sys
3
4   pygame.init()
5   bgcolor = (200, 200, 100)
6   surf = pygame.display.set_mode((400,400))
7
8   circle_color = (0, 255, 255)
9   x, y = 200, 300
10  circle_rad = 50
11
12  pygame.display.set_caption("My Pygame Window")
13
14  while True:
15      for event in pygame.event.get():
```

```
16              if event.type == pygame.QUIT:
17                  sys.exit()
18          elif event.type == pygame.KEYDOWN:
19              if event.key == pygame.K_UP:
20                  y -= 10
21              elif event.key == pygame.K_DOWN:
22                  y += 10
23              elif event.key == pygame.K_RIGHT:
24                  x += 10
25              elif event.key == pygame.K_LEFT:
26                  x -= 10
27
28      circle_pos = (x, y)
29
30      surf.fill(bgcolor)
31      pygame.draw.circle(surf, circle_color ,
32                          circle_pos , circle_rad)
33      pygame.display.flip()
```

2. The first line imports the `pygame` package. On line 4, the modules within this `pygame` package are initialized. An instance of class `Surface` is created using `display.set_mode` method. This is the main PyGame window inside which the images will be drawn. To ensure that this window is constantly displayed on the screen, we need to add a `while` loop that will run forever, until the window is closed by the user. In this simple application everything we need is placed inside the `while` loop. The background color of the PyGame window represented by object `surf` is set on line 30.

3. A circular shape is drawn in the PyGame surface by the code on line 31. The arguments to `draw.circle` are `(Surface, color, position, radius)`. This creates a circle at the position specified by the argument `circle_pos`. The instance of class `Surface` is sent as the first argument to this method.

4. The code block 16-26 captures certain *events*. An *event* occurs when, for instance, a mouse button or a key is pressed. In this example, we instruct the program to do certain things when the arrow keys are pressed. When the RIGHT arrow key is pressed, the circle is drawn with the x coordinate offset by 10 pixels to the previous position. As a result, the circle appears to be moving towards right whenever you press the RIGHT arrow key. When the PyGame window is closed, the `pygame.QUIT` event occurs. Here, we simply exit the application by calling `sys.exit()` as done on line 17.

5. Finally, we need to ensure that everything drawn on the `Surface` is visible. This is accomplished by the code on line 31. If you disable this line, incompletely drawn images may appear on the screen.

6. Execute the program from a terminal window. It will show a new graphics window containing a circular shape. If you press the arrow keys on the keyboard, the circle will move in the direction indicated by the arrow key. The next illustration shows the screenshot of the original circle position (left) and when it is moved using the UP and RIGHT arrow keys.

A simple PyGame application with a circle drawn within the Surface (window). The image on the right side is a screenshot taken after maneuvering the position of the circle with the help of arrow keys:

What just happened?

We used PyGame to create a simple user interactive application. The purpose of this example was to introduce some of the basic concepts behind animation and game programming. It was just a preview of what is coming next! Later in this book we will use Pyglet framework to create some interesting 2D animations.

QT Phonon

When one thinks of a media player, it is almost always associated with a graphical user interface. Of course one can work with command-line multimedia players. But a media player with a GUI is a clear winner as it provides an easy to use, intuitive user interface to stream a media and control its playback. The next screenshot shows the user interface of an audio player developed using QT Phonon.

An Audio Player application developed with QT Phonon:

QT is an open source GUI framework. 'Phonon' is a multimedia package within QT that supports audio and video playback. Note that, Phonon is meant for simple media player functionality. For complex audio/video player functionality, you should use multimedia frameworks like GStreamer. Phonon depends on a platform-specific backend for media processing. For example, on Windows platform the backend framework is DirectShow. The supported functionality may vary depending on the platform.

To develop a media processing application, a media graph is created in Phonon. This media graph contains various interlinked media nodes. Each media node does a portion of media processing. For example, an effects node will add an audio effect, such as echo to the media. Another node will be responsible for outputting the media from an audio or video device and so on. In chapter 8, we will develop audio and video player applications using Phonon framework. The next illustration shows a video player streaming a video. It is developed using QT Phonon. We will be developing this application in *Chapter 8*.

Using various built-in modules of QT Phonon, it is very easy to create GUI-based audio and video players. This example shows a video player in action:

Other multimedia libraries

Python bindings for several other multimedia libraries are available on various platforms. Some of the popular libraries are mentioned below.

Snack Sound Toolkit

Snack is an audio toolkit that is used to create cross-platform audio applications. It includes audio analysis and input-output functionality and it has support for audio visualization as well. The official website for Snack Sound Toolkit is `http://www.speech.kth.se/snack/`.

PyAudiere

PyAudiere (`http://pyaudiere.org/`) is an open source audio library. It provides an API to easily implement the audio functionality in various applications. It is based on Audiere Sound Library.

Summary

This chapter served as an introduction to multimedia processing using Python.

Specifically, in this chapter we covered:

♦ An overview of multimedia processing. It introduced us to digital image, audio, and video processing.

♦ We learned about a number of freely available multimedia frameworks that can be used for multimedia processing.

Now that we know what multimedia libraries and frameworks are out there, we're ready to explore these to develop exciting multimedia applications!

2
Working with Images

In this chapter, we will learn basic image conversion and manipulation techniques using the Python Imaging Library. The chapter ends with an exciting project where we create an image processing application.

In this chapter, we shall:

- ◆ Learn various image I/O operations for reading and writing images using the **Python Imaging Library (PIL)**
- ◆ With the help of several examples and code snippets, perform some basic manipulations on the image, such as resizing, rotating/ flipping, cropping, pasting, and so on.
- ◆ Write an image-processing application by making use of PIL
- ◆ Use the QT library as a frontend (GUI) for this application

So let's get on with it!

Installation prerequisites

Before we jump in to the main chapter, it is necessary to install the following packages.

Python

In this book we will use Python Version 2.6, or to be more specific, Version 2.6.4. It can be downloaded from the following location:
`http://python.org/download/releases/`

Windows platform

For Windows, just download and install the platform-specific binary distribution of Python 2.6.4.

Other platforms

For other platforms, such as Linux, Python is probably already installed on your machine. If the installed version is not 2.6, build and install it from the source distribution. If you are using a package manager on a Linux system, search for Python 2.6. It is likely that you will find the Python distribution there. Then, for instance, Ubuntu users can install Python from the command prompt as:

```
$sudo apt-get python2.6
```

Note that for this, you must have administrative permission on the machine on which you are installing Python.

Python Imaging Library (PIL)

We will learn image-processing techniques by making extensive use of the Python Imaging Library (PIL) throughout this chapter. As mentioned in *Chapter 1*, PIL is an open source library. You can download it from `http://www.pythonware.com/products/pil/`. Install the PIL Version 1.1.6 or later.

Windows platform

For Windows users, installation is straightforward—use the binary distribution PIL 1.1.6 for Python 2.6.

Other platforms

For other platforms, install PIL 1.1.6 from the source. Carefully review the README file in the source distribution for the platform-specific instructions. Libraries listed in the following table are required to be installed before installing PIL from the source. For some platforms like Linux, the libraries provided in the OS should work fine. However, if those do not work, install a pre-built "libraryName-devel" version of the library. For example, for JPEG support, the name will contain "jpeg-devel-", and something similar for the others. This is generally applicable to rpm-based distributions. For Linux flavors like Ubuntu, you can use the following command in a shell window.

```
$sudo apt-get install python-imaging.
```

However, you should make sure that this installs Version 1.1.6 or later. Check PIL documentation for further platform-specific instructions. For Mac OSX, see if you can use `fink` to install these libraries. See `http://www.finkproject.org/` for more details. You can also check the website `http://pythonmac.org` or Darwin ports website `http://darwinports.com/` to see if a binary package installer is available. If such a pre-built version is not available for any library, install it from the source.

The PIL prerequisites for installing PIL from source are listed in the following table:

Library	URL	Version	Installation options (a) or (b)
`libjpeg` (JPEG support)	`http://www.ijg.org/files`	7 or 6a or 6b	(a) Pre-built version. For example: `jpeg-devel-7` Check if you can do: `sudo apt-install libjpeg` (works on some flavors of Linux) (b) Source tarball. For example: `jpegsrc.v7.tar.gz`
`zib` (PNG support)	`http://www.gzip.org/zlib/`	1.2.3 or later	(a) Pre-built version. For example: `zlib-devel-1.2.3..` (b) Install from the source.
`freetype2` (OpenType /TrueType support)	`http://www.freetype.org`	2.1.3 or later	(a) Pre-built version. For example: `freetype2-devel-2.1.3..` (b) Install from the source.

PyQt4

This package provides Python bindings for Qt libraries. We will use PyQt4 to generate GUI for the image-processing application that we will develop later in this chapter. The GPL version is available at: `http://www.riverbankcomputing.co.uk/software/pyqt/download`.

Windows platform

Download and install the binary distribution pertaining to Python 2.6. For example, the executable file's name could be 'PyQt-Py2.6-gpl-4.6.2-2.exe'. Other than Python, it includes everything needed for GUI development using PyQt.

Other platforms

Before building PyQt, you must install SIP Python binding generator. For further details, refer to the SIP homepage: `http://www.riverbankcomputing.com/software/sip/`.

After installing SIP, download and install PyQt 4.6.2 or later, from the source tarball. For Linux/Unix source, the filename will start with `PyQt-x11-gpl-..` and for Mac OS X, `PyQt-mac-gpl-...` Linux users should also check if PyQt4 distribution is already available through the package manager.

Summary of installation prerequisites

Package	Download location	Version	Windows platform	Linux/Unix/OS X platforms
Python	`http://python.org/download/releases/`	2.6.4 (or any 2.6.x)	Install using binary distribution	(a) Install from binary; Also install additional developer packages (For example, with `python-devel` in the package name in the rpm systems) OR
				(b) Build and install from the source tarball.
				(c) MAC users can also check websites such as `http://darwinports.com/` or `http://pythonmac.org/`.
PIL	`www.pythonware.com/products/pil/`	1.1.6 or later	Install PIL 1.1.6 (binary) for Python 2.6	(a) Install prerequisites if needed. Refer to Table #1 and the README file in PIL source distribution.
				(b) Install PIL from source.
				(c) MAC users can also check websites like `http://darwinports.com/` or `http://pythonmac.org/`.
PyQt4	`http://www.riverbankcomputing.co.uk/software/pyqt/download`	4.6.2 or later	Install using binary pertaining to Python 2.6	(a) First install SIP 4.9 or later.
				(b) Then install PyQt4.

Reading and writing images

To manipulate an existing image, we must open it first for editing and we also require the ability to save the image in a suitable file format after making changes. The `Image` module in PIL provides methods to read and write images in the specified image file format. It supports a wide range of file formats.

To open an image, use `Image.open` method. Start the Python interpreter and write the following code. You should specify an appropriate path on your system as an argument to the `Image.open` method.

```
>>>import Image
>>>inputImage = Image.open("C:\\PythonTest\\image1.jpg")
```

This will open an image file by the name `image1.jpg`. If the file can't be opened, an `IOError` will be raised, otherwise, it returns an instance of class `Image`.

For saving image, use the `save` method of the `Image` class. Make sure you replace the following string with an appropriate `/path/to/your/image/file`.

```
>>>inputImage.save("C:\\PythonTest\\outputImage.jpg")
```

You can view the image just saved, using the `show` method of `Image` class.

```
>>>outputImage = Image.open("C:\\PythonTest\\outputImage.jpg")
>>>outputImage.show()
```

Here, it is essentially the same image as the input image, because we did not make any changes to the output image.

Time for action – image file converter

With this basic information, let's build a simple image file converter. This utility will batch-process image files and save them in a user-specified file format.

To get started, download the file `ImageFileConverter.py` from the Packt website, `www.packtpub.com`. This file can be run from the command line as:

```
python ImageConverter.py [arguments]
```

Here, [arguments] are:

- `--input_dir`: The directory path where the image files are located.
- `--input_format`: The format of the image files to be converted. For example, jpg.

- ◆ --output_dir: The location where you want to save the converted images.
- ◆ --output_format: The output image format. For example, jpg, png, bmp, and so on.

The following screenshot shows the image conversion utility in action on Windows XP, that is, running image converter from the command line.

Here, it will batch-process all the .jpg images within C:\PythonTest\images and save them in png format in the directory C:\PythonTest\images\OUTPUT_IMAGES.

```
Command Prompt                                                        _ □ ×

C:\PythonTest\src>python ImageFileConverter.py --input_dir=C:\PythonTest\images
                                              --input_format=jpg
                                              --output_format=png
('--input_dir', 'C:\\PythonTest\\images')
('--input_format', 'jpg')
('--output_format', 'png')

 Converting images..

 Done!

  8 image(s) written to directory:        C:\PythonTest\images\OUTPUT_IMAGES

 Approximate time required for conversion:         4.2007 seconds
C:\PythonTest\src>
```

The file defines class ImageConverter . We will discuss the most important methods in this class.

- ◆ def processArgs : This method processes all the command-line arguments listed earlier. It makes use of Python's built-in module getopts to process these arguments. Readers are advised to review the code in the file ImageConverter.py in the code bundle of this book for further details on how these arguments are processed.

- ◆ def convertImage : This is the workhorse method of the image-conversion utility.

```
1   def convertImage(self):
2     pattern = "*." + self.inputFormat
3     filetype = os.path.join(self.inputDir, pattern)
4     fileList = glob.glob(filetype)
5     inputFileList = filter(imageFileExists, fileList)
6
7     if not len(inputFileList):
8       print "\n No image files with extension %s located \
9       in dir %s"%(self.outputFormat, self.inputDir)
10        return
11      else:
```

```
12          # Record time before beginning image conversion
13          starttime = time.clock()
14          print "\n Converting images.."
15
16      # Save image into specified file format.
17      for imagePath in inputFileList:
18          inputImage = Image.open(imagePath)
19          dir, fil = os.path.split(imagePath)
20          fil, ext = os.path.splitext(fil)
21          outPath = os.path.join(self.outputDir,
22                       fil + "." + self.outputFormat)
23          inputImage.save(outPath)
24
25      endtime = time.clock()
26      print "\n Done!"
27      print "\n %d image(s) written to directory:\
28      %s" % (len(inputFileList), self.outputDir)
29      print "\n Approximate time required for conversion: \
30      %.4f seconds" % (endtime - starttime)
```

Now let's review the preceding code.

1. Our first task is to get a list of all the image files to be saved in a different format. This is achieved by using `glob` module in Python. Line 4 in the code snippet finds all the file path names that match the pattern specified by the local variable `fileType`. On line 5, we check whether the image file in `fileList` exists. This operation can be efficiently performed over the whole list using the built-in `filter` functionality in Python.

2. The code block between lines 7 to 14 ensures that one or more images exist. If so, it will record the time before beginning the image conversion.

3. The next code block (lines 17-23) carries out the image file conversion. On line 18, we use `Image.open` to open the image file. Line 18 creates an `Image` object. Then the appropriate output path is derived and finally the output image is saved using the `save` method of the `Image` module.

What just happened?

In this simple example, we learned how to open and save image files in a specified image format. We accomplished this by writing an image file converter that batch-processes a specified image file. We used PIL's `Image.open` and `Image.save` functionality along with Python's built-in modules such as `glob` and `filter`.

Now we will discuss other key aspects related to the image reading and writing.

Creating an image from scratch

So far we have seen how to open an existing image. What if we want to create our own image? As an example, it you want to create fancy text as an image, the functionality that we are going to discuss now comes in handy. Later in this book, we will learn how to use such an image containing some text to embed into another image. The basic syntax for creating a new image is:

```
foo = Image.new(mode, size, color)
```

Where, new is the built-in method of class Image. Image.new takes three arguments, namely, mode, size, and color. The mode argument is a string that gives information about the number and names of image bands. Following are the most common values for mode argument: L (gray scale) and RGB (true color). The size is a tuple specifying dimensions of the image in pixels, whereas, color is an optional argument. It can be assigned an RGB value (a 3-tuple) if it's a multi-band image. If it is not specified, the image is filled with black color.

Time for action – creating a new image containing some text

As already stated, it is often useful to generate an image containing only some text or a common shape. Such an image can then be pasted onto another image at a desired angle and location. We will now create an image with text that reads, "Not really a fancy text!"

1. Write the following code in a Python source file:

    ```
    1 import Image
    2 import ImageDraw
    3 txt = "Not really a fancy text!"
    4 size = (150, 50)
    5 color = (0, 100, 0)
    6 img = Image.new('RGB', size, color)
    7 imgDrawer = ImageDraw.Draw(img)
    8 imgDrawer.text((5, 20), txt)
    9 img.show()
    ```

2. Let's analyze the code line by line. The first two lines import the necessary modules from PIL. The variable txt is the text we want to include in the image. On line 7, the new image is created using Image.new. Here we specify the mode and size arguments. The optional color argument is specified as a tuple with RGB values pertaining to the "dark green" color.

3. The `ImageDraw` module in PIL provides graphics support for an `Image` object. The function `ImageDraw.Draw` takes an image object as an argument to create a `Draw` instance. In output code, it is called `imgDrawer`, as used on line 7. This `Draw` instance enables drawing various things in the given image.

4. On line 8, we call the text method of the Draw instance and supply position (a `tuple`) and the text (stored in the string `txt`) as arguments.

5. Finally, the image can be viewed using `img.show()` call. You can optionally save the image using `Image.save` method. The following screenshot shows the resultant image.

What just happened?

We just learned how to create an image from scratch. An empty image was created using the `Image.new` method. Then, we used the `ImageDraw` module in PIL to add text to this image.

Reading images from archive

If the image is part of an archived container, for example, a TAR archive, we can use the `TarIO` module in PIL to open it and then call `Image.open` to pass this `TarIO` instance as an argument.

Time for action – reading images from archives

Suppose there is an archive file `images.tar` containing image file `image1.jpg`. The following code snippet shows how to read `image1.jpg` from the tarball.

```
>>>import TarIO
>>>import Images
>>>fil = TarIO.TarIO("images.tar", "images/image1.jpg")
>>>img = Image.open(fil)
>>>img.show()
```

What just happened?

We learned how to read an image located in an archived container.

Modify the image conversion code so that it supports the following new functionality, which:

1. Takes a ZIP file containing images as input
2. Creates a TAR archive of the converted images

Basic image manipulations

Now that we know how to open and save images, let's learn some basic techniques to manipulate images. PIL supports a variety of geometric manipulation operations, such as resizing an image, rotating it by an angle, flipping it top to bottom or left to right, and so on. It also facilitates operations such as cropping, cutting and pasting pieces of images, and so on.

Resizing

Changing the dimensions of an image is one of the most frequently used image manipulation operations. The image resizing is accomplished using `Image.resize` in PIL. The following line of code explains how it is achieved.

```
foo = img.resize(size, filter)
```

Here, `img` is an image (an instance of class `Image`) and the result of resizing operation is stored in `foo` (another instance of class `Image`). The `size` argument is a `tuple` (`width`, `height`). Note that the `size` is specified in pixels. Thus, resizing the image means modifying the number of pixels in the image. This is also known as **image re-sampling**. The `Image.resize` method also takes `filter` as an optional argument. A `filter` is an interpolation algorithm used while re-sampling the given image. It handles deletion or addition of pixels during re-sampling, when the resize operation is intended to make image smaller or larger in size respectively. There are four filters available. The resize filters in the increasing order of quality are `NEAREST`, `BILINEAR`, `BICUBIC`, and `ANTIALIAS`. The default filter option is `NEAREST`.

Time for action – resizing

Let's now resize images by modifying their pixel dimensions and applying various filters for re-sampling.

1. Download the file `ImageResizeExample.bmp` from the Packt website. We will use this as the reference file to create scaled images. The original dimensions of `ImageResizeExample.bmp` are `200 x 212` pixels.

2. Write the following code in a file or in Python interpreter. Replace the `inPath` and `outPath` strings with the appropriate image path on your machine.

```
1 import Image
2 inPath = "C:\\images\\ImageResizeExample.jpg"
3 img = Image.open(inPath)
4 width , height = (160, 160)
5 size = (width, height)
6 foo = img.resize(size)
7 foo.show()
8 outPath = "C:\\images\\foo.jpg"
9 foo.save(outPath)
```

3. The image specified by the `inPath` will be resized and saved as the image specified by the `outPath`. Line 6 in the code snippet does the resizing job and finally we save the new image on line 9. You can see how the resized image looks by calling `foo.show()`.

4. Let's now specify the `filter` argument. In the following code, on line 14, the `filterOpt` argument is specified in the `resize` method. The valid `filter` options are specified as values in the dictionary `filterDict`. The keys of `filterDict` are used as the filenames of the output images. The four images thus obtained are compared in the next illustration. You can clearly notice the difference between the ANTIALIAS image and the others (particularly, look at the flower petals in these images). When the processing time is not an issue, choose the ANTIALIAS filter option as it gives the best quality image.

```
1 import Image
2 inPath = "C:\\images\\ImageResizeExample.jpg"
3 img = Image.open(inPath)
4 width , height = (160, 160)
5 size = (width, height)
6 filterDict = {'NEAREST':Image.NEAREST,
7          'BILINEAR':Image.BILINEAR,
8          'BICUBIC':Image.BICUBIC,
9          'ANTIALIAS':Image.ANTIALIAS }
10
11 for k in filterDict.keys():
12    outPath= "C:\\images\\" + k + ".jpg"
13    filterOpt = filterDict[k]
14    foo = img.resize(size, filterOpt)
15    foo.save(outPath)
```

The resized images with different filter options appear as follows. Clockwise from left, `Image.NEAREST`, `Image.BILENEAR`, `Image.BICUBIC`, and `Image.ANTIALIAS`:

5. The `resize` functionality illustrated here, however, doesn't preserve the aspect ratio of the resulting image. The image will appear distorted if one dimension is stretched more or stretched less in comparison with the other dimension. PIL's `Image` module provides another built-in method to fix this. It will override the larger of the two dimensions, such that the aspect ratio of the image is maintained.

```
import Image
inPath = "C:\\images\\ResizeImageExample.jpg"
img = Image.open(inPath)
width , height = (100, 50)
size = (width, height)
outPath = "C:\\images\\foo.jpg"
img.thumbnail(size, Image.ANTIALIAS)
img.save(outPath)
```

6. This code will override the maximum pixel dimension value (`width` in this case) specified by the programmer and replace it with a value that maintains the aspect ratio of the image. In this case, we have an image with pixel dimensions (47, 50). The resultant images are compared in the following illustration.

It shows the comparison of output images for methods `Image.thumbnail` and `Image.resize`.

What just happened?

We just learned how image resizing is done using PIL's `Image` module, by writing a few lines of code. We also learned different types of filters used in image resizing (re-sampling). And finally, we also saw how to resize an image while still keeping the aspect ratio intact (that is, without distortion), using the `Image.thumbnail` method.

Rotating

Like image resizing, rotating an image about its center is another commonly performed transformation. For example, in a composite image, one may need to rotate the text by certain degrees before embedding it in another image. For such needs, there are methods such as `rotate` and `transpose` available in PIL's `Image` module. The basic syntax to rotate an image using `Image.rotate` is as follows:

```
foo = img.rotate(angle, filter)
```

Where, the `angle` is provided in degrees and `filter`, the optional argument, is the image-re-sampling filter. The valid `filter` value can be NEAREST, BILINEAR, or BICUBIC. You can rotate the image using `Image.transpose` only for 90-, 180-, and 270-degree rotation angles.

Time for action – rotating

1. Download the file `Rotate.png` from the Packt website. Alternatively, you can use any supported image file of your choice.

2. Write the following code in Python interpreter or in a Python file. As always, specify the appropriate path strings for `inPath` and `outPath` variables.

```
1 import Image
2 inPath = "C:\\images\\Rotate.png"
3 img = Image.open(inPath)
4 deg = 45
5 filterOpt = Image.BICUBIC
6 outPath = "C:\\images\\Rotate_out.png"
7 foo = img.rotate(deg, filterOpt)
8 foo.save(outPath)
```

3. Upon running this code, the output image, rotated by 45 degrees, is saved to the `outPath`. The filter option `Image.BICUBIC` ensures highest quality. The next illustration shows the original and the images rotated by 45 and 180 degrees respectively—the original and rotated images.

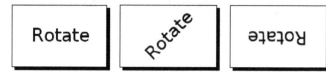

4. There is another way to accomplish rotation for certain angles by using the `Image.transpose` functionality. The following code achieves a 270-degree rotation. Other valid options for rotation are `Image.ROTATE_90` and `Image.ROTATE_180`.

```
import Image
inPath = "C:\\images\\Rotate.png"
img = Image.open(inPath)
outPath = "C:\\images\\Rotate_out.png"
foo = img.transpose(Image.ROTATE_270)
foo.save(outPath)
```

What just happened?

In the previous section, we used `Image.rotate` to accomplish rotating an image by the desired angle. The image filter `Image.BICUBIC` was used to obtain better quality output image after rotation. We also saw how `Image.transpose` can be used for rotating the image by certain angles.

Flipping

There are multiple ways in PIL to flip an image horizontally or vertically. One way to achieve this is using the `Image.transpose` method. Another option is to use the functionality from the `ImageOps` module . This module makes the image-processing job even easier with some ready-made methods. However, note that the PIL documentation for Version 1.1.6 states that `ImageOps` is still an experimental module.

Time for action – flipping

Imagine that you are building a symmetric image using a bunch of basic shapes. To create such an image, an operation that can flip (or mirror) the image would come in handy. So let's see how image flipping can be accomplished.

1. Write the following code in a Python source file.

```
1 import Image
2 inPath = "C:\\images\\Flip.png"
3 img = Image.open(inPath)
4 outPath = "C:\\images\\Flip_out.png"
5 foo = img.transpose(Image.FLIP_LEFT_RIGHT)
6 foo.save(outPath)
```

2. In this code, the image is flipped horizontally by calling the `transpose` method. To flip the image vertically, replace line 5 in the code with the following:

```
foo = img.transpose(Image.FLIP_TOP_BOTTOM)
```

3. The following illustration shows the output of the preceding code when the image is flipped horizontally and vertically.

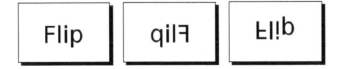

4. The same effect can be achieved using the `ImageOps` module. To flip the image horizontally, use `ImageOps.mirror`, and to flip the image vertically, use `ImageOps.flip`.

```
import ImageOps

# Flip image horizontally
foo1 = ImageOps.mirror(img)
# Flip image vertically
foo2 = ImageOps.flip(img)
```

What just happened?

With the help of example, we learned how to flip an image horizontally or vertically using `Image.transpose` and also by using methods in class `ImageOps`. This operation will be applied later in this book for further image processing such as preparing composite images.

Capturing screenshots

How do you capture the desktop screen or a part of it using Python? There is `ImageGrab` module in PIL. This simple line of code will capture the whole screen.

```
img = ImageGrab.grab()
```

Where, `img` is an instance of class `Image`.

However, note that in PIL Version 1.1.6, the `ImageGrab` module supports screen grabbing only for Windows platform.

Time for action – capture screenshots at intervals

Imagine that you are developing an application, where, after certain time interval, the program needs to automatically capture the whole screen or a part of the screen. Let's develop code that achieves this.

1. Write the following code in a Python source file. When the code is executed, it will capture part of the screen after every two seconds. The code will run for about three seconds.

```
1 import ImageGrab
2 import time
3 startTime = time.clock()
4 print "\n The start time is %s sec" % startTime
5 # Define the four corners of the bounding box.
6 # (in pixels)
7 left = 150
```

```
8 upper = 200
9 right = 900
10 lower = 700
11 bbox = (left, upper, right, lower)
12
13 while time.clock() < 3:
14   print " \n Capturing screen at time %.4f sec" \
15      %time.clock()
16   screenShot = ImageGrab.grab(bbox)
17   name = str("%.2f"%time.clock())+ "sec.png"
18   screenShot.save("C:\\images\\output\\" + name)
19   time.sleep(2)
```

2. We will now review the important aspects of this code. First, import the necessary modules. The `time.clock()` keeps track of the time spent. On line 11, a bounding box is defined. It is a `4-tuple` that defines the boundaries of a rectangular region. The elements in this `tuple` are specified in pixels. In PIL, the origin (0, 0) is defined in the top-left corner of an image. The next illustration is a representation of a bounding box for image cropping; see how left, upper and right, lower are specified as the ends of a diagonal of rectangle.

Example of a bounding box used for image cropping.

3. The `while` loop runs till the `time.clock()` reaches three seconds. Inside the loop, the part of the screen bounded within `bbox` is captured (see line 16) and then the image is saved on line 18. The image name corresponds to the time at which it is taken.

4. The `time.sleep(2)` call suspends the execution of the application for two seconds. This ensures that it grabs the screen every two seconds. The loop repeats until the given time is reached.

5. In this example, it will capture two screenshots, one when it enters the loop for the first time and the next after a two-second time interval. In the following illustration, the two images grabbed by the code are shown. Notice the time and console prints in these images.

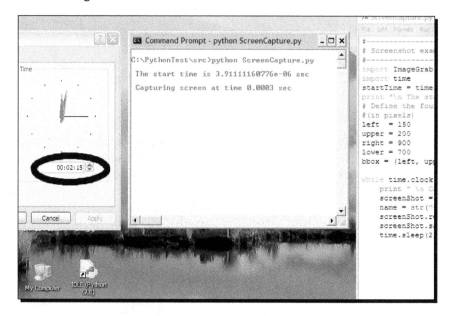

The preceding screenshot is taken at time 00:02:15 as shown dialog. The next screenshot is taken after 2 seconds, at wall clock time, 00:02:17.

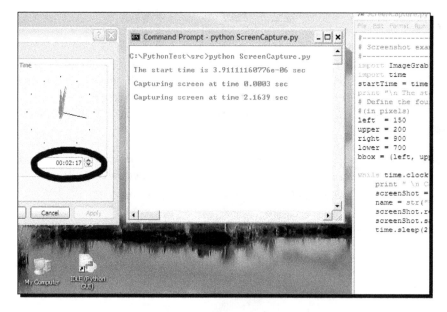

What just happened?

In the preceding example, we wrote a simple application that captures the screen at regular time intervals. This helped us to learn how to grab a screen region using `ImageGrab`.

Cropping

In previous section, we learned how to grab a part of the screen with `ImageGrab`. Cropping is a very similar operation performed on an image. It allows you to modify a region within an image.

Time for action – cropping an image

This simple code snippet crops an image and applies some changes on the cropped portion.

1. Download the file `Crop.png` from Packt website. The size of this image is `400 x 400` pixels. You can also use your own image file.

2. Write the following code in a Python source file. Modify the path of the image file to an appropriate path.

```
import Image
img = Image.open("C:\\images\\Crop.png")
left = 0
upper = 0
right = 180
lower = 215
bbox = (left, upper, right, lower)
img = img.crop(bbox)
img.show()
```

3. This will crop a region of the image bounded by bbox. The specification of the bounding box is identical to what we have seen in the *Capturing screenshots* section. The output of this example is shown in the following illustration.

   Original image (left) and its cropped region (right).

What just happened?

In the previous section, we used `Image.crop` functionality to crop a region within an image and save the resultant image. In the next section, we will apply this while pasting a region of an image onto another.

Pasting

Pasting a copied or cut image onto another one is a commonly performed operation while processing images. Following is the simplest syntax to paste one image on another.

```
img = img.paste(image, box)
```

Here `image` is an instance of class `Image` and `box` is a rectangular bounding box that defines the region of `img`, where the `image` will be pasted. The `box` argument can be a 4-tupleError: Reference source not found or a 2-tuple. If a 4-tuple `box` is specified, the size of the image to be pasted must be same as the size of the region. Otherwise, PIL will throw an error with a message `ValueError: images do not match`. The 2-tuple on the other hand, provides pixel coordinates of the upper-left corner of the region to be pasted.

Now look at the following line of code. It is a copy operation on an image.

```
img2 = img.copy(image)
```

The copy operation can be viewed as pasting the whole image onto a new image. This operation is useful when, for instance, you want to keep the original image unaltered and make alterations to the copy of the image.

Time for action – pasting: mirror the smiley face!

Consider the example in earlier section where we cropped a region of an image. The cropped region contained a smiley face. Let's modify the original image so that it has a 'reflection' of the smiley face.

1. If not already, download the file `Crop.png` from the Packt website.

2. Write this code by replacing the file path with appropriate file path on your system.

```
1 import Image
2 img = Image.open("C:\\images\\Crop.png")
3 # Define the elements of a 4-tuple that represents
4 # a bounding box ( region to be cropped)
5 left = 0
6 upper = 25
7 right = 180
```

```
8 lower = 210
9 bbox = (left, upper, right, lower)
10 # Crop the smiley face from the image
11 smiley = img.crop(bbox_1)
12 # Flip the image horizontally
13 smiley = smiley.transpose(Image.FLIP_TOP_BOTTOM)
14 # Define the box as a 2-tuple.
15 bbox_2 = (0, 210)
16 # Finally paste the 'smiley' on to the image.
17 img.paste(smiley, bbox_2)
18 img.save("C:\\images\\Pasted.png")
19 img.show()
```

3. First we open an image and crop it to extract a region containing the smiley face. This was already done in section Error: Reference source not found 'Cropping'. The only minor difference you will notice is the value of the tuple element upper. It is intentionally kept as 25 pixels from the top to make sure that the crop image has a size that can fit in the blank portion below the original smiley face.

4. The cropped image is then flipped horizontally with code on line 13.

5. Now we define a box, bbox_2, for pasting the cropped smiley face back on to the original image. Where should it be pasted? We intend to make a 'reflection' of the original smiley face. So the coordinate of the top-right corner of the pasted image should be greater than or equal to the bottom y coordinate of the cropped region, indicated by 'lower' variable (see line 8) . The bounding box is defined on line 15, as a 2-tuple representing the upper-left coordinates of the smiley.

6. Finally, on line 17, the paste operation is performed to paste the smiley on the original image. The resulting image is then saved with a different name.

7. The original image and the output image after the paste operation is shown in the next illustration.

The illustration shows the comparison of original and resulting images after the paste operation.

What just happened?

Using a combination of `Image.crop` and `Image.paste`, we accomplished cropping a region, making some modifications, and then pasting the region back on the image.

Project: Thumbnail Maker

Let's take up a project now. We will apply some of the operations we learned in this chapter to create a simple Thumbnail Maker utility. This application will accept an image as an input and will create a resized image of that image. Although we are calling it a thumbnail maker, it is a multi-purpose utility that implements some basic image-processing functionality.

Before proceeding further, make sure that you have installed all the packages discussed at the beginning of this chapter. The screenshot of the Thumbnail Maker dialog is show in the following illustration.

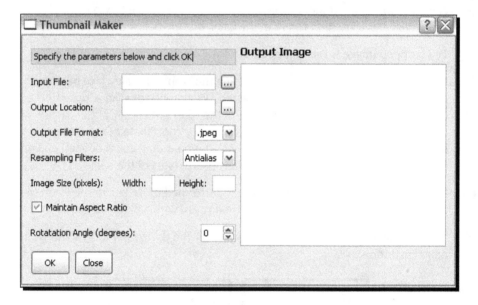

The Thumbnail Maker GUI has two components:

1. The left panel is a 'control area', where you can specify certain image parameters along with options for input and output paths.

2. A graphics area on the right-hand side where you can view the generated image.

In short, this is how it works:

1. The application takes an image file as an input.

2. It accepts user input for image parameters such as dimensions in pixel, filter for re-sampling and rotation angle in degrees.

3. When the user clicks the **OK** button in the dialog, the image is processed and saved at a location indicated by the user in the specified output image format.

Time for action – play with Thumbnail Maker application

First, we will run the Thumbnail Maker application as an end user. This warm-up exercise intends to give us a good understanding of how the application works. This, in turn, will help us develop/learn the involved code quickly. So get ready for action!

1. Download the files `ThumbnailMaker.py`, `ThumbnailMakeDialog.py`, and `Ui_ThumbnailMakerDialog.py` from Packt website. Place these files in some directory.

2. From the command prompt, change to this directory location and type the following command:

```
python ThumbnailMakerDialog.py
```

The Thumbnail Maker dialog that pops up was shown in the earlier screenshot. Next, we will specify the input-output paths and various image parameters. You can open any image file of your choice. Here, the flower image shown in some previous sections will be used as an input image. To specify an input image, click on the small button with three dots .... It will open a file dialog. The following illustration shows the dialog with all the parameters specified.

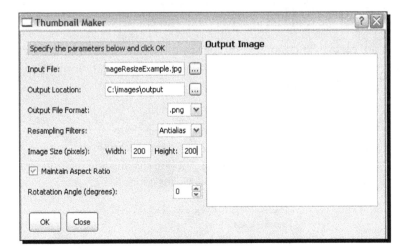

3. If **Maintain Aspect Ratio** checkbox is checked, internally it will scale the image dimension so that the aspect ratio of the output image remains the same. When the **OK** button is clicked, the resultant image is saved at the location specified by the **Output Location** field and the saved image is displayed in the right-hand panel of the dialog. The following screenshot shows the dialog after clicking **OK** button.

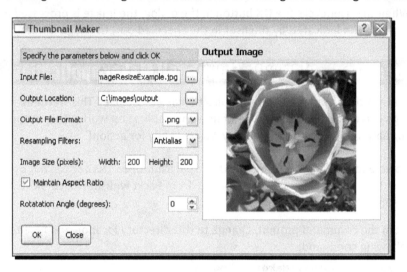

4. You can now try modifying different parameters such as output image format or rotation angle and save the resulting image.

5. See what happens when the **Maintain Aspect Ratio** checkbox is unchecked. The aspect ratio of the resulting image will not be preserved and the image may appear distorted if the width and height dimensions are not properly specified.

6. Experiment with different re-sampling filters; you can notice the difference between the quality of the resultant image and the earlier image.

7. There are certain limitations to this basic utility. It is required to specify reasonable values for all the parameters fields in the dialog. The program will print an error if any of the parameters is not specified.

What just happened?

We got ourselves familiar with the user interface of the thumbnail maker dialog and saw how it works for processing an image with different dimensions and quality. This knowledge will make it easier to understand the Thumbnail Maker code.

Generating the UI code

The Thumbnail Maker GUI is written using PyQt4 (Python bindings for Qt4 GUI framework). Detailed discussion on how the GUI is generated and how the GUI elements are connected to the main functions is beyond the scope of this book. However, we will cover certain main aspects of this GUI to get you going. The GUI-related code in this application can simply be used 'as-is' and if this is something that interests you, go ahead and experiment with it further! In this section, we will briefly discuss how the UI code is generated using PyQt4.

Time for action – generating the UI code

PyQt4 comes with an application called QT Designer. It is a GUI designer for QT-based applications and provides a quick way to develop a graphical user interface containing some basic widgets. With this, let's see how the Thumbnail Maker dialog looks in QT Designer and then run a command to generate Python source code from the .ui file.

1. Download the thumbnailMaker.ui file from the Packt website.

2. Start the QT Designer application that comes with PyQt4 installation.

3. Open the file thumbnailMaker.ui in QT Designer. Notice the red-colored borders around the UI elements in the dialog. These borders indicate a 'layout' in which the widgets are arranged. Without a layout in place, the UI elements may appear distorted when you run the application and, for instance, resize the dialog. Three types of QLayouts are used, namely Horizontal, Vertical, and Grid layout.

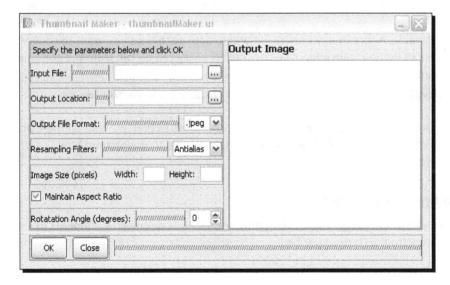

4. You can add new UI elements, such as a QCheckbox or a QLabel, by dragging and dropping it from the 'Widget Box' of QT Designer. It is located in the left panel by default.

5. Click on the field next to the label "Input file". In the right-hand panel of QT Designer, there is a Property Editor that displays the properties of the selected widget (in this case it's a QLineEdit). This is shown in the following illustration. The Property Editor allows us to assign values to various attributes such as the objectName, width, and height of the widget, and so on.

   Qt Designer shows the details of the selected widget in Property Editor.

6. QT designer saves the file with extension .ui. To convert this into Python source code, PyQt4 provides a conversion utility called pyuic4. On Windows XP, for standard Python installation, it is present at the following location—C:\Python26\ Lib\site-packages\PyQt4\pyuic4.bat. Add this path to your environment variable. Alternatively specify the whole path each time you want to convert ui file to Python source file. The conversion utility can be run from the command prompt as:

   ```
   pyuic4 thumbnailMaker.ui -o Ui_ThumbnailMakerDialog.py
   ```

7. This script will generate Ui_ThumbnailMakerDialog.py with all the GUI elements defined. You can further review this file to understand how the UI elements are defined.

What just happened?

We learned how to autogenerate the Python source code defining UI elements of Thumbnail Maker Dialog from a Qt designer file.

Have a go hero – tweak UI of Thumbnail Maker dialog

Modify the `thumbnailMaker.ui` file in QT Designer and implement the following list of things in the Thumbnail Maker dialog.

1. Change the color of all the line edits in the left panel to pale yellow.

2. Tweak the default file extension displayed in the **Output file Format** combobox such that the first option is `.png` instead of `.jpeg`

> Double click on this combobox to edit it.

3. Add new option `.tiff` to the output format combobox.

4. Align the **OK** and **Cancel** buttons to the right corner.

> You will need to break layouts, move the spacer around, and recreate the layouts.

5. Set the range of rotation angle 0 to 360 degrees instead of the current -180 to +180 degrees.

After this, create `Ui_ThumbnailMakerDialog.py` by running the `pyuic4` script and then run the Thumbnail Maker application.

Connecting the widgets

In the earlier section, the Python source code representing UI was automatically generated using the `pyuic4` script. This, however, only has the widgets defined and placed in a nice layout. We need to teach these widgets what they should do when a certain event occurs. To do this, QT's slots and signals will be used. A signal is emitted when a particular GUI event occurs. For example, when the user clicks on the **OK** button, internally, a `clicked()` signal is emitted. A slot is a function that is called when a particular signal is emitted. Thus, in this example, it will call a specified method, whenever the **OK** button is clicked. See PyQt4 documentation for a complete list of available signals for various widgets.

Time for action – connecting the widgets

You will notice several different widgets in the dialog. For example, the field which accepts the input image path or the output directory path is a QLineEdit. The widget where image format is specified is a QCombobox. On similar lines, the **OK** and **Cancel** buttons are QPushButton. As an exercise, you can open up the thumbnailMaker.ui file and click on each element to see the associated QT class from the Property Editor.

With this, let's learn how the widgets are connected.

1. Open the file ThumbnailMakerDialog.py. The _connect method of class ThumbnailMakerDialog is copied. The method is called in the constructor of this class.

```
def _connect(self):
    """
    Connect slots with signals.
    """
    self.connect(self._dialog.inputFileDialogButton,
    SIGNAL("clicked()"), self._openFileDialog)

    self.connect(self._dialog.outputLocationDialogButton,
    SIGNAL("clicked()"), self._outputLocationPath)

    self.connect(self._dialog.okPushButton,
    SIGNAL("clicked()"), self._processImage)

    self.connect(self._dialog.closePushButton,
    SIGNAL("clicked()"), self.close)

    self.connect(self._dialog.aspectRatioCheckBox,
            SIGNAL('stateChanged(int)'),
            self._aspectRatioOptionChanged)
```

2. self._dialog is an instance of class Ui_ThumbnailMakerDialog. self.connect is the inherited method of Qt class QDialog. Here, it takes the following arguments (QObject, signal, callable), where QObject is any widget type (all inherit QObject), signal is the QT SIGNAL that tells us about what event occurred and callable is any method handling this event.

3. For example, consider the highlighted lines of the code snippet. They connect the **OK** button to a method that handles image processing. The first argument , self._dialog.okPushButton refers to the button widget defined in class Ui_ThumbnailMakerDialog. Referring to QPushButton documentation, you will find there is a "clicked()" signal that it can emit. The second argument SIGNAL("clicked()") tells Qt that we want to know when that button is clicked by the user. The third argument is the method self._processImage that gets called when this signal is emitted.

4. Similarly, you can review the other connections in this method. Each of these connects a widget to a method of the class `ThumbnailMakerDialog`.

What just happened?

We reviewed `ThumbnailMakerDialog._connect()` method to understand how the UI elements are connected to various internal methods. The previous two sections helped us learn some preliminary concepts of GUI programming using QT.

Developing the image processing code

The previous sections were intended to get ourselves familiar with the application as an end user and to understand some basic aspects of the GUI elements in the application. With all necessary pieces together, let's focus our attention on the class that does all the main image processing in the application.

The class `ThumbnailMaker` handles the pure image processing code. It defines various methods to achieve this. For example, the class methods such as `_rotateImage`, `_makeThumbnail`, and `_resizeImage` manipulate the given image to accomplish rotation, thumbnail generation, and resizing respectively. This class accepts input from `ThumbnailMakerDialog`. Thus, no QT related UI code is required here. If you want to use some other GUI framework to process input, you can do that easily. Just make sure to implement the public API methods defined in class `ThumbnailMakerDialog`, as those are used by the `ThumbnailMaker` class.

Time for action – developing image processing code

Thus, with `ThumbnailMakerDialog` at your disposal, you can develop your own code in scratch, in class `ThumbnailMaker`. Just make sure to implement the method `processImage` as this is the only method called by `ThumbnailMakerDialog`.

Let's develop some important methods of class `ThumbnailMaker`.

1. Write the constructor for class `ThumbnailMaker`. It takes `dialog` as an argument. In the constructor, we only initialize `self._dialog`, which is an instance of class `ThumbnailMakerDialog`. Here is the code.

```
def __init__(self, dialog):
    """
    Constructor for class ThumbnailMaker.
    """
    # This dialog can be an instance of
    # ThumbnailMakerDialog class. Alternatively, if
    # you have some other way to process input,
```

```
# it will be that class. Just make sure to implement
# the public API methods defined in
# ThumbnailMakerDialog class!
self._dialog = dialog
```

2. Next, write the `processImage` method in class `ThumbnailMaker`. The code is as follows:

 Note: You can download the file `ThumbnailMaker.py` from Packt website. The code written is from this file. The only difference is that some code comments are removed here.

```
1 def processImage(self):
2     filePath = self._dialog.getInputImagePath()
3     imageFile = Image.open(filePath)
4
5     if self._dialog.maintainAspectRatio:
6       resizedImage = self._makeThumbnail(imageFile)
7     else:
8       resizedImage = self._resizeImage(imageFile)
9
10    rotatedImage = self._rotateImage(resizedImage)
11
12    fullPath = self._dialog.getOutImagePath()
13
14    # Finally save the image.
15    rotatedImage.save(fullPath)
```

3. On line 2, it gets the full path of the input image file. Note that it relies on `self._dialog` to provide this information.

4. Then the image file is opened the usual way. On line 4, it checks a flag that decides whether or not to process the image by maintaining the aspect ratio. Accordingly, `_makeThumbnail` or `_resizeImage` methods are called.

5. On line 10, it rotates the image resized earlier, using the `_rotateImage` method.

6. Finally, on line 15, the processed image is saved at a path obtained from the `getOutImagePath` method of class `ThumbnailMakerDialog`.

7. We will now write the `_makeThumbnail` method.

```
1 def _makeThumbnail(self, imageFile):
2     foo = imageFile.copy()
3     size = self._dialog.getSize()
4     imageFilter = self._getImageFilter()
5     foo.thumbnail(size, imageFilter)
6     return foo
```

8. First a copy of the original image is made. We will manipulate this copy and the method will return it for further processing.

9. Then the necessary parameters such as the image dimension and filter for re-sampling are obtained from `self._dialog` and `_getImageFilter` respectively.

10. Finally the thumbnail is created on line 5 and then method returns this image instance.

11. We have already discussed how to resize and rotate image. The related code is straightforward to write and the readers are suggested to write it as an exercise. You will need to review the code from file `ThumbnailMakerDialog.py` for getting appropriate parameters. Write remaining routines namely, `_resizeImage, _rotateImage` and `_getImageFilter`.

12. Once all methods are in place, run the code from the command line as:

```
python Thumbnailmaker.py
```

13. It should show our application dialog. Play around with it to make sure everything works!

What just happened?

In the previous section, we completed an exciting project. Several things learned in this chapter, such as image I/O, resizing, and so on, were applied in the project. We developed a GUI application where some basic image manipulation features, such as creating thumbnails, were implemented. This project also helped us gain some insight into various aspects of GUI programming using QT.

Have a go hero – enhance the ThumbnailMaker application

Want to do something more with the Thumbnail Maker. Here you go! As you will add more features to this application, the first thing you would need to do is to change its name—at least from the caption of the dialog that pops up! Edit the `thumbnailMaker.ui` file in QT designer, change the name to something like "Image Processor", and recreate the corresponding `.py` file. Next, add the following features to this application.

 If you don't want to deal with any UI code, that is fine too! You can write a class similar to `ThumbnailMakerDialog`. Do the input argument processing in your own way. All that class `ThumbnailMaker` requires is implementation of certain public methods in this new class, to get various input parameters.

1. Accept output filename from the user. Currently, it gives the same name as the input file.

    Edit the `.ui` file. You would need to break the layouts before adding a `QLineEdit` and its `QLabel` and then recreate the layouts.

2. If there is a previously created output image file in the output directory, clicking **OK** would simply overwrite that file. Add a checkbox reading, "Overwrite existing file (if any)". If the checkbox in deselected, it should pop up a warning dialog and exit.

    For the latter part, there is a commented out code block in `ThumbnailMakerDialog._processImage`. Just enable the code.

3. Add a feature that can add specified text in the lower-left corner of the output image.

4. Create an image with this text, and use the combination of crop and paste to achieve desired results. For user input, you will need to add a new `QLineEdit` for accepting text input and then connect signals with a callable method in `ThumbnailMakerDialog._connect`.

Summary

We learned a lot in this chapter about basic image manipulation.

Specifically, we covered image input-output operations that enable reading and writing of images, and creation of images from scratch.

With the help of numerous examples and code snippets, we learned several image manipulation operations. Some of them are:

◆ How to resize an image with or without maintaining aspect ratio

◆ Rotating or flipping an image

◆ Cropping an image, manipulating it using techniques learned earlier in the chapter, and then pasting it on the original image

◆ Creating an image with a text

◆ We developed a small application that captures a region of your screen at regular time intervals

◆ We created an interesting project implementing some image processing functionality learned in this chapter

With this basic image manipulation knowledge, we are ready to learn how to add some cool effects to an image. In the next chapter, we will see how to enhance an image.

3
Enhancing Images

In the previous chapter, we learned a lot about day-to-day image processing. We accomplished the learning objective of performing basic image manipulation by working on several examples and small projects. In this chapter, we will move a step further by learning how to add special effects to an image. The special effects added to the image serve several purposes. These not only give a pleasing appearance to the image but may also help you to understand important information presented by the image.

In this chapter, we shall:

- ◆ Learn how to adjust brightness and contrast levels of an image
- ◆ Add code to selectively modify the color of an image and create gray scale images and negatives
- ◆ Use PIL functionality to combine two images together and add transparency effects to the image
- ◆ Apply various image-enhancement filters to an image to achieve effects such as smoothing, sharpening, embossing, and so on
- ◆ Undertake a project to develop a tool to add a watermark or text or a date stamp to an image

So let's get on with it.

Installation and download prerequisites

The installation prerequisites for this chapter are same as the ones in *Chapter 2, Working with Images*. Please refer to that chapter for further details.

It is important to download all the images required for this chapter from the Packt website at `http://www.packtpub.com/`. We will be using these images throughout this chapter in the image processing code. Additionally, please download the PDF file, `Chapter 3 Supplementary Material.pdf` from Packt website. This is very important if you are reading a hard copy of this book which is printed in black and white. In the upcoming sections such as "Tweaking Colors", we compare the images before and after processing. In the black and white edition, you won't be able to see the difference between the compared images. For example, the effects such as changed image color, modified contrast, and so on, won't be noticeable. The PDF file contains all these image comparisons. So please keep this file handy while working on the examples in this chapter!

Adjusting brightness and contrast

One often needs to tweak the brightness and contrast level of an image. For example, you may have a photograph that was taken with a basic camera, when there was insufficient light. How would you correct that digitally? The brightness adjustment helps make the image brighter or darker whereas the contrast adjustments emphasize differences between the color and brightness level within the image data. The image can be made lighter or darker using the `ImageEnhance` module in PIL. The same module provides a class that can auto-contrast an image.

Time for action – adjusting brightness and contrast

Let's learn how to modify the image brightness and contrast. First, we will write code to adjust brightness. The `ImageEnhance` module makes our job easier by providing `Brightness` class.

1. Download image `0165_3_12_Before_BRIGHTENING.png` and rename it to `Before_BRIGHTENING.png`.

2. Use the following code:

```
1 import Image
2 import ImageEnhance
3
4 brightness = 3.0
5 peak = Image.open( "C:\\images\\Before_BRIGHTENING.png ")
6 enhancer = ImageEnhance.Brightness(peak)
7 bright = enhancer.enhance(brightness)
8 bright.save( "C:\\images\\BRIGHTENED.png ")
9 bright.show()
```

3. On line 6 in the code snippet, we created an instance of the class `Brightness`. It takes `Image` instance as an argument.

4. Line 7 creates a new image `bright` by using the specified `brightness` value. A value between `0.0` and less than `1.0` gives a darker image, whereas a value greater than `1.0` makes it brighter. A value of `1.0` keeps the brightness of the image unchanged.

5. The original and resultant image are shown in the next illustration.

Comparison of images before and after brightening.

6. Let's move on and adjust the contrast of the brightened image. We will append the following lines of code to the code snippet that brightened the image.

```
10 contrast = 1.3
11 enhancer = ImageEnhance.Contrast(bright)
12 con = enhancer.enhance(contrast)
13 con.save( "C:\\images\\CONTRAST.png ")
14 con.show()
```

7. Thus, similar to what we did to brighten the image, the image contrast was tweaked by using the `ImageEnhance.Contrast` class. A contrast value of `0.0` creates a black image. A value of `1.0` keeps the current contrast.

8. The resultant image is compared with the original in the following illustration.

NOTE: As mentioned in the *Installation and Download Prerequisites* section, the images compared in the following illustration will appear identical if you are reading a hard copy of this book. Please download and refer to the supplementary PDF file Chapter 3 Supplementary Material.pdf. Here, the color images are provided, which will help you see the difference.

The original image with the image displaying the increasing contrast.

9. In the preceding code snippet, we were required to specify a contrast value. If you prefer PIL for deciding an appropriate contrast level, there is a way to do this. The ImageOps.autocontrast functionality sets an appropriate contrast level. This function normalizes the image contrast. Let's use this functionality now.

10. Use the following code:

```
import ImageOps
bright = Image.open( "C:\\images\\BRIGHTENED.png ")
con = ImageOps.autocontrast(bright, cutoff = 0)
con.show()
```

11. The highlighted line in the code is where contrast is automatically set. The autocontrast function computes histogram of the input image. The cutoff argument represents the percentage of lightest and darkest pixels to be trimmed from this histogram. The image is then remapped.

What just happened?

Using the classes and functionality in ImageEnhance module, we learned how to increase or decrease the brightness and the contrast of the image. We also wrote code to auto-contrast an image using functionality provided in the ImageOps module. The things we learned here will be useful in the upcoming sections in this chapter.

Tweaking colors

Another useful operation performed on the image is adjusting the colors within an image. The image may contain one or more bands, containing image data. The image mode contains information about the depth and type of the image pixel data. The most common *modes* we will use in this chapter are RGB (true color, 3x8 bit pixel data), RGBA (true color with transparency mask, 4x8 bit) and L (black and white, 8 bit).

In PIL, you can easily get the information about the bands data within an image. To get the name and number of bands, the getbands() method of the class Image can be used. Here, img is an instance of class Image.

```
>>> img.getbands()
('R', 'G', 'B', 'A')
```

Time for action – swap colors within an image!

To understand some basic concepts, let's write code that just swaps the image band data.

1. Download the image 0165_3_15_COLOR_TWEAK.png and rename it as COLOR_TWEAK.png.

2. Type the following code:

```
1 import Image
2
3 img = Image.open( "C:\\images\\COLOR_TWEAK.png ")
4 img = img.convert('RGBA')
5 r, g, b, alpha = img.split()
6 img = Image.merge( "RGBA ", (g, r, b, alpha))
7 img.show()
```

3. Let's analyze this code now. On line 2, the Image instance is created as usual. Then, we change the mode of the image to RGBA.

> Here we should check if the image already has that mode or if this conversion is possible. You can add that check as an exercise!

4. Next, the call to Image.split() creates separate instances of Image class, each containing a single band data. Thus, we have four Image instances—r, g, b, and alpha corresponding to red, green, and blue bands, and the alpha channel respectively.

5. The code in line 6 does the main image processing. The first argument that `Image.merge` takes `mode` as the first argument whereas the second argument is a tuple of image instances containing band information. It is required to have same size for all the bands. As you can notice, we have swapped the order of band data in `Image` instances `r` and `g` while specifying the second argument.

6. The original and resultant image thus obtained are compared in the next illustration. The color of the flower now has a shade of green and the grass behind the flower is rendered with a shade of red.

 As mentioned in the *Installation and Download Prerequisites* section, the images compared in the following illustration will appear identical if you are reading a hard copy of this book. Please download and refer to the supplementary PDF file `Chapter 3 Supplementary Material.pdf`. Here, the color images are provided that will help you see the difference.

Original (left) and the color swapped image (right).

What just happened?

We accomplished creating an image with its band data swapped. We learned how to use PIL's `Image.split()` and `Image.merge()` to achieve this. However, this operation was performed on the whole image. In the next section, we will learn how to apply color changes to a specific color region.

Changing individual image band

In the previous section, we saw how to change the data represented by the whole band. As a result of this band swapping, the color of the flower was changed to a shade of green and the grass color was rendered as a shade of red. What if we just want to change the color of the flower and keep the color of the grass unchanged? To do this, we will make use of `Image.point` functionality along with `Image.paste` operation discussed in depth in the previous chapter.

However, note that we need to be careful in specifying the color region that needs to be changed. It may also depend on the image. Sometimes, it will select some other regions matching the specified color range, which we don't want.

Time for action – change the color of a flower

We will make use of the same flower image used in the previous section. As mentioned earlier, our task is to change the color of the flower while keeping the grass color unchanged.

1. Add this code in a Python source file.

    ```
    1 import Image
    2
    3 img = Image.open( "C:\\images\\COLOR_TWEAK.png ")
    4 img = img.convert('RGBA')
    5 r, g, b, alpha = img.split()
    6 selection = r.point(lambda i: i > 120 and 150)
    7 selection.save( "C:\\images\\COLOR_BAND_MASK.png ")
    8 r.paste(g, None, selection)
    9 img = Image.merge( "RGBA ", (r, g, b, alpha))
    10 img.save( "C:\\images\\COLOR_CHANGE_BAND.png ")
    11 img.show()
    ```

2. Lines 1 to 5 remain the same as seen earlier. On line 5, we split the original image, creating four `Image` instances, each holding a single band data.

3. A new `Image` instance 'selection' is created on line 6. This is an important operation that holds the key to selectively modify color! So let's see what this line of code does. If you observe the original image, the flower region (well, most of it) is rendered with a shade of red color. So, we have called the `point (function)` method on `Image` instance `r`. The `point` method takes a single function and an argument maps the image through this function. It returns a new `Image` instance.

4. What does this lambda function on line 6 do? Internally, PIL's point function does something of this sort:

```
lst = map(function, range(256)) * no_of_bands
```

In this example, function is nothing but the lambda function. The no_of_bands for the image is 1. Thus, line 6 is used to select a region where the red value is greater than 120. The lst is a list which, in this case has the first 120 values as False whereas the remaining values as 150. The value of 150 plays a role in determining the final color when we perform the paste operation.

5. The image mask thus created after the application of point operation is shown in the following illustration. The white region in this image represents the region captured by the point operation that we just performed. Only the white region will undergo change when we perform paste operation next.

6. On line 8, we perform a paste operation discussed in the last chapter. Here, the image g is pasted onto image r using mask selection. As a result, the band data of image r is modified.

7. Finally, a new Image instance is created using the merge operation, by making use of the individual r, g, b, and alpha image instances containing the new band information.

8. The original and final processed images are compared in the next illustration. The new flower color looks as cool as the original color, doesn't it?

As mentioned in the *Installation and download prerequisites* section, the images compared in the following illustration will appear identical if you are reading a hard copy of this book. Please download and refer to the supplementary PDF file Chapter 3 Supplementary Material.pdf. The color images are provided that will help you see the difference.

What just happened?

We worked out an example that modified a selective color region. Individual image band data was processed to accomplish this task. With the help of point, paste, and merge operations in PIL's Image module, we accomplished changing the color of the flower in the provided image.

Gray scale images

If you want to give a nostalgic effect to an image, one of the many things that you can do is to convert it to gray scale. There is more than one way to create a gray scale image in PIL. When the *mode* is specified as L, the resultant image is gray scale. The basic syntax to convert color images to black and white is:

```
img = img.convert('L')
```

Alternatively, we can use functionality provided in the ImageOps module.

```
img = ImageOps.grayscale(img)
```

If you are creating the image from scratch, the syntax is:

```
img = Image.new('L', size)
```

The following illustration shows the original and the converted gray scale images created using one of these techniques.

Please download and refer to the supplementary PDF file Chapter 3 Supplementary Material.pdf. The color images are provided that will help you see the difference between the following images.

Original and gray scale images of a bridge:

Cook up negatives

Creating a negative of an image is straightforward. We just need to invert each color pixel. Therefore, if you have a color x at a pixel, the negative image will have $(255 - x)$ at that pixel. The ImageOps module makes it very simple. The following line of code creates a negative of an image.

```
img = ImageOps.invert(img)
```

Here is the result of this operation:

Original image (left) and its negative (right).

Blending

Have you ever wished to see yourself in a family photo, taken at a time when you were not around? Or what if you just want to see yourself at the top of Mount Everest at least in a picture? Well, it is possible to do this digitally, using the functionality provided in PIL such as blending, composite image processing, and so on.

In this section, we will learn how to blend images together. As the name suggests, blending means mixing two compatible images to create a new image. The `blend` functionality in PIL creates a new image using two input images of the same `size` and `mode`. Internally, the two input images are interpolated using a constant value of alpha.

In the PIL documentation, it is formulated as:

```
blended_image = in_image1 * (1.0 - alpha) + in_image2 * alpha
```

Looking at this formula, it is clear that `alpha = 1.0` will make the blended image the same as 'n_image2 whereas `alpha = 0.0` returns `in_image1` as the blended image.

Time for action – blending two images

Sometimes, the combined effect of two images mixed together makes a big impact compared to viewing the same images differently. Now it's time to give way to your imagination by blending two pictures together. In this example, our resultant image shows birds flying over the Mackinac bridge in Michigan. However, where did they come from? The birds were not there in the original image of the bridge.

1. Download the following files from Packt website: `0165_3_28_BRIDGE2.png` and `0165_3_29_BIRDS2.png`. Rename these files as `BRIDGE2.png` and `BIRDS2.png` respectively.

2. Add the following code in a Python source file.

```
1 import Image
2
3 img1 = Image.open( "C:\\images\\BRIDGE2.png ")
4 img1 = img1.convert('RGBA')
5
6 img2 = Image.open( "C:\\images\\BIRDS2.png ")
7 img2 = img2.convert('RGBA')
8
9 img = Image.blend(img1, img2, 0.3)
10 img.show()
11 img.save( "C:\\images\\BLEND.png")
```

3.   The next illustration shows the two images before blending, represented by `img1` and `img2` in the code.

Individual images of a bridge and flying birds, before blending.

4.   The lines 3 to 7 open the two input images to be blended. Notice that we have converted both the images RGBA. It need not be necessarily RGBA mode. We can specify the modes such as 'RGB' or 'L'. However, it is required to have both the images with same `size` and `mode`.

5.   The images are blended on line 9 using the `Image.blend` method in PIL. The first two arguments in the `blend` method are two `Image` objects representing the two images to be blended. The third argument defines the transparency factor `alpha`. In this example, the image of the bridge is the main image we want to focus on. Thus, the factor `alpha` is defined such that more transparency is applied to the image of the flying birds while creating the final image. The `alpha` factor can have a value between `0.0` to `1.0`. Note that, while rendering the output image, the second image, `img2`, is multiplied by this `alpha` value whereas the first image is multiplied by `1 - alpha`. This can be represented by the following equation.

```
blended_img = img1 * (1 - alpha) + img2* alpha
```

Thus, if we select an `alpha` factor of, for instance, `0.8`, it means that the birds will appear more opaque compared to the bridge. Try changing the `alpha` factor to see how it changes the resultant image. The resultant image with `alpha` = `0.3` is:

Blended image showing birds flying over a bridge.

6. The picture appears a bit dull due to the transparency effect applied while creating the image. If you convert the input images to mode `L`, the resultant image will look better—however, it will be rendered as gray scale. This is shown in the next illustration.

Blended gray scale image when both the input images have mode `L`.

What just happened?

Blending is an important image enhancement feature. With the help of examples, we accomplished creating blended images. We learned using the `Image.blend` method and applied the transparency factor `alpha` to achieve this task. The technique learned in this chapter will be very useful throughout this chapter. In the next section, we will apply the blending technique to create a transparent image.

Creating transparent images

In the previous section, we learned how to blend two images together. In this section, we will go one step further and see how the same `blend` functionality can be used to create a transparent image! The images with mode RGBA define an `alpha` band. The transparency of the image can be changed by tweaking this band data. `Image.putalpha()` method allows defining new data for the `alpha` band of an image. We will see how to perform point operation to achieve the same effect.

Time for action – create transparency

Let's write a few lines of code that add the transparency effects to an input image.

1. We will use one of the images used in *Chapter 2*. Download `0165_3_25_SMILEY.png` and rename it to `SMILEY.png`.

2. Use the following code:

```
1 import Image
2
3 def addTransparency(img, factor = 0.7 ):
4   img = img.convert('RGBA')
5   img_blender = Image.new('RGBA', img.size, (0,0,0,0))
6   img = Image.blend(img_blender, img, factor)
7   return img
8
9 img = Image.open( "C:\\images\\SMILEY.png ")
10
11 img = addTransparency(img, factor =0.7)
```

3. In this example, the `addTransparency()` function takes the `img` instance as input and returns a new image instance with the desired level of transparency.

4. Now let's see how this function works. On line 4, we first convert the image mode to RGBA. As discussed in an earlier section, you can add a conditional here to see if the image is already in the RGBA mode.

5. Next, we create a new Image class instance, image_blender, using the Image.new method. It has the same size and mode as the input image. The third argument represents the color. Here, we specify the transparency as 0.

6. On line 6, two images, img (input image) and img_blender, are blended together by applying a constant alpha value. The function then returns this modified Image instance.

7. The original image and the one with the transparency effect are compared. The images are the screenshots of the images opened in the GIMP editor. This is done so that you clearly understand the effect of transparency. The checkered pattern in these images represents the canvas. Notice how the canvas appears in the transparent image.

8. There is another simple way to add transparency to an image, using the Image.point functionality! Enter the following code in a Python source file and execute it.

```
1 import Image
2 img = Image.open( "C:\\images\\SMILEY.png ")
3 r, g, b, alpha = img.split()
4 alpha = alpha.point(lambda i: i>0 and 178)
5 img.putalpha(alpha)
6 img.save( "C:\\images\\Transparent_SMILEY.png ")
```

9. In this new code, we split the original image into four new image instance, each having one of the image band data (r, g, b, or alpha). Note that we are assuming here that the mode of the image is RGBA. If it is not, you need to convert this image to RGBA! As an exercise, you can add that check in the code.

10. Next, on line 4, the Image.point method is called. The lambda function operates on the alpha band data. It sets the value as 178. This is roughly equal to the alpha factor of 0.7 that we set earlier. It is computed here as int(255*0.7)). In the *Changing individual image band* section, where we learned modifying colors within images, the point operation was thoroughly discussed.

11. On line 5, we put back the new `alpha` band data in `img`. The resultant images using `blend` and `point` functionality are shown in the next illustration.

Image before and after adding transparency.

What just happened?

We accomplished adding transparency effect to an image. This is a very useful image enhancement that we need from time to time. We learned how to create a transparent image using two different techniques, namely, using `Image.blend` functionality and `Image.point` operation. The knowledge gained in this section will be applied later in this chapter.

Making composites with image mask

So far, we have already seen how to blend two images together. It was done using the `Image.blend` operation where the two input images were blended by using a constant `alpha` transparency factor. In this section, we will learn another technique to combine two images together. Here, instead of a constant `alpha` factor, an image instance that defines the transparency mask is used as the third argument. Another difference is that the input images need not have the same `mode`. For instance, the first image can be with mode `L` and the second with mode `RGBA`. The syntax to create composite images is:

```
outImage = Image.composite(img1, img2, mask)
```

Here, the arguments to the composite method are `Image` instances. The mask is specified as `alpha`. The mode for mask image instance can be 1, `L`, or `RGBA`.

Time for action – making composites with image mask

We will mix the same two images blended in another section. Just to try out something different, in the composite image, we will focus on the flying birds instead of the bridge.

1. We will use the same set of input images as used in the *Blending* section.

```
1 import Image
2
3 img1 = Image.open( "C:\\images\\BRIDGE2.png ")
4 img1 = img1.convert('RGBA')
5
6 img2 = Image.open( "C:\\images\\BIRDS2.png ")
7 img2 = img2.convert('RGBA')
8
9 r, g, b, alpha = img2.split()
10 alpha = alpha.point(lambda i: i>0 and 204)
11
12 img = Image.composite(img2, img1, alpha)
13 img.show()
```

2. The code until line 7 is identical to the one illustrated in the blending example. Note that the two input images need not have the same mode. On line 10, the Image. point method is called. The lambda function operates on the alpha band data. The code on lines 9 and 10 is similar to that illustrated in the section *Creating Transparent Images*. Please refer to that section for further details. The only difference is that the pixel value is set as 204. This modifies the band data in the image instance alpha. This value of 204 is roughly equivalent to the alpha factor of 0.7 if the image were to be blended. What this implies is the bridge will have a fading effect and the flying birds will appear prominently in the composite image.

3. One thing you will notice here is we are not putting the modified alpha band data back in img2. Instead, on line 12, the composite image is created using the mask as alpha.

4. The resultant composite image is shown in the next illustration—with emphasis on the image of the flying birds.

What just happened?

We learned how to create an image combining two images, using an `alpha` mask. This was accomplished by using `Image.composite` functionality.

Project: Watermark Maker Tool

We have now learned enough image enhancement techniques to take up a simple project applying these techniques. Let's create a simple command line utility, a "Watermark Maker Tool". Although we call it a "Watermark Maker ", it actually provides some more useful features. Using this utility, you can add the date stamp to the image (the date on which the image was enhanced using this tool). It also enables embedding custom text within an image. The tool can be run on the command line using the following syntax:

```
python WaterMarkMaker.py [options]
```

Where, the [options] are as follows:

- ◆ --image1: The file path of the main image that provides canvas.
- ◆ --waterMark: The file path of the watermark image (if any).
- ◆ --mark_pos: The coordinates of top-left corner of the watermark image to be embedded. The values should be specified in double quotes, like **100, 50**.
- ◆ --text: The text that should appear in the output image.
- ◆ --text_pos: The coordinates of top-left corner of the TEXT to be embedded. The values should be specified in double quotes, like **100, 50**.
- ◆ --transparency: The transparency factor for the watermark (if any)
- ◆ --dateStamp: Flag (True or False) that determines whether to insert date stamp in the image. If True, the date stamp at the time this image was processed will be inserted.

The following is an example that shows how to run this tool with all the options specified.

```
python WaterMarkMaker.py --image1= "C:\foo.png "
        --watermark= "C:\watermark.png "
        --mark_pos= "200, 200 "
        --text= "My Text "
        --text_pos= "10, 10 "
        --transparency=0.4
        --dateStamp=True
```

This creates an output image file WATERMARK.png, with a watermark and text at the specified anchor point within the image.

Time for action – Watermark Maker Tool

Think about all the methods we would need to accomplish this. The first thing that comes to mind is a function that will process the command-line arguments mentioned earlier. Next, we need to write code that can add a watermark image to the main image. Let's call this addWaterMark(). On similar lines, we will need methods that add text and date stamp to the image. We will call this addText() and addDateStamp() respectively. With this information, we will develop code to make this work. In this project, we will encapsulate this functionality in a class, but it is not necessary. We do so to make this tool extensible for future use.

1. Download the file WaterMarkMaker.py. This has the code required in this project. Just keep it for further use. Some of the methods will not be discussed in this section. If you encounter difficulties while developing those methods, you can always go back and refer to this file.

2. Open a new Python source file and declare the following class and its methods. Just create empty methods for now. We will expand these in as we proceed along.

```python
import Image, ImageDraw, ImageFont
import os, sys
import getopt
from datetime import date

class WaterMarkMaker:
 def __init__(self):
  pass
 def addText(self):
  pass
 def addDateStamp(self):
  pass
 def _addTextWorker(self, txt, dateStamp = False):
  pass
 def addWaterMark(self):
  pass
 def addTransparency(self, img):
  pass
 def createImageObjects(self):
  pass
 def _getMarkPosition(self, canvasImage, markImage):
  return
 def processArgs(self):
  pass
 def printUsage(self):
  pass
```

3. Next, we will write code in the constructor of this class.

```python
def __init__(self):
 # Image paths
 self.waterMarkPath = ''
 self.mainImgPath = ''
 # Text to be embedded
 self.text = ''
 # Transparency Factor
 self.t_factor = 0.5
 # Anchor point for embedded text
 self.text_pos = (0, 0)
 # Anchor point for watermark.
 self.mark_pos = None

 # Date stamp
 self.dateStamp = False
 # Image objects
 self.waterMark = None
 self.mainImage = None
```

```
    self.processArgs()
    self.createImageObjects()
    self.addText()
    self.addWaterMark()

    if self.dateStamp:
     self.addDateStamp()
     self.mainImage.save( "C:\\images\\WATERMARK.png ")
     self.mainImage.show()
```

4.   The code is self-explanatory. First, all the necessary attributes are initialized and then the relevant methods are called to create the image with watermark and/or the embedded text. Let's write the methods in the order in which they are called in the constructor.

5.   The `processArgs()` method processes the command-line arguments. You can write this method as an exercise. Alternatively, you can use code in the `WaterMarkMaker.py` file from the Packt website. The process arguments method should take the assignments as shown in the following table. In the reference files, `getopt` module is used to process these arguments. Alternatively, you can use `OptionParser` in the `optparse` module of Python.

Argument	Value	Argument	Value
image1	self.mainImgPath	text_pos	self.text_pos
waterMark	self.waterMarkPath	transparency	self.t_factor
mark_pos	self.mark_pos	dateStamp	self.dateStamp
text	self.text		

6.   The `printUsage()` method just prints how to run this tool. You can easily write that method.

7.   Let's review the `addText()` and `_addTextWorker()` methods now. Note that some of the code comments are removed from the code samples for clarity. You can refer to the code in `WaterMarkMaker.py` for detailed comments.

```
def addText(self):
 if not self.text:
  return
 if self.mainImage is None:
  print "\n Main Image not defined.Returning. "
  return
 txt = self.text
 self._addTextWorker(txt)
```

The `addText()` method simply calls `_addTextWorker()` by providing the `self.text` argument received from the command line.

8. The `_addTextWorker()` does the main processing that embeds the text within the image. This method is used in the following code:

```
1 def _addTextWorker(self, txt, dateStamp = False):
2  size = self.mainImage.size
3  color = (0, 0, 0)
4  textFont = ImageFont.truetype( "arial.ttf ", 50)
5
6  # Create an ImageDraw instance to draw the text.
7  imgDrawer = ImageDraw.Draw(self.mainImage)
8  textSize = imgDrawer.textsize(txt, textFont)
9
10  if dateStamp:
11   pos_x = min(10, size[0])
12   pos_y = size[1] - textSize[0]
13   pos = (pos_x, pos_y)
14  else:
15   # We need to add text. Use self.text_pos
16   pos = self.text_pos
17  #finally add the text
18  imgDrawer.text(pos, txt, font=textFont)
19
20  if ( textSize[0] > size[0]
21   or textSize[1] > size[1] ):
22   print ( "\n Warning, the specified text "
23     "going out of bounds. " )
```

In *Chapter 2*, we created a new image containing a text string. It read "Not really a fancy text ". Do you remember? Here, we have written similar code with some improvements. The function `ImageDraw.Draw` takes the `self.mainImage` (an `Image` instance) as an argument to create a `Draw` instance, `imgDrawer`.

On line 18, the text is embedded onto the given position using a given font. The `text()` method of `Draw` instance takes three arguments, namely, `position`, `text`, and the `font`. In the previous chapter, we already made use of the first two arguments. The third argument `font` is an instance of class `ImageFont` in PIL.

On line 4, we create this instance specifying a font type (`arial.ttf`) and the font size (=50). The given text string is now added on to the main image!

9. The next method we will discuss is `addDateStamp()`. It calls the same `_addTextWorker()` in the end. However, the placement of this date stamp is fixed at the bottom left corner of the image and of course we create our date string by using Python's `datetime` module. The code is illustrated below along with the import statement declared earlier.

```
from datetime import date

def addDateStamp(self):
 today = date.today()
 time_tpl = today.timetuple()
 year, month, day = map(str, time_tpl)
 datestamp = "%s/%s/%s "%(year,month, day)
 self._addTextWorker(datestamp, dateStamp = True)
```

The first line of the code in this method creates a date instance `today` with today's date provided as a `3-tuple`. Something like this: `datetime.date(2010, 1, 20)`. Next, we call the `timetuple` method of `date` instance. The first three values in this tuple are `year`, `month`, and `day` respectively.

The rest of the code is just the processing of the date stamp as a text string and then calling the main worker method just discussed.

10. Now we will review the code in the `addWaterMark()` method. A **watermark** is typically a semi-transparent image that appears in the main image. There are two different approaches to accomplish creating a watermark. The following code considers both these approaches.

```
1 def addWaterMark(self):
2  # There are more than one way to achieve creating a
3  # watermark. The following flag,if True, will use
4  # Image.composite to create the watermark instead of a
5  # simple Image.paste
6  using_composite = False
7
8  if self.waterMark is None:
9   return
10  # Add Transparency
11  self.waterMark = self.addTransparency(self.waterMark)
12  # Get the anchor point
13  pos_x, pos_y = self._getMarkPosition(self.mainImage,
14          self.waterMark)
15  # Create the watermark
16  if not using_composite:
17   # Paste the image using the transparent
18   # watermark image as the mask.
```

```
19    self.mainImage.paste(self.waterMark,
20          (pos_x, pos_y),
21          self.waterMark)
22   else:
23    # Alternate method to create water mark.
24    # using Image.composite create a new canvas
25    canvas = Image.new('RGBA',
26          self.mainImage.size,
27          (0,0,0,0))
28    # Paste the watermark on the canvas
29    canvas.paste(self.waterMark, (pos_x, pos_y))
30    # Create a composite image
31    self.mainImage = Image.composite(canvas,
32          self.mainImage,
33          canvas)
```

11. To add a watermark, first we make the image transparent. This is accomplished by calling the `addTransparency()` method. This method also changes the `mode` of the image to `RGBA`. This method is shown here. It is almost identical to the one we developed in an earlier section where an image was made transparent using blending functionality of PIL.

```
def addTransparency(self, img):
  img = img.convert('RGBA')
  img_blender = Image.new('RGBA',
        img.size,
        (0,0,0,0))
  img = Image.blend(img_blender,
        img,
        self.t_factor)
  return img
```

Next, on line 13, we determine the anchor point on the main image, where the top-left corner of the watermark will appear. By default, we will match the bottom-left corner of the watermark with the main image. You can review the code for method `_getMarkPosition()` in the file `WaterMarkMaker.py` to see how this is done. Moving forward, the code block between lines 16-21 creates the watermark using the paste functionality. This is one way to create the image with a watermark. The arguments provided in the `Image.paste` function are `image to be pasted`, `anchor point`, and `mask`. The `mask` is selected as the watermark image itself so as to consider the transparency. Otherwise, the watermark image will appear opaque. The resultant image with and without image mask specification is compared in the following illustration.

Resultant images using Image.paste operation created with and without mask.

Next, in the `else` condition block (lines 22 to 33), we use `Image.composite` functionality in PIL to embed the watermark. The dimensions of the example watermark image used here are 200x200 pixels, whereas the dimensions of the main image are 800x600 pixels. To use the `composite()` method, we need to make these images of the same size, and yet, make sure to paste the watermark at the specified position. How to achieve this? The first thing to do is to create a canvas image to hold the watermark. The canvas image is of the same size as that of the main image. The code block 25-29 creates the canvas and pastes the watermark at an appropriate location.

Finally, on line 31, the composite image is created using the `canvas` image instance as the alpha mask.

12. Now lets run this tool! You can use your own image files for main image or the watermark. Alternatively, you can use the image `0165_3_34_KokanPeak_for_WATERMARK.png` as the main image and `0165_3_38_SMILEY_small.png` as the watermark image. The command-line arguments for this run are:

```
python WaterMarkMaker.py
--image1= "C:\images\KokanPeak_for_WATERMARK.png "
--text= "Peak "
--text_pos= "10, 10 "
--waterMark= "C:\\images\\SMILEY_small.png "
--dateStamp=True
```

13. The resultant image with text, date stamp, and the watermark is shown in the next illustration.

Final processed image with text, date stamp, and a watermark.

What just happened?

We created a very useful utility that can add a watermark and/or a text string and/or a date stamp to an input image. We used several of the image processing techniques learned in this as well as in an earlier chapter on image processing. Especially, image enhancement features such as blending, creating composite images, and adding transparency were applied to accomplish this task. Additionally we made use of common functionality such as pasting an image, drawing text onto the image, and so on.

Have a go hero – do more with Watermark Maker Tool

Our Watermark Maker tool needs an upgrade. Extend this application so that it supports following the features:

1. The text or the date stamp color is currently hardcoded. Add a new command-line argument so that a text color can be specified as an optional argument.

2. Add some standard default options for specifying anchor position for text, date stamp, and the watermark image. These options can be TOP_RIGHT, TOP_LEFT, BOTTOM_RIGHT, and BOTTOM_LEFT.

3. The command-line options list is too long. Add code so that all arguments can be read from a text file.

4. Add support so that it can batch-process images to create desired effect.

Applying image filters

In the previous chapter, `filter` argument was used while performing the image resize operation. This `filter` determined the quality of the output image. However, there were only four `filter` options available and the scope was limited to a resize operation. In this section, some additional image enhancement filters will be introduced. These are predefined filters and can be directly used on any input image. Following is a basic syntax used for applying a filter.

```
img = Image.open('foo.jpg')
filtered_image = img.filter(FILTER)
```

Here, we created a new image `filtered_image` by filtering image `img` . The FILTER argument can be one of the predefined filters in the `ImageFilter` module of PIL for filtering the image data. PIL offers several predefined image enhancement filters. These can be broadly classified into the following categories. With the help of examples, we will learn some of these in the coming sections.

◆ **Blurring and sharpening**: BLUR, SHARPEN, SMOOTH, SMOOTH_MORE

◆ **Edge detection and enhancement**: EDGE_ENHANCE, EDGE_ENHANCE_MORE, FIND_EDGES, CONTOUR

◆ **Distortion/special effects**: EMBOSS

The file `ImageFilter.py` in the PIL source code defines the-mentioned filter classes. You can create your own custom filter by tweaking various arguments in these filter classes.

```
filterargs = size, scale, offset, kernel
```

Where, `kernel` is the *convolution kernel*. Here, the '*convolution*' is a mathematical operation, on the image matrix by the '*kernel*' matrix to produce a resultant matrix.

The size of matrix is specified by the *size* argument. It is specified in the form (width, height). This can either be (3, 3) or (5, 5) size in the current PIL version. The result of each pixel is divided by `scale` argument. This is an optional argument. The `offset` value, if specified, has its value is added to the result *after* dividing it by the scale argument.

In some of the image enhancement filter examples, we will create our own custom filter.

Smoothing

Smoothing an image means reducing the *noise* within the image data. For this, certain mathematical approximation is applied on the image data to recognize the important patterns within the image. The `ImageFilter` module defines `class SMOOTH` for smoothing an image. PIL specifies the following default filter arguments for the image-smoothing filter.

```
filterargs = (3, 3),
    13,
    0,
    (1, 1, 1,
     1, 5, 1,
     1, 1, 1)
```

Time for action – smoothing an image

Let's work out an example where a smoothing filter will be applied to an image.

1. Download the image file `0165_3_Before_SMOOTHING.png` from the Packt website and save it as `Before_SMOOTHING.png`.

2. This is a low-resolution image scanned from a developed photograph. As you can see, there is a lot of *salt-and-pepper* noise in the image. We will apply smoothing filter to reduce some of this noise in the image data.

3. Add the following code in a Python file.
    ```python
    import ImageFilter
    import Image

    img = Image.open( "C:\\images\\Before_SMOOTH.png ")
    img = img.filter(ImageFilter.SMOOTH)
    img.save( "C:\\images\\ch3\\After_SMOOTH.png")
    img.show()
    ```

4. The highlighted line in the code is where the smoothing filter is applied to the image. The results are shown in the next illustration.

Picture before and after smoothing:

5. To reduce the noise further down, you can use `ImageFilter.SMOOTH_MORE` or try reapplying the `ImageFilter.SMOOTH` multiple times until you get the desired effect.

```
import ImageFilter
import Image

img = Image.open( "C:\\images\\0165_3_2_Before_SMOOTH.png ")
i = 0
while i < 5:
  img = img.filter(ImageFilter.SMOOTH)
  i += 1
img.save( "C:\\images\\0165_3_3_After_SMOOTH_5X.png")
img.show()
```

As you can observe in the illustration, the noise is further reduced but the image appears a little bit hazy. Thus, one has to determine an appropriate level of smoothness.

Comparison of the resultant image with single and multiple smoothing filters.

What just happened?

We learned how to reduce high-level noise from the image data using the smoothing filter in the `ImageFilter` module.

Sharpening

In the earlier section, we learned image-smoothing techniques. If you want to view the finer details within an image, a sharpening filter can be applied over the image. Like image-smoothing filters, PIL provides predefined filters for sharpening called `ImageFilter.SHARPEN`. The basic syntax to sharpen an image is as follows:

```
img = img.filter(ImageFilter.SHARPEN)
```

You can try this filter on the image that was smoothed multiple times in the earlier section.

Blurring

In general, blurring makes an image lose its focus. In PIL, the predefined filter for this is `ImageFilter.BLUR`. This is typically useful if you want to fade out the background to highlight some object in the foreground. The syntax is similar to the one used for other filters.

```
img = img.filter(ImageFilter.BLUR)
```

The following illustration shows the effect of this filter.

Image before and after application of blurring filter:

Edge detection and enhancements

In this section, we will learn some general edge detection and enhancement filters. The edge enhance filter improves the edge contrast. It increases the contrast of the region very close to the edge. This makes the edge stand out. The edge detection algorithm looks for discontinuities within the pixel data of the image. For example, it looks for sharp change in the brightness to identify an edge.

Time for action – detecting and enhancing edges

Let's see how the edge detection and enhancement filters modify the data of a picture. The photograph that we will use is a close-up of a leaf. The original photo is shown in the next illustration. Applying an edge detection filter on this image creates a cool effect where only edges are highlighted and the remaining portion of the image is rendered as black.

1. Download the image `0165_3_6_Before_EDGE_ENHANCE.png` from the Packt website and save it as `Before_EDGE_ENHANCE.png`.

2. Add the following code in a Python file.

```
1 import Image
2 import ImageFilter
3 import os
4 paths = [ "C:\images\Before_EDGE_ENHANCE.png ",
5     "C:\images\After_EDGE_ENHANCE.png ",
6     "C:\images\EDGE_DETECTION_1.png ",
7     "C:\images\EDGE_DETECTION_2.png "
8     ]
9 paths = map(os.path.normpath, paths)
10
```

```
11 ( imgPath ,outImgPath1,
12 outImgPath2, outImgPath3) = paths
13 img = Image.open(imgPath)
14 img1 = img.filter(ImageFilter.FIND_EDGES)
15 img1.save(outImgPath1)
16
17 img2 = img.filter(ImageFilter.EDGE_ENHANCE)
18 img2.save(outImgPath2)
19
20 img3 = img2.filter(ImageFilter.FIND_EDGES)
21 img3.save(outImgPath3)
```

3. Line 14 modifies the image data using the FIND_EDGES filter and then the resulting image is saved.

4. Next, we modify the original image data, so that more veins within the leaf become visible. This is accomplished by the application of ENHANCE_EDGES filter (line 17).

5. On line 20, the FIND_EDGES filter is applied on the edge-enhanced image. The resultant images are compared in the next illustration.

a) First row: Images before and after application of edge enhancement filter b) Second row: The edges detected by ImageFilter.FIND_EDGES filter.

What just happened?

We created an image with enhanced edges by applying the EDGE_ENHANCE filter in the ImageFilter module. We also learned how to detect edges within the image using the edge detection filter. In the next section, we will apply a special form of the edge filter that highlights or darkens the detected edges within an image. It is called an embossing filter.

Embossing

In image processing, embossing is a process that gives an image a 3-D appearance. The edges within the image appear raised above the image surface. This optical illusion is accomplished by highlighting or darkening edges within the image. The following illustration shows original and embossed images. Notice how the edges along the characters in the embossed image are either highlighted or darkened to give the desired effect.

The ImageFiltermodule provides a predefined filter, ImageFilter.EMBOSS, to achieve the embossing effect for an image. The convolution kernel of this filter is of a (3, 3) size and the default filter arguments are:

```
filterargs = (3, 3), 1, 128, (
  -1, 0, 0,
  0, 1, 0,
  0, 0, 0
  )
```

Time for action – embossing

1. Download the image 0165_3_4_Bird_EMBOSS.png from the Packt website and save it as Bird_EMBOSS.png.

2. Add the following code in a Python file:
```
1 import os, sys
2 import Image
3 import ImageFilter
4 imgPath = "C:\images\Bird_EMBOSS.png "
5 outImgPath = "C:\images\Bird_EMBOSSED.png "
6 imgPath = os.path.normpath(imgPath)
```

```
 6 outImgPath = os.path.normpath(outImgPath)
 7 bird = Image.open(imgPath)
 8 bird = bird.filter(ImageFilter.EMBOSS)
 9 bird.save(outImgPath)
10 bird.show()
```

3. On line 9, the embossing filter `ImageFilter.EMBOSS` is applied to the image object `bird`. The resultant embossed image of the bird is shown in the next illustration.

Original and embossed images of a bird using `ImageFilter.EMBOSS`.

 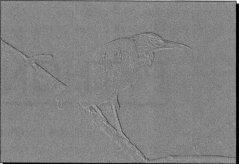

What just happened?

We applied an embossing filter on an image and created an embossed image. As seen in previous section, the filter modified the brightness of various edges to make them appear highlighted or darkened. This created an optical illusion where the image appeared raised above the surface.

Adding a border

How would you prefer viewing a family photo? As a bare picture or enclosed in a nice photo frame? In `ImageOps` module, PIL provides a preliminary functionality to add a plain border around the image. Here is the syntax to achieve this:

```
img = ImageOps.expand(img, border, fill)
```

This code creates a border around the image. Internally, PIL just creates an image that has dimesions such that:

```
new_width = ( right_border_thickness + image_width +
    left_border_thickness )

new_height = ( top_border_thickness + image_height +
    bottom_border_thickness )
```

Then, the original image is pasted onto this new image to create the border effect. The `border` argument in the preceding code suggests border thickness in pixels. It is uniform in this example and is set to 20 pixels for left, right, top, and bottom borders. The `fill` argument specifies the border color. It can be a number in the range 0 to 255 indicating the pixel color, where 0 is for 'black' and 255 for 'white' border. Alternatively, you can specify a string representing a color, such as 'red' for red color, and so on.

Time for action – enclosing a picture in a photoframe

Let's develop code that adds a frame around a picture.

1. Download the image `0165_3_15_COLOR_TWEAK.png` and rename it to `FLOWER.png`.

2. Add the following code in a Python source file. Make sure to modify the code to specify in the input and output paths appropriately.

```
1 import Image, ImageOps
2 img = Image.open( "C:\\images\\FLOWER.png ")
3 img = ImageOps.expand(img, border=20, fill='black')
4 img = ImageOps.expand(img, border=40, fill='silver')
5 img = ImageOps.expand(img, border=2, fill='black')
6 img.save( "C:\\images\\PHOTOFRAME.png ")
7 img.show()
```

3. In this code snippet, three stacked borders are created. The innermost border layer is rendered with black color. This is intentionally chosen darker.

4. Next, there is a middle layer of border, rendered with a lighter color (silver color in this case). This is done by the code on line 4. It is thicker than the innermost border.

5. The outermost border is created by code on line 5. It is a very thin layer rendered as black.

6. Together, these three layers of borders create an optical illusion of a photo frame, by making the border appear raised above the original image.

7. The following image shows the result of adding this border to the specified input image—it shows the image before and after enclosing in a 'photo frame'.

What just happened?

We learned how to create a simple border around an image. By calling `ImageOps.expand` multiple times, we created a multi-layered border having each layer of variable thickness and color. With this, we accomplished creating an optical illusion where the picture appears to be enclosed within a simple photo frame.

Summary

This chapter taught us several important image enhancement techniques, specifically:

- With the help of ample examples, we learned how to adjust the color, brightness, and contrast of an image.

- We learned how to blend images together create composites using image mask and how to add transparency.

- We applied blending, pasting, and other techniques learned to develop an interesting tool. We implemented features in this tool that enabled inserting a watermark, text, or date stamp to an image.

- A number of image enhancement filters were discussed. Using code snippets we learned how to reduce high-level noise from image, enhance edges, add sharpening or blurring effects, emboss an image, and so on.

- We learned miscellaneous other useful image enhancements such as creating negatives and adding border effects to the image.

4
Fun with Animations

Cartoons have always fascinated the young and old alike. An animation is where the imaginary creatures become alive and take us to a totally different world.

Animation is a sequence of frames displayed quickly one after the other. This creates an optical illusion where the objects, for instance, appear to be moving around. This chapter will introduce you to the fundamentals of developing animations using Python and Pyglet multimedia application development frameworks. Pyglet is designed to do 3D operations, but we will use it for developing very simple 2D animations in this book.

In this chapter, we shall:

- ◆ Learn the basics of Pyglet framework. This will be used to develop code to create or play animations.

- ◆ Learn how to play an existing animation file and create animations using a sequence of images.

- ◆ Work on project 'Bowling animation', where animations can be controlled using inputs from the keyboard.

- ◆ Develop code to create an animation using different *regions* of a single image.

- ◆ Work on an exciting project that animates a car moving in a thunderstorm. This project will cover many important things covered throughout this chapter.

So let's get on with it.

Installation prerequisites

We will cover the prerequisites for the installation of Pyglet in this section.

Pyglet

Pyglet provides an API for multimedia application development using Python. It is an OpenGL-based library, which works on multiple platforms. It is primarily used for developing gaming applications and other graphically-rich applications. Pyglet can be downloaded from `http://www.pyglet.org/download.html`. Install Pyglet version 1.1.4 or later. The Pyglet installation is pretty straightforward.

Windows platform

For Windows users, the Pyglet installation is straightforward—use the binary distribution `Pyglet 1.1.4.msi` or later.

 You should have Python 2.6 installed. For Python 2.4, there are some more dependencies. We won't discuss them in this book, because we are using Python 2.6 to build multimedia applications.

If you install Pyglet from the source, see the instructions under the next sub-section, *Other platforms*.

Other platforms

The Pyglet website provides a binary distribution file for Mac OS X. Download and install `pyglet-1.1.4.dmg` or later.

On Linux, install Pyglet 1.1.4 or later if it is available in the package repository of your operating system. Otherwise, it can be installed from source tarball as follows:

- Download and extract the tarball `pyglet-1.1.4.tar.gz` or a later version.
- Make sure that `python` is a recognizable command in shell. Otherwise, set the `PYTHONPATH` environment variable to the correct Python executable path.
- In a shell window, change to the mentioned extracted directory and then run the following command:

  ```
  python setup.py install
  ```

- Review the succeeding installation instructions using the README/install instruction files in the Pyglet source tarball.

If you have the package setuptools (http://pypi.python.org/pypi/setuptools) installed, the Pyglet installation should be very easy. However, for this, you will need a runtime egg of Pyglet. But the egg file for Pyglet is not available at http://pypi.python.org. If you get hold of a Pyglet egg file, it can be installed by running the following command on Linux or Mac OS X. You will need administrator access to install the package:

`$sudo easy_install -U pyglet`

Summary of installation prerequisites

The following table illustrates installation prerequisites depending on the version and platform.

Package	Download location	Version	Windows platform	Linux/Unix/OS X platforms
Python	http://python.org/download/releases/	2.6.4 (or any 2.6.x)	Install using binary distribution	◆ Install from binary; also install additional developer packages (For example, with python-devel in the package name in a rpm-based Linux distribution). ◆ Build and install from the source tarball.
Pyglet	http://www.pyglet.org/download.html	1.1.4 or later	Install using binary distribution (the .msi file)	◆ **Mac**: Install using disk image file (.dmg file). ◆ **Linux**: Build and install using the source tarball.

Testing the installation

Before proceeding further, ensure that Pyglet is installed properly. To test this, just start Python from the command line and type the following:

`>>>import pyglet`

If this import is successful, we are all set to go!

A primer on Pyglet

Pyglet provides an API for multimedia application development using Python. It is an OpenGL-based library that works on multiple platforms. It is primarily used for developing gaming and other graphically-rich applications. We will cover some important aspects of Pyglet framework.

Important components

We will briefly discuss some of the important modules and packages of Pyglet that we will use. Note that this is just a tiny chunk of the Pyglet framework. Please review the Pyglet documentation to know more about its capabilities, as this is beyond the scope of this book.

Window

The `pyglet.window.Window` module provides the user interface. It is used to create a window with an OpenGL context. The `Window` class has API methods to handle various events such as mouse and keyboard events. The window can be viewed in normal or full screen mode. Here is a simple example of creating a `Window` instance. You can define a size by specifying `width` and `height` arguments in the constructor.

```
win = pyglet.window.Window()
```

The background color for the image can be set using OpenGL call `glClearColor`, as follows:

```
pyglet.gl.glClearColor(1, 1, 1, 1)
```

This sets a white background color. The first three arguments are the red, green, and blue color values. Whereas, the last value represents the alpha. The following code will set up a gray background color.

```
pyglet.gl.glClearColor(0.5, 0.5, 0.5, 1)
```

The following illustration shows a screenshot of an empty window with a gray background color.

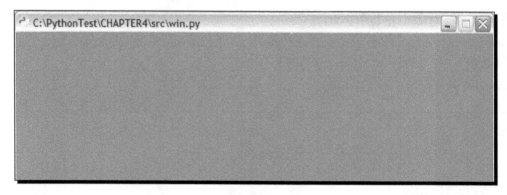

Image

The `pyglet.image` module enables the drawing of images on the screen. The following code snippet shows a way to create an image and display it at a specified position within the Pyglet window.

```
img = pyglet.image.load('my_image.bmp')
x, y, z = 0, 0, 0
img.blit(x, y, z)
```

A later section will cover some important operations supported by the `pyglet.image` module.

Sprite

This is another important module. It is used to display an image or an animation frame within a Pyglet window discussed earlier. It is an image instance that allows us to position an image anywhere within the Pyglet window. A `sprite` can also be rotated and scaled. It is possible to create multiple sprites of the same image and place them at different locations and with different orientations inside the window.

Animation

`Animation` module is a part of `pyglet.image` package. As the name indicates, `pyglet.image.Animation` is used to create an animation from one or more image frames. There are different ways to create an animation. For example, it can be created from a sequence of images or using `AnimationFrame` objects. We will study these techniques later in the chapter. An animation sprite can be created and displayed within the Pyglet window.

AnimationFrame

This creates a single frame of an animation from a given image. An animation can be created from such `AnimationFrame` objects. The following line of code shows an example.

```
animation = pyglet.image.Animation(anim_frames)
```

`anim_frames` is a list containing instances of `AnimationFrame`.

Clock

Among many other things, this module is used for scheduling functions to be called at a specified time. For example, the following code calls a method `moveObjects` ten times every second.

```
pyglet.clock.schedule_interval(moveObjects, 1.0/10)
```

Displaying an image

In the *Image* sub-section, we learned how to load an image using image.blit. However, image *blitting* is a less efficient way of drawing images. There is a better and preferred way to display the image by creating an instance of Sprite. Multiple Sprite objects can be created for drawing the same image. For example, the same image might need to be displayed at various locations within the window. Each of these images should be represented by separate Sprite instances. The following simple program just loads an image and displays the Sprite instance representing this image on the screen.

```
1  import pyglet
2
3  car_img= pyglet.image.load('images/car.png')
4  carSprite = pyglet.sprite.Sprite(car_img)
5  window = pyglet.window.Window()
6  pyglet.gl.glClearColor(1, 1, 1, 1)
7
8  @window.event
9  def on_draw():
10     window.clear()
11     carSprite.draw()
12
13 pyglet.app.run()
```

On line 3, the image is opened using pyglet.image.load call. A Sprite instance corresponding to this image is created on line 4. The code on line 6 sets white background for the window. The on_draw is an API method that is called when the window needs to be redrawn. Here, the image sprite is drawn on the screen. The next illustration shows a loaded image within a Pyglet window.

In various examples in this chapter and others, the file path strings are hardcoded. We have used forward slashes for the file path. Although this works on Windows platform, the convention is to use backward slashes. For example, images/car.png is represented as images\car.png. Additionally, you can also specify a complete path to the file by using the os.path.join method in Python. Regardless of what slashes you use, the os.path.normpath will make sure it modifies the slashes to fit to the ones used for the platform. The use of os.path.normpath is illustrated in the following snippet:

```
import os
original_path = 'C:/images/car.png"
new_path = os.path.normpath(original_path)
```

The preceding image illustrates Pyglet window showing a still image.

Mouse and keyboard controls

The `Window` module of Pyglet implements some API methods that enable user input to a playing animation. The API methods such as `on_mouse_press` and `on_key_press` are used to capture mouse and keyboard events during the animation. These methods can be overridden to perform a specific operation.

Adding sound effects

The `media` module of Pyglet supports audio and video playback. The following code loads a media file and plays it during the animation.

```
1 background_sound = pyglet.media.load(
2                 'C:/AudioFiles/background.mp3',
3                 streaming=False)
4 background_sound.play()
```

The second optional argument provided on line 3 decodes the media file completely in the memory at the time the media is loaded. This is important if the media needs to be played several times during the animation. The API method `play()` starts streaming the specified media file.

Animations with Pyglet

The Pyglet framework provides a number of modules required to develop animations. Many of these were discussed briefly in earlier sections. Lets now learn techniques to create 2D animations using Pyglet.

Viewing an existing animation

If you already have an animation in, for example, `.gif` file format, it can be loaded and displayed directly with Pyglet. The API method to use here is `pyglet.image.load_animation`.

Time for action – viewing an existing animation

This is going to be a short exercise. The goal of this section is to develop a primary understanding on use of Pyglet for viewing animations. So let's get on with it.

1. Download the file `SimpleAnimation.py` from the Packt website. Also download the file `SimpleAnimation.gif` and place it in a sub-directory `images`. The code is illustrated as follows:

```
1 import pyglet
2
3 animation = pyglet.image.load_animation(
4                "images/SimpleAnimation.gif")
5
6 # Create a sprite object as an instance of this animation.
7 animSprite = pyglet.sprite.Sprite(animation)
8
9 # The main pyglet window with OpenGL context
10 w = animSprite.width
11 h = animSprite.height
12 win = pyglet.window.Window(width=w, height=h)
13
14 # r,g b, color values and transparency for the background
15 r, g, b, alpha = 0.5, 0.5, 0.8, 0.5
16
17 # OpenGL method for setting the background.
18 pyglet.gl.glClearColor(r, g, b, alpha)
19
20 # Draw the sprite in the API method on_draw of
21 # pyglet.Window
22 @win.event
23 def on_draw():
24     win.clear()
25     animSprite.draw()
26
27 pyglet.app.run()
```

The code is self-explanatory. On line 3, the API method `image.load_animation` creates an instance of class `image.Animation` using the specified animation file. For this animation, a `Sprite` object is created on line 7. The Pyglet window created on line 12 will be used to display the animation. The size of this window is specified by the `height` and `width` of the `animSprite`. The background color for the window is set using OpenGL call `glClearColor`.

2. Next, we need to draw this animation sprite into the Pyglet window. The `pyglet.window` defines API method `on_draw` which gets called when an event occurs. The call to the `draw()` method of animation `Sprite` is made on line 25 to render the animation on screen. The code on line 22 is important. The `decorator`, `@win.event` allows us to modify the `on_draw` API method of `pyglet.window.Window` when an event occurs. Finally code on line 27 runs this application.

You can create your own animation file like `SimpleAnimation.gif` using freely available image editing software packages like GIMP. This animation file was created using GIMP 2.6.7, by drawing each of the characters on a separate layer and then blending all the layers using **Filters | Animation | Blend**.

3. Put the file `SimpleAnimation.py` along with the animation file `SimpleAnimation.gif` in the same directory and then run the program as follows:

```
$python SimpleAnimation.py
```

This will show the animation in a Pyglet window. You can use a different animation file instead of `SimpleAnimation.gif`. Just modify the related code in this file or add code to accept any GIF file as a command-line argument for this program. The next illustration shows some of the frames from this animation at different time intervals.

The preceding image is a screen capture of a running animation at different time intervals.

What just happened?

We worked out an example where an already created animation file was loaded and viewed using Pyglet. This short exercise taught us some preliminary things about viewing animations using Pyglet. For example, we learned how to create a Pyglet window and load an animation using `pyglet.Sprite` object. These fundamentals will be used throughout this chapter.

Animation using a sequence of images

The API method `Animation.from_image_sequence` enables creation of an animation using a bunch of sequential images. Each of the images is displayed as a frame in the animation, one after the other. The time for which each frame is displayed can be specified as an argument while creating the animation object. It can also be set after the animation instance is created.

Time for action – animation using a sequence of images

Let's develop a tool that can create an animation and display it on the screen. This tool will create and display the animation using the given image files. Each of the image files will be displayed as a frame in the animation for a specified amount of time. This is going to be a fun little animation that shows a grandfather clock with a pendulum. We will animate the pendulum oscillations with other things, including making the dial remaining still. This animation has only three image frames; two of them show the pendulum at opposite extremes. These images are sequenced as shown in the next illustration.

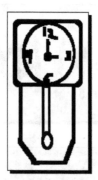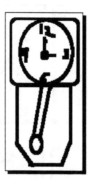

Clock image frames to be animated appear in the preceding image.

1. Download the file ImageSequenceAnimation.py from the Packt website.

2. The code in this file is presented below.

```
1 import pyglet
2
3 image_frames = ('images/clock1.png',
4              'images/clock2.png',
5              'images/clock3.png')
6
7 # Create the list of pyglet images
8 images = map(lambda img: pyglet.image.load(img),
9               image_frames)
10
11 # Each of the image frames will be displayed for 0.33
12 # seconds
13 # 0.33 seconds chosen so that the 'pendulam in the clock
14 # animation completes one oscillation in ~ 1 second !
15
16 animation = pyglet.image.Animation.from_image_sequence(
17                      images, 0.33)
18 # Create a sprite instance.
19 animSprite = pyglet.sprite.Sprite(animation)
20
21 # The main pyglet window with OpenGL context
22 w = animSprite.width
23 h = animSprite.height
24 win = pyglet.window.Window(width=w, height=h)
25
26 # Set window background color to white.
27 pyglet.gl.glClearColor(1, 1, 1, 1)
28
29 # The @win.event is a decorator that helps modify the API
30 # methods such as
31 # on_draw called when draw event occurs.
32 @win.event
33 def on_draw():
34   win.clear()
35   animSprite.draw()
36
37 pyglet.app.run()
```

The `tuple`, `image_frames` contains the paths for the images. The `map` function call on line 8 creates `pyglet.image` objects corresponding to each of the image paths and stores the resultant images in a `list`. On line 16, the `animation` is created using the API method `Animation.from_image_sequence`. This method takes the list of image objects as an argument. The other optional argument is the time in seconds for which each of the frames will be shown. We set this time as `0.33` seconds per image so that the total time for a complete animation loop is nearly 1 second. Thus, in the animation, one complete oscillation of the pendulum will be complete in about one second. We already discussed the rest of the code in an earlier section.

3. Place the image files in a sub-directory `images` within the directory in which file `ImageSequenceAnimation.py` is placed. Then run the program using:

```
$python ImageSequenceAnimation.py
```

You will see a clock with an oscillating pendulum in the window. The animation will continue in a loop and closing the window will end it.

What just happened?

By rapidly displaying still images, we just created something like a 'flipbook' cartoon! We developed a simple utility that takes a sequence of images as an input and creates an animation using Pyglet. To accomplish this task, we used `Animation.from_image_sequence` to create the animation and re-used most of the framework from the *Viewing an existing animation* section.

Single image animation

Imagine that you are creating a cartoon movie where you want to animate the motion of an arrow or a bullet hitting a target. In such cases, typically it is just a single image. The desired animation effect is accomplished by performing appropriate translation or rotation of the image.

Time for action – bouncing ball animation

Lets create a simple animation of a 'bouncing ball'. We will use a single image file, `ball.png`, which can be downloaded from the Packt website. The dimensions of this image in pixels are 200x200, created on a transparent background. The following screenshot shows this image opened in GIMP image editor. The three dots on the ball identify its side. We will see why this is needed. Imagine this as a ball used in a bowling game.

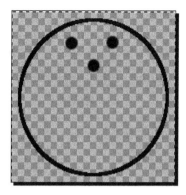

The image of a ball opened in GIMP appears as shown in the preceding image. The ball size in pixels is 200x200.

1. Download the files SingleImageAnimation.py and ball.png from the Packt website. Place the ball.png file in a sub-directory 'images' within the directory in which SingleImageAnimation.py is saved.

2. The following code snippet shows the overall structure of the code.

```
1 import pyglet
2 import time
3
4 class SingleImageAnimation(pyglet.window.Window):
5   def __init__(self, width=600, height=600):
6     pass
7   def createDrawableObjects(self):
8     pass
9   def adjustWindowSize(self):
10     pass
11   def moveObjects(self, t):
12     pass
13   def on_draw(self):
14     pass
15 win = SingleImageAnimation()
16 # Set window background color to gray.
17 pyglet.gl.glClearColor(0.5, 0.5, 0.5, 1)
18
19 pyglet.clock.schedule_interval(win.moveObjects, 1.0/20)
20
21 pyglet.app.run()
```

Although it is not required, we will encapsulate event handling and other functionality within a class `SingleImageAnimation`. The program to be developed is short, but in general, it is a good coding practice. It will also be good for any future extension to the code. An instance of `SingleImageAnimation` is created on line 14. This class is inherited from `pyglet.window.Window`. It encapsulates the functionality we need here. The API method `on_draw` is overridden by the class. `on_draw` is called when the window needs to be redrawn. Note that we no longer need a `decorator` statement such as `@win.event` above the `on_draw` method because the window API method is simply overridden by this inherited class.

3. The constructor of the class `SingleImageAnimation` is as follows:

```
1 def __init__(self, width=None, height=None):
2    pyglet.window.Window.__init__(self,
3                      width=width,
4                      height=height,
5                      resizable = True)
6    self.drawableObjects = []
7    self.rising = False
8    self.ballSprite = None
9    self.createDrawableObjects()
10   self.adjustWindowSize()
```

As mentioned earlier, the class `SingleImageAnimation` inherits `pyglet.window.Window`. However, its constructor doesn't take all the arguments supported by its super class. This is because we don't need to change most of the default argument values. If you want to extend this application further and need these arguments, you can do so by adding them as `__init__` arguments. The constructor initializes some instance variables and then calls methods to create the animation sprite and resize the window respectively.

4. The method `createDrawableObjects` creates a sprite instance using the `ball.png` image.

```
1 def createDrawableObjects(self):
2    """
3    Create sprite objects that will be drawn within the
4    window.
5    """
6    ball_img= pyglet.image.load('images/ball.png')
7    ball_img.anchor_x = ball_img.width / 2
8    ball_img.anchor_y = ball_img.height / 2
9
```

```
10    self.ballSprite = pyglet.sprite.Sprite(ball_img)
11    self.ballSprite.position = (
12       self.ballSprite.width + 100,
13       self.ballSprite.height*2 - 50)
14    self.drawableObjects.append(self.ballSprite)
```

The `anchor_x` and `anchor_y` properties of the image instance are set such that the image has an anchor exactly at its center. This will be useful while rotating the image later. On line 10, the sprite instance `self.ballSprite` is created. Later, we will be setting the width and height of the Pyglet window as twice of the sprite width and thrice of the sprite height. The position of the image within the window is set on line 11. The initial position is chosen as shown in the next screenshot. In this case, there is only one `Sprite` instance. However, to make the program more general, a list of *drawable* objects called `self.drawableObjects` is maintained.

5. To continue the discussion from the previous step, we will now review the `on_draw` method.

```
def on_draw(self):
    self.clear()
    for d in self.drawableObjects:
        d.draw()
```

As mentioned previously, the `on_draw` function is an API method of class `pyglet.window.Window` that is called when a window needs to be redrawn. This method is overridden here. The `self.clear()` call clears the previously drawn contents within the window. Then, all the `Sprite` objects in the list `self.drawableObjects` are drawn in the `for` loop.

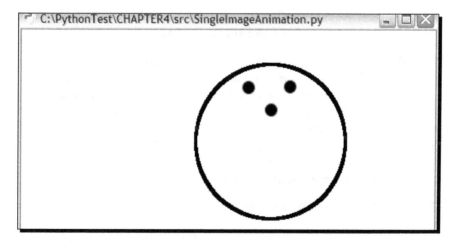

The preceding image illustrates the initial ball position in the animation.

6. The method `adjustWindowSize` sets the `width` and `height` parameters of the Pyglet window. The code is self-explanatory:

```
def adjustWindowSize(self):
  w = self.ballSprite.width * 3
  h = self.ballSprite.height * 3
  self.width = w
  self.height = h
```

7. So far, we have set up everything for the animation to play. Now comes the fun part. We will change the position of the sprite representing the image to achieve the animation effect. During the animation, the image will also be rotated, to give it the natural feel of a bouncing ball.

```
1 def moveObjects(self, t):
2    if self.ballSprite.y - 100 < 0:
3       self.rising = True
4    elif self.ballSprite.y > self.ballSprite.height*2 - 50:
5       self.rising = False
6
7    if not self.rising:
8       self.ballSprite.y -= 5
9       self.ballSprite.rotation -= 6
10   else:
11      self.ballSprite.y += 5
12      self.ballSprite.rotation += 5
```

This method is scheduled to be called 20 times per second using the following code in the program.

```
pyglet.clock.schedule_interval(win.moveObjects, 1.0/20)
```

To start with, the ball is placed near the top. The animation should be such that it gradually falls down, hits the bottom, and bounces back. After this, it continues its upward journey to hit a boundary somewhere near the top and again it begins its downward journey. The code block from lines 2 to 5 checks the current y position of `self.ballSprite`. If it has hit the upward limit, the flag `self.rising` is set to `False`. Likewise, when the lower limit is hit, the flag is set to `True`. The flag is then used by the next code snippet to increment or decrement the y position of `self.ballSprite`.

8. The highlighted lines of code rotate the `Sprite` instance. The current rotation angle is incremented or decremented by the given value. This is the reason why we set the image anchors, `anchor_x` and `anchor_y` at the center of the image. The `Sprite` object honors these image anchors. If the anchors are not set this way, the ball will be seen wobbling in the resultant animation.

9. Once all the pieces are in place, run the program from the command line as:

```
$python SingleImageAnimation.py
```

This will pop up a window that will play the bouncing ball animation. The next illustration shows some intermediate frames from the animation while the ball is falling down.

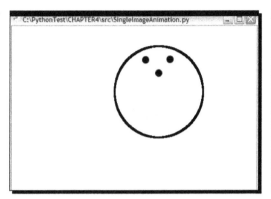 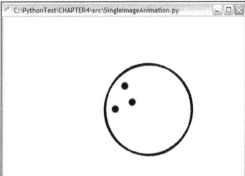

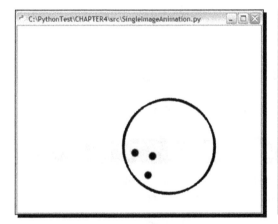 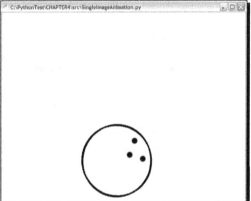

What just happened?

We learned how to create an animation using just a single image. The image of a ball was represented by a sprite instance. This sprite was then translated and rotated on the screen to accomplish a bouncing ball animation. The whole functionality, including the event handling, was encapsulated in the class SingleImageAnimation.

Project: a simple bowling animation

It's time for a small project. We will re-use most of the code we used in the *Single Image Animation* section and some more stuff to create an animation where a rolling ball hits a pin in a bowling game. Although this chapter covers animation, this project will give you a preliminary understanding on how to turn an animation into a game. This is not a real game as such, but it will involve some user interactions to control the animation.

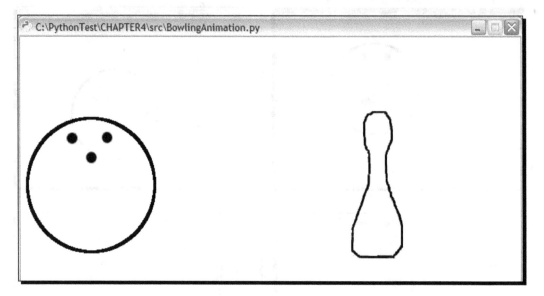

The starting position in the bowling animation, showing ball and pin images.

Time for action – a simple bowling animation

Let's develop the code for this application. As mentioned earlier, a big chunk of the code comes from the *Single Image Animation* section. So we will only discuss the new and modified methods needed to create a bowling animation.

1. Download the Python source file `BowlingAnimation.py` from the Packt website. The overall class design is the same as the one developed in the *Single Image Animation* section. We will only discuss the new and modified methods. You can review the rest of the code from this file.

2. Also, download the image files used in this project. These files are `ball.png` and `pin.png`. Place these files in a sub-directory `images`. The `images` directory should be placed in the directory in which the above Python source file is located.

3. The `__init__` method of the class is identical to that of class `SingleImageAnimation`. The only change here is that it initializes the following flags:

```
self.paused = False
self.pinHorizontal = False
```

The flag `self.pinHorizontal` is used later to check if the pin is knocked out by the ball. Whereas, `self.paused` is used to pause or resume the animation depending on its value.

4. The `createDrawable` object method is modified to create a sprite instance for the pin image. Also, the position of the ball and pin sprites are adjusted for our animation needs. The code is presented as follows:

```
1  def createDrawableObjects(self):
2      ball_img= pyglet.image.load('images/ball.png')
3      ball_img.anchor_x = ball_img.width / 2
4      ball_img.anchor_y = ball_img.height / 2
5
6      pin_img = pyglet.image.load('images/pin.png')
7      pin_img.anchor_x = pin_img.width / 2
8      pin_img.anchor_y = pin_img.height / 2
9
10     self.ballSprite = pyglet.sprite.Sprite(ball_img)
11     self.ballSprite.position = (0 + 100,
12                 self.ballSprite.height)
13
14     self.pinSprite = pyglet.sprite.Sprite(pin_img)
15     self.pinSprite.position = (
16             (self.ballSprite.width*2 + 100,
17             self.ballSprite.height) )
18
19     # Add these sprites to the list of drawables
20     self.drawableObjects.append(self.ballSprite)
21     self.drawableObjects.append(self.pinSprite)
```

The code block 6-8 creates an `image` instance for the pin image and then sets the image anchor at its center. The `Sprite` instances representing ball and pin images are created on lines 10 and 14 respectively. Their positions are set such that the initial positions appear as shown in the earlier illustration. Finally these sprites are added to the list of drawable objects that are drawn in `on_draw` method.

5. Next, let's review the `moveObjects` method. As before, this method is called every `0.05` seconds.

```
1 def moveObjects(self, t):
2   if self.pinHorizontal:
3     self.ballSprite.x = 100
4     self.pinSprite.x -= 100
5
6   if self.ballSprite.x < self.ballSprite.width*2:
7     if self.ballSprite.x == 100:
8       time.sleep(1)
9       self.pinSprite.rotation = 0
10      self.pinHorizontal = False
11
12    self.ballSprite.x += 5
13    self.ballSprite.rotation += 5
14
15  if self.ballSprite.x >= self.ballSprite.width*2:
16    self.pinSprite.rotation = 90
17    self.pinSprite.x += 100
18    self.pinHorizontal = True
```

The `if` block, from lines 6 to 13, is called for when the x position of the ball sprite is between 100 pixels to twice the width of the `self.ballSprite`. On line 12, the x position of `self.ballSprite` is incremented by 5 pixels. Also, the sprite is rotated by 5 degrees. The combination of these two transforms creates an effect where we see the ball rolling horizontally, from left to right, inside the Pyglet window. As seen earlier, the center of the pin is located at x = `self.ballSprite.width*2 + 100` and y = `self.ballSprite.height`.

The `if` block from lines 15 to 18 is where the ball appears to have hit the pin. That is, the x coordinate of ball sprite center is about 100 pixels away from the center of the pin. The 100-pixel value is chosen to account for the ball radius. Therefore, once the ball hits the pin, the pin image is rotated by 90 degrees (line 16). This creates a visual effect where the pin appears to be knocked down by the ball. The x coordinate of the pin is incremented by 100 pixels so that, after the pin rotation, the ball and pin images don't overlap. You can do some more improvement here. Shift the y position of the pin sprite further down, so that the pin appears lying on the ground. In this `if` block, we also set the flag `self.pinHorizontal` to `True`. When the `moveObjects` method is called the next time, the first thing that is checked is whether the pin is vertical or horizontal. If the pin is horizontal, the original positions of the ball and pin are restored by the code on lines 2 to 4. This is a preparation for the next animation loop. On line 9, the pin is rotated back to 0 degree, whereas on line 10, the flag `self.pinHorizontal` is reset to `False`.

6. With the code we developed so far, and with the remaining code from class `SingleImageAnimation`, if you run the program, it will show the bowling animation. Now let's add some *controls* to this animation. A flag, `self.paused`, was initialized in the constructor. It will be used here. Just like `on_draw`, `on_key_press` is another API method of `pyglet.window.Window`. It is overridden here to implement pause and resume controls.

```
1 def on_key_press(self, key, modifiers):
2    if key == pyglet.window.key.P and not self.paused:
3       pyglet.clock.unschedule(self.moveObjects)
4       self.paused = True
5    elif key == pyglet.window.key.R and self.paused:
6       pyglet.clock.schedule_interval(
7                 self.moveObjects, 1.0/20)
8       self.paused = False
```

The `key` argument is one of the keyboard keys pressed by the user. The `if` block from lines 2 to 4 pauses the animation when P key is pressed. The method `self.moveObjects` is scheduled to be called every `0.05` seconds. The scheduled callback to this method is canceled using the `pyglet.clock.unschedule` method. To resume the animation, the `schedule_interval` method is called on line 6. The `self.paused` flag ensures that the multiple keypresses won't have any undesirable effect on the animation. For example, if you press the R key multiple times, the code will just ignore the keypress events that follow.

7. Refer to the file BowlingAnimation.py to review or develop the rest of the code and then run the program from the command line as:

```
$python BowlingAnimation.py
```

This will pop up a window in which the animation will be played. Press the *P* key on the keyboard to pause the animation. To resume a paused animation, press the *R* key. The next illustration shows a few intermediate frames in this animation.

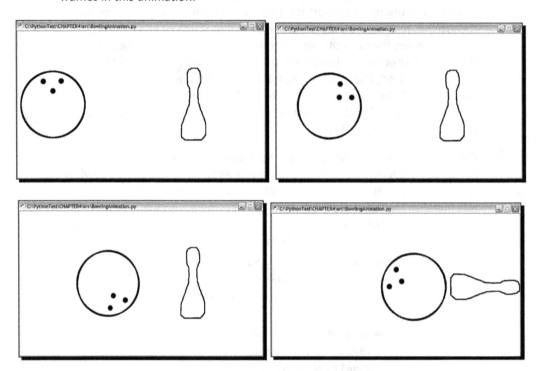

The intermediate frames in the bowling animation appear as shown in the preceding image.

What just happened?

We completed a simple but exciting project where an animation of a bowl hitting a pin was developed. This was accomplished by moving and rotating the image sprites on the screen. Several methods from the SingleImageAnimation class were re-used. Additionally, we learned how to control the animation by overriding the on_key_press API method.

Animations using different image regions

It is possible to create an animation using different regions of a single image. Each of these regions can be treated as a separate animation frame. In order to achieve the desired animation effect, it is important to properly create the image with regions. In the following example, the animation will be created using such regions. We will also be using the default position parameters for each of the regions within that image. Thus, our main task in this section is simply to use these regions in their original form and create animation frames out of them. We will first see how the image looks. The following illustration shows this image.

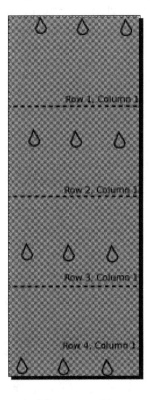

A single image file with an imaginary 'grid' on top of it appears in the previous image.

The horizontal dotted lines overlaying this image indicate how an imaginary image grid divides the image into different regions. Here we have four rows and just a single column. Thus, during the animation, each of these image regions will be shown as a single animation frame. Notice how the droplet images are drawn. In the first row, the four droplets are drawn at the top. Then in the next row, these images are slightly offset to the south-west direction compared to the droplets in the first row. This offset is increased further in the third and fourth rows.

Time for action – raindrops animation

Let's create an animation of falling raindrops by using different regions of a single image.

1. Download the Python source file `RainDropsAnimation.py` and the image file `droplet.png` from the Packt website. As done before, place the image file in a sub-directory `images`. The `images` directory should be placed in the directory in which the Python source file is located.

2. The `__init__` method of the class `RainDropsAnimation` is presented.

```
1 def __init__(self, width=None, height=None):
2    pyglet.window.Window.__init__(self,
3                    width=width,
4                    height=height)
5    self.drawableObjects = []
6    self.createDrawableObjects()
```

The code is self-explanatory. The class `RainDropsAnimation` inherits `pyglet.window.Window`. The constructor of the class calls the method that creates the `Sprite` instance for displaying the animation on the screen.

3. Let's review the `createDrawableObjects` method.

```
1 def createDrawableObjects(self):
2    num_rows = 4
3    num_columns = 1
4    droplet = 'images/droplet.png'
5    animation = self.setup_animation(droplet,
6                    num_rows,
7                    num_columns)
8
9    self.dropletSprite = pyglet.sprite.Sprite(animation)
10   self.dropletSprite.position = (0,0)
11
12   # Add these sprites to the list of drawables
13   self.drawableObjects.append(self.dropletSprite)
```

The `pyglet.image.Animation` instance is created on line 5, by calling `setup_animation` method. On line 9, the `Sprite` instance is created for this `animation` object.

4. The `setup_animation` method is the main worker method that uses *regions* within the image file to create individual animation frames.

```
1 def setup_animation(self, img, num_rows, num_columns):
2    base_image = pyglet.image.load(img)
3    animation_grid = pyglet.image.ImageGrid(base_image,
4                        num_rows,
5                        num_columns)
6    image_frames = []
7
8    for i in range(num_rows*num_columns, 0, -1):
9      frame = animation_grid[i-1]
10      animation_frame = (
11              pyglet.image.AnimationFrame(frame,
12                          0.2))
13      image_frames.append(animation_frame)
14
15    animation = pyglet.image.Animation(image_frames)
16    return animation
```

First, the instance of `image` is created on line 2. The `ImageGrid` is an imaginary grid placed over the droplet image. Each '*cell*' or the '*image region*' within this image grid can be viewed as a separate image frame in an animation. The `ImageGrid` instance is constructed by providing the image object and the number of rows and columns as arguments. The number of rows in this case is 4 and there is only a single column. Thus, there will be four such image frames in the animation corresponding to each of these rows in the `ImageGrid`. The `AnimationFrame` object is created on line 10. The code on line 8 increments the value of `i` from maximum to minimum region or cell of the imaginary grid. Line 9 gets the specific image region and this is then used to create the `pyglet.image.AnimationFrame` instance, as we did on line 10. The second argument is the time for which each frame will be displayed on the screen. Here, we are displaying each frame for `0.2` seconds. All such animation frame forms are stored in a list `image_frames` and then the `pyglet.image.Animation` instance is created using this list.

5. Refer to the file `RainDropsAnimation.py` to review the rest of the code and then run the program from the command line as:

```
$python RainDropsAnimation.py
```

This animation displays four image regions of a single image, one after another. The next illustration shows these four images.

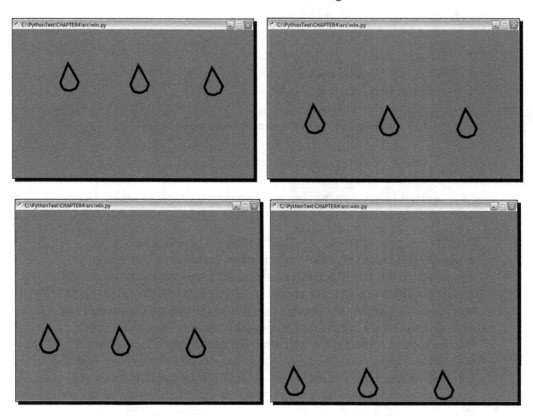

The four image frames that display different regions of a single image appear in the previous illustration. These four image frames are repeated in the animation loop.

What just happened?

We created an animation using different regions of a single image. Each of these regions was treated as a separate animation frame. The creation of an image used in this animation was briefly discussed. Among many other things, we learned how to create and use Pyglet classes such as `ImageGrid` and `AnimationFrame`.

Project: drive on a rainy day!

This project is essentially a summary of what we have learned so far in this chapter. Additionally, it will cover a few other things such as adding sound effects to an animation, showing or hiding certain image sprites while the animation is being played, and so on. In this animation, there will be a stationary cloud image. We will re-use the code from the *raindrops animation* section to animate falling rain. There will be an image sprite to animate lightning effect. Finally, a car cartoon will be shown passing by from left to right in this heavy rain. The following snapshot is an animation frame that captures all these component images.

Component images of animation *drive on a rainy day* illustrated in the preceding image.

Time for action – drive on a rainy day!

It's time to write the code for this animation.

1. Download the Python source file `RainyDayAnimation.py`. We will discuss some of the important methods from this file. You can go through the rest of the code from this file.

2. Download the image files, `droplet.png`, `cloud.png`, `car.png`, and `lightening.png` from the Packt website. Place these image files in a sub-directory called `images`. The `images` directory should be placed in the directory where the Python source file is located.

3. The constructor of the class is written as follows:

```
1 def __init__(self, width=None, height=None):
2   pyglet.window.Window.__init__(self,
3                      width=width,
4                      height=height,
5                      resizable=True)
6   self.drawableObjects = []
7   self.paused = False
8
9
10   self.createDrawableObjects()
11   self.adjustWindowSize()
12   # Make sure to replace the following media path to
13   # with an appropriate path on your computer.
14   self.horn_sound = (
15       pyglet.media.load('C:/AudioFiles/horn.wav',
16               streaming=False) )
```

The code is same as the one developed in the raindrops animation. The media file `horn.wav` is decoded on line 14. The flag streaming is set to `False` so that the media can be played multiple times during the animation. Make sure you specify an appropriate audio file path on your computer on line 15.

4. Let's review the `createDrawableObjects` method:

```
1 def createDrawableObjects(self):
2
3     num_rows = 4
4     num_columns = 1
5     droplet = 'images/droplet.png'
6     animation = self.setup_animation(droplet,
7                       num_rows,
8                       num_columns)
9
10    self.dropletSprite = pyglet.sprite.Sprite(animation)
11    self.dropletSprite.position = (0,200)
12
13    cloud = pyglet.image.load('images/cloud.png')
14    self.cloudSprite = pyglet.sprite.Sprite(cloud)
15    self.cloudSprite.y = 100
16
17    lightening = pyglet.image.load('images/lightening.png')
18    self.lSprite = pyglet.sprite.Sprite(lightening)
19    self.lSprite.y = 200
20
21    car = pyglet.image.load('images/car.png')
22    self.carSprite = pyglet.sprite.Sprite(car, -500, 0)
23
24    # Add these sprites to the list of drawables
25    self.drawableObjects.append(self.cloudSprite)
26    self.drawableObjects.append(self.lSprite)
27    self.drawableObjects.append(self.dropletSprite)
28    self.drawableObjects.append(self.carSprite)
```

The code block from lines 3 to 10 is identical to the one developed in the raindrops animation. The `self.dropletSprite` image is placed at an appropriate position. Next, we just create sprites to load images of clouds, lightning, and car in the Pyglet window. These sprites are placed at appropriate locations within the window. For example, the starting position of the car is off the screen. It is anchored at $x = -500$ and $y = 0$. The code block from lines 24 to 28 adds all the `Sprite` instances to `self.drawableObjects`. The `draw()` method of each one of these instances is called in `on_draw` method.

5. To achieve the desired animation effect, we have to move around various sprites during the animation. This is done by scheduling a few methods to be called at specified time intervals. These methods update the coordinates of the sprite or toggle its visibility when the Pyglet window is redrawn. The code is illustrated as follows:

```
# Schedule the method RainyDayAnimation.moveObjects to be
# called every 0.05 seconds.
pyglet.clock.schedule_interval(win.moveObjects, 1.0/20)

# Show the lightening every 1 second
pyglet.clock.schedule_interval(win.show_lightening, 1.0)
```

We have already seen an example of the moveObjects method in earlier sections. In this project, we schedule another method, RainyDayAnimation.show_lightening, to be called every second. This method created an animation effect where lightning strikes every second at different positions.

6. We will now review the method show_lightening.

```
1 def show_lightening(self, t):
2    if self.lSprite.visible:
3      self.lSprite.visible = False
4    else:
5      if(self.lSprite.x == 100):
6        self.lSprite.x += 200
7      else:
8        self.lSprite.x = 100
9
10      self.lSprite.visible = True
```

self.lSprite is the sprite representing the lightning image. Our target is to create an animation effect where the lightning flashes for a moment and then disappears. This can be accomplished by toggling the Sprite. visible property. When this property is set to False, the lightning is not shown. When it is set to True, the else block 4-10 is executed. The position of self.lSprite is changed so that the lightning appears at different locations the next time this method is called.

7. The `moveObjects` method is scheduled to be called every `0.05` seconds.

```
1 def moveObjects(self, t):
2   if self.carSprite.x <= self.cloudSprite.width:
3     self.carSprite.x += 10
4   else:
5     self.carSprite.x = -500
6     self.horn_sound.play()
```

Every time it is called, it moves the position of the `Sprite` representing the car by 10 pixels in the positive direction of x axis. However, if the `x` coordinate of the `self.carSprite` exceeds its width, the car is reset to its original position. Also, at the starting position of the car, the horn sound is played.

8. Review the rest of the code from file `RainyDayAnimation.py`. Make sure to replace the audio file path for `self.horn_sound` with an appropriate file path on your computer. Once everything is all set, run the program from the command line as:

```
$python RainyDayAnimation.py
```

This will pop up a window that will play the animation in which a fun car cruises along in a thunderstorm. The next illustration shows some intermediate frames from the animation.

Intermediate frames from an animation where a car drives along on a rainy day appear in the preceding image.

What just happened?

The animation developed in this project used four different images. We learned how to add sound effects and change the visibility of the image sprites during the animation. Some of the images were translated or made intermittently visible to achieve the desired animation effect. Different regions of a single image were used to animate raindrops. Overall, this fun project covered most of the things we learned throughout this book.

Have a go hero – add more effects

1. Additional sound effects—whenever lightning strikes in the animation, play a thunderstorm sound.

2. In the code presented earlier, the lightning image position is toggled between two fixed locations. Use random module in Python to get a random coordinate between 0 to `self.cloudSprite.width` and use that as the x coordinate of `self.lSprite`.

3. Add keyboard controls to change the speed of the car, the frequency of lightning, and so on.

Summary

We learned a lot in this chapter about creating 2D animations in Python using Pyglet. Specifically, we:

♦   Learned some fundamental components of the Pyglet framework for creating animations. Modules such as `Window`, `Image`, `Animation`, `Sprite`, `AnimationFrame`, `ImageGrid`, and so on were discussed.

♦   Wrote code to create an animation using a sequence of images or to play a pre-created animation.

♦   Learned things such as modifying the position of the Pyglet sprite, adding keyboard and mouse controls and adding sound effects to the animation.

♦   Worked on a cartoon animation project 'Drive on a Rainy Day'. Here we applied several of the techniques learned throughout the chapter.

5
Working with Audios

Decades ago, silent movies lit up the screen—but later, it was audio effect that brought life into them. We deal with digital audio processing quite frequently— when just playing a CD track, recording your own voice or converting songs into a different audio format. There are many libraries or multimedia frameworks available for audio processing. This chapter teaches some common digital audio processing techniques using Python bindings of a popular multimedia framework called GStreamer.

In this chapter, we shall:

- Learn basic concepts behind GStreamer multimedia framework
- Use GStreamer API for audio processing
- Develop some simple audio processing tools for 'everyday use'. We will develop tools that will batch convert audio file formats, record an audio, and play audio files

So let's get on with it!

Installation prerequisites

Since we are going to use an external multimedia framework, it is necessary to install the packages mentioned in this section.

GStreamer

GStreamer is a popular open source multimedia framework that supports audio/video manipulation of a wide range of multimedia formats. It is written in the C programming language and provides bindings for other programming languages including Python. Several open source projects use GStreamer framework to develop their own multimedia application. Throughout this chapter, we will make use of the GStreamer framework for audio handling. In order to get this working with Python, we need to install both GStreamer and the Python bindings for GStreamer.

Windows platform

The binary distribution of GStreamer is not provided on the project website `http://www.gstreamer.net/`. Installing it from the source may require considerable effort on the part of Windows users. Fortunately, *GStreamer WinBuilds* project provides pre-compiled binary distributions. Here is the URL to the project website: `http://www.gstreamer-winbuild.ylatuya.es`

The binary distribution for GStreamer as well as its Python bindings (Python 2.6) are available in the **Download** area of the website:
`http://www.gstreamer-winbuild.ylatuya.es/doku.php?id=download`

You need to install two packages. First, the GStreamer and then the Python bindings to the GStreamer. Download and install the GPL distribution of GStreamer available on the GStreamer WinBuilds project website. The name of the GStreamer executable is `GStreamerWinBuild-0.10.5.1.exe`. The version should be 0.10.5 or higher. By default, this installation will create a folder `C:\gstreamer` on your machine. The `bin` directory within this folder contains runtime libraries needed while using GStreamer.

Next, install the Python bindings for GStreamer. The binary distribution is available on the same website. Use the executable `Pygst-0.10.15.1-Python2.6.exe` pertaining to Python 2.6. The version should be 0.10.15 or higher.

GStreamer WinBuilds appears to be an independent project. It is based on the OSSBuild developing suite. Visit `http://code.google.com/p/ossbuild/` for more information. It could happen that the GStreamer binary built with Python 2.6 is no longer available on the mentioned website at the time you are reading this book. Therefore, it is advised that you should contact the developer community of OSSBuild. Perhaps they might help you out!

Alternatively, you can build GStreamer from source on the Windows platform, using a Linux-like environment for Windows, such as Cygwin (http://www.cygwin.com/). Under this environment, you can first install dependent software packages such as Python 2.6, gcc compiler, and others. Download the gst-python-0.10.17.2.tar.gz package from the GStreamer website http://www.gstreamer.net/. Then extract this package and install it from sources using the Cygwin environment. The INSTALL file within this package will have installation instructions.

Other platforms

Many of the Linux distributions provide GStreamer package. You can search for the appropriate gst-python distribution (for Python 2.6) in the package repository. If such a package is not available, install gst-python from the source as discussed in the earlier the *Windows platform* section.

If you are a Mac OS X user, visit http://py26-gst-python.darwinports.com/. It has detailed instructions on how to download and install the package Py26-gst-python version 0.10.17 (or higher).

> Mac OS X 10.5.x (Leopard) comes with the Python 2.5 distribution. If you are using packages using this default version of Python, GStreamer Python bindings using Python 2.5 are available on the darwinports website: http://gst-python.darwinports.com/

PyGobject

There is a free multiplatform software utility library called 'GLib'. It provides data structures such as hash maps, linked lists, and so on. It also supports the creation of threads. The 'object system' of GLib is called **GObject**. Here, we need to install the Python bindings for GObject. The Python bindings are available on the PyGTK website at: http://www.pygtk.org/downloads.html.

Windows platform

The binary installer is available on the PyGTK website. The complete URL is: http://ftp.acc.umu.se/pub/GNOME/binaries/win32/pygobject/2.20/. Download and install version 2.20 for Python 2.6.

Other platforms

For Linux, the source tarball is available on the PyGTK website. There could even be binary distribution in the package repository of your Linux operating system. The direct link to the Version 2.21 of PyGObject (source tarball) is: http://ftp.gnome.org/pub/GNOME/sources/pygobject/2.21/.

If you are a Mac user and you have Python 2.6 installed, a distribution of PyGObject is available at `http://py26-gobject.darwinports.com/`. Install version 2.14 or later.

Summary of installation prerequisites

The following table summarizes the packages needed for this chapter.

Package	Download location	Version	Windows platform	Linux/Unix/OS X platforms
GStreamer	`http://www.gstreamer.net/`	0.10.5 or later	Install using binary distribution available on the Gstreamer WinBuild website: `http://www.gstreamer-winbuild.ylatuya.es/doku.php?id=download` Use `GStreamerWinBuild-0.10.5.1.exe` (or later version if available).	Linux: Use GStreamer distribution in package repository. Mac OS X: Download and install by following instructions on the website: `http://gstreamer.darwinports.com/`.
Python Bindings for GStreamer	`http://www.gstreamer.net/`	0.10.15 or later for Python 2.6	Use binary provided by GStreamer WinBuild project. See `http://www.gstreamer-winbuild.ylatuya.es` for details pertaining to Python 2.6.	Linux: Use gst-python distribution in the package repository. Mac OS X: Use this package (if you are using Python2.6): `http://py26-gst-python.darwinports.com/`. Linux/Mac: Build and install from the source tarball.
Python bindings for GObject "PyGObject"	Source distribution: `http://www.pygtk.org/downloads.html`	2.14 or later for Python 2.6	Use binary package from `pygobject-2.20.0.win32-py2.6.exe`	Linux: Install from source if pygobject is not available in the package repository. Mac: Use this package on darwinports (if you are using Python2.6) See `http://py26-gobject.darwinports.com/` for details.

Testing the installation

Ensure that the GStreamer and its Python bindings are properly installed. It is simple to test this. Just start Python from the command line and type the following:

```
>>>import pygst
```

If there is no error, it means the Python bindings are installed properly.

Next, type the following:

```
>>>pygst.require("0.10")
>>>import gst
```

If this import is successful, we are all set to use GStreamer for processing audios and videos!

If `import gst` fails, it will probably complain that it is unable to work some required DLL/shared object. In this case, check your environment variables and make sure that the PATH variable has the correct path to the `gstreamer/bin` directory. The following lines of code in a Python interpreter show the typical location of the `pygst` and `gst` modules on the Windows platform.

```
>>> import pygst
>>> pygst
<module 'pygst' from 'C:\Python26\lib\site-packages\pygst.pyc'>
>>> pygst.require('0.10')
>>> import gst
>>> gst
<module 'gst' from 'C:\Python26\lib\site-packages\gst-0.10\gst\__init__
.pyc'>
```

Next, test if PyGObject is successfully installed. Start the Python interpreter and try importing the `gobject` module.

```
>>import gobject
```

If this works, we are all set to proceed!

A primer on GStreamer

In this chapter, we will be using GStreamer multimedia framework extensively. Before we move on to the topics that teach us various audio processing techniques, a primer on GStreamer is necessary.

So what is GStreamer? It is a framework on top of which one can develop multimedia applications. The rich set of libraries it provides makes it easier to develop applications with complex audio/video processing capabilities. Fundamental components of GStreamer are briefly explained in the coming sub-sections.

Comprehensive documentation is available on the GStreamer project website. GStreamer Application Development Manual is a very good starting point. In this section, we will briefly cover some of the important aspects of GStreamer. For further reading, you are recommended to visit the GStreamer project website: `http://www.gstreamer.net/documentation/`

gst-inspect and gst-launch

We will start by learning the two important GStreamer commands. GStreamer can be run from the command line, by calling `gst-launch-0.10.exe` (on Windows) or `gst-launch-0.10` (on other platforms). The following command shows a typical execution of GStreamer on Linux. We will see what a `pipeline` means in the next sub-section.

`$gst-launch-0.10 pipeline_description`

GStreamer has a plugin architecture. It supports a huge number of plugins. To see more details about any plugin in your GStreamer installation, use the command `gst-inspect-0.10` (`gst-inspect-0.10.exe` on Windows). We will use this command quite often. Use of this command is illustrated here.

`$gst-inspect-0.10 decodebin`

Here, `decodebin` is a plugin. Upon execution of the preceding command, it prints detailed information about the plugin `decodebin`.

Elements and pipeline

In GStreamer, the data flows in a pipeline. Various elements are connected together forming a pipeline, such that the output of the previous element is the input to the next one.

A pipeline can be logically represented as follows:

`Element1 ! Element2 ! Element3 ! Element4 ! Element5`

Here, `Element1` through to `Element5` are the element objects chained together by the symbol `!`. Each of the elements performs a specific task. One of the element objects performs the task of reading input data such as an audio or a video. Another element decodes the file read by the first element, whereas another element performs the job of converting this data into some other format and saving the output. As stated earlier, linking these element objects in a proper manner creates a pipeline.

The concept of a pipeline is similar to the one used in Unix. Following is a Unix example of a pipeline. Here, the vertical separator | defines the pipe.

```
$ls -la | more
```

Here, the `ls -la` lists all the files in a directory. However, sometimes, this list is too long to be displayed in the shell window. So, adding | `more` allows a user to navigate the data.

Now let's see a realistic example of running GStreamer from the command prompt.

```
$ gst-launch-0.10 -v filesrc location=path/to/file.ogg ! decodebin !
audioconvert ! fakesink
```

For a Windows user, the `gst` command name would be `gst-launch-0.10.exe`. The pipeline is constructed by specifying different elements. The !symbol links the adjacent elements, thereby forming the whole pipeline for the data to flow. For Python bindings of GStreamer, the abstract base class for pipeline elements is `gst.Element`, whereas `gst.Pipeline` class can be used to created pipeline instance. In a pipeline, the data is sent to a separate thread where it is processed until it reaches the end or a termination signal is sent.

Plugins

GStreamer is a plugin-based framework. There are several plugins available. A plugin is used to encapsulate the functionality of one or more GStreamer elements. Thus we can have a plugin where multiple elements work together to create the desired output. The plugin itself can then be used as an abstract element in the GStreamer pipeline. An example is `decodebin`. We will learn about it in the upcoming sections. A comprehensive list of available plugins is available at the GStreamer website `http://gstreamer.freedesktop.org`. In this book, we will be using several of them to develop audio/video processing applications. For example, a plugin `Playbin` will be used for audio playback. In almost all applications to be developed, `decodebin` plugin will be used. For audio processing, the functionality provided by plugins such as `gnonlin`, `audioecho`, `monoscope`, `interleave`, and so on will be used.

Bins

In GStreamer, a bin is a container that manages the element objects added to it. A bin instance can be created using gst.Bin class. It is inherited from `gst.Element` and can act as an abstract element representing a bunch of elements within it. A GStreamer plugin decodebin is a good example representing a bin. The decodebin contains decoder elements. It auto-plugs the decoder to create the decoding pipeline.

Pads

Each element has some sort of *connection points* to handle data input and output. GStreamer refers to them as *pads*. Thus an element object can have one or more "receiver pads" termed as **sink pads** that accept data from the previous element in the pipeline. Similarly, there are 'source pads' that take the data out of the element as an input to the next element (if any) in the pipeline. The following is a very simple example that shows how source and sink pads are specified.

```
>gst-launch-0.10.exe fakesrc num-bufferes=1 ! fakesink
```

The `fakesrc` is the first element in the pipeline. Therefore, it only has a source pad. It transmits the data to the next `linkedelement`, that is `fakesink` which only has a sink pad to accept elements. Note that, in this case, since these are `fakesrc` and `fakesink`, just empty buffers are exchanged. A pad is defined by the class `gst.Pad`. A pad can be attached to an element object using the `gst.Element.add_pad()` method.

The following is a diagrammatic representation of a GStreamer element with a pad. It illustrates two GStreamer elements within a pipeline, having a single source and sink pad.

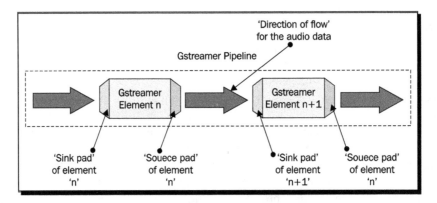

Now that we know how the pads operate, let's discuss some of special types of pads. In the example, we assumed that the pads for the element are always 'out there'. However, there are some situations where the element doesn't have the pads available all the time. Such elements request the pads they need at runtime. Such a pad is called a dynamic pad. Another type of pad is called ghost pad. These types are discussed in this section.

Dynamic pads

Some objects such as `decodebin` do not have pads defined when they are created. Such elements determine the type of pad to be used at the runtime. For example, depending on the media file input being processed, the `decodebin` will create a pad. This is often referred to as **dynamic pad** or sometimes the **available pad** as it is not always available in elements such as `decodebin`.

Ghost pads

As stated in the *Bins* section a **bin** object can act as an abstract element. How is it achieved? For that, the bin uses 'ghost pads' or 'pseudo link pads'. The ghost pads of a bin are used to connect an appropriate element inside it. A ghost pad can be created using gst.GhostPad class.

Caps

The element objects send and receive the data by using the pads. The type of media data that the element objects will handle is determined by the **caps** (a short form for **capabilities**). It is a structure that describes the media formats supported by the element. The caps are defined by the class gst.Caps.

Bus

A bus refers to the object that delivers the message generated by GStreamer. A message is a gst.Message object that informs the application about an event within the pipeline. A message is put on the bus using the gst.Bus.gst_bus_post() method. The following code shows an example usage of the bus.

```
1 bus = pipeline.get_bus()
2 bus.add_signal_watch()
3 bus.connect("message", message_handler)
```

The first line in the code creates a gst.Bus instance. Here the pipeline is an instance of gst.PipeLine. On the next line, we add a signal watch so that the bus gives out all the messages posted on that bus. Line 3 connects the signal with a Python method. In this example, the message is the signal string and the method it calls is message_handler.

Playbin/Playbin2

Playbin is a GStreamer plugin that provides a high-level audio/video player. It can handle a number of things such as automatic detection of the input media file format, auto-determination of decoders, audio visualization and volume control, and so on. The following line of code creates a playbin element.

```
playbin = gst.element_factory_make("playbin")
```

It defines a property called uri. The **URI (Uniform Resource Identifier)** should be an absolute path to a file on your computer or on the Web. According to the GStreamer documentation, Playbin2 is just the latest unstable version but once stable, it will replace the Playbin.

A Playbin2 instance can be created the same way as a Playbin instance.

```
gst-inspect-0.10 playbin2
```

With this basic understanding, let us learn about various audio processing techniques using GStreamer and Python.

Playing music

Given an audio file, one the first things you will do is to play that audio file, isn't it? In GStreamer, what basic elements do we need to play an audio? The essential elements are listed as follows.

- The first thing we need is to open an audio file for reading

- Next, we need a decoder to transform the encoded information

- Then, there needs to be an element to convert the audio format so that it is in a 'playable' format required by an audio device such as speakers

- Finally, an element that will enable the actual playback of the audio file

How will you play an audio file using the command-line version of GStreamer? One way to execute it using command line is as follows:

```
$gstlaunch-0.10 filesrc location=/path/to/audio.mp3 ! decodebin !
audioconvert ! autoaudiosink
```

The autoaudiosink automatically detects the correct audio device on your computer to play the audio. This was tested on a machine with Windows XP and it worked fine. If there is any error playing an audio, check if the audio device on your computer is working properly. You can also try using element sdlaudiosink that outputs to the sound card via SDLAUDIO . If this doesn't work, and you want to install a plugin for audiosink—here is a partial list of GStreamer plugins:
http://www.gstreamer.net/data/doc/gstreamer/head/gst-plugins-good-plugins/html/

Mac OS X users can try installing osxaudiosink if the default autoaudiosink doesn't work.

The audio file should start playing with this command unless there are any missing plugins.

Time for action – playing an audio: method 1

There are a number of ways to play an audio using Python and GStreamer. Let's start with a simple one. In this section, we will use a command string, similar to what you would specify using the command-line version of GStreamer. This string will be used to construct a `gst.Pipeline` instance in a Python program.

So, here we go!

1. Start by creating an `AudioPlayer` class in a Python source file. Just define the empty methods illustrated in the following code snippet. We will expand those in the later steps.

```
1 import thread
2 import gobject
3 import pygst
4 pygst.require("0.10")
5 import gst
6
7 class AudioPlayer:
8   def __init__(self):
9     pass
10  def constructPipeline(self):
11    pass
12  def connectSignals(self):
13    pass
14  def play(self):
15    pass
16  def message_handler(self):
17    pass
18
19 # Now run the program
20 player = AudioPlayer()
21 thread.start_new_thread(player.play, ())
22 gobject.threads_init()
23 evt_loop = gobject.MainLoop()
24 evt_loop.run()
```

Lines 1 to 5 in the code import the necessary modules. As discussed in the *Installation prerequisites* section, the package `pygst` is imported first. Then we call `pygst.require` to enable the import of `gst` module.

2. Now focus on the code block between lines 19 to 24. It is the main execution code. It enables running the program until the music is played. We will use this or similar code throughout this book to run our audio application.

On line 21, the `thread` module is used to create a new thread for playing the audio. The method `AudioPlayer.play` is sent on this thread. The second argument of `thread.start_new_thread` is the list of arguments to be passed to the method `play`. In this example, we do not support any command-line arguments. Therefore, an empty *tuple* is passed. Python adds its own thread management functionality on top of the operating system threads. When such a thread makes calls to external functions (such as C functions), it puts the 'Global Interpreter Lock' on other threads until, for instance, the C function returns a value.

The `gobject.threads_init()` is an initialization function for facilitating the use of Python threading within the `gobject` modules. It can enable or disable threading while calling the C functions. We call this before running the main event loop. The main event loop for executing this program is created using `gobject` on line 23 and this loop is started by the call `evt_loop.run()`.

3. Next, fill the `AudioPlayer` class methods with the code. First, write the constructor of the class.

```
1 def __init__(self):
2    self.constructPipeline()
3    self.is_playing = False
4    self.connectSignals()
```

The pipeline is constructed by the method call on line 2. The flag `self.is_playing` is initialized to `False`. It will be used to determine whether the audio being played has reached the end of the stream. On line 4, a method `self.connectSignals` is called, to capture the messages posted on a bus. We will discuss both these methods next.

4. The main driver for playing the sound is the following `gst` command:

```
"filesrc location=C:/AudioFiles/my_music.mp3 "\
```

```
"! decodebin ! audioconvert ! autoaudiosink"
```

The preceding string has four elements separated by the symbol `!`. These elements represent the components we briefly discussed earlier.

5. The first element `filesrc location=C:/AudioFiles/my_music.mp3` defines the source element that loads the audio file from a given location. In this string, just replace the audio file path represented by `location` with an appropriate file path on your computer. You can also specify a file on a disk drive.

If the filename contains namespaces, make sure you specify the path within quotes. For example, if the filename is my sound.mp3, specify it as follows:
```
filesrc location =\"C:/AudioFiles/my sound.mp3\"
```

6. The next element loads the file. This element is connected to a decodebin. As discussed earlier, the decodebin is a plugin to GStreamer and it inherits gst.Bin. Based on the input audio format, it determines the right type of decoder element to use.

   The third element is audioconvert. It translates the decoded audio data into a format playable by the audio device.

   The final element, autoaudiosink, is a plugin; it automatically detects the audio sink for the audio output.

   We have sufficient information now to create an instance of gst. Pipeline. Write the following method.

```
1 def constructPipeline(self):
2   myPipelineString = \
3   "filesrc location=C:/AudioFiles/my_music.mp3 "\
4   "! decodebin ! audioconvert ! autoaudiosink"
5   self.player = gst.parse_launch(myPipelineString)
```

   An instance of gst.Pipeline is created on line 5, using the gst.parse_launch method.

7. Now write the following method of class AudioPlayer.

```
1 def connectSignals(self):
2   # In this case, we only capture the messages
3   # put on the bus.
4   bus = self.player.get_bus()
5   bus.add_signal_watch()
6   bus.connect("message", self.message_handler)
```

   On line 4, an instance of gst.Bus is created. In the introductory section on GStreamer, we already learned what the code between lines 4 to 6 does. This bus has the job of delivering the messages posted on it from the streaming threads. The add_signal_watch call makes the bus emit the message signal for each message posted. This signal is used by the method message_handler to take appropriate action.

Write the following method:

```
1 def play(self):
2    self.is_playing = True
3    self.player.set_state(gst.STATE_PLAYING)
4    while self.is_playing:
5       time.sleep(1)
6    evt_loop.quit()
```

On line 2, we set the state of the gst pipeline to gst.STATE_PLAYING to start the audio streaming. The flag self.is_playing controls the while loop on line 4. This loop ensures that the main event loop is not terminated before the end of the audio stream is reached. Within the loop the call to time.sleep just buys some time for the audio streaming to finish. The value of flag is changed in the method message_handler that watches for the messages from the bus. On line 6, the main event loop is terminated. This gets called when the end of stream message is emitted or when some error occurs while playing the audio.

8. Next, develop method AudioPlayer.message_handler. This method sets the appropriate flag to terminate the main loop and is also responsible for changing the playing state of the pipeline.

```
1  def message_handler(self, bus, message):
2    # Capture the messages on the bus and
3    # set the appropriate flag.
4    msgType = message.type
5    if msgType == gst.MESSAGE_ERROR:
6       self.player.set_state(gst.STATE_NULL)
7       self.is_playing = False
8       print "\n Unable to play audio. Error: ", \
9       message.parse_error()
10   elif msgType == gst.MESSAGE_EOS:
11      self.player.set_state(gst.STATE_NULL)
12      self.is_playing = False
```

In this method, we only check two things: whether the message on the bus says the streaming audio has reached its end (gst.MESSAGE_EOS) or if any error occurred while playing the audio stream (gst.MESSAGE_ERROR). For both these messages, the state of the gst pipeline is changed from gst.STATE_PLAYING to gst.STATE_NULL. The self.is_playing flag is updated to instruct the program to terminate the main event loop.

We have defined all the necessary code to play the audio. Save the file as `PlayingAudio.py` and run the application from the command line as follows:

```
$python PlayingAudio.py
```

This will begin playback of the input audio file. Once it is done playing, the program will be terminated. You can press *Ctrl + C* on Windows or Linux to interrupt the playing of the audio file. It will terminate the program.

What just happened?

We developed a very simple audio player, which can play an input audio file. The code we wrote covered some of the most important components of GStreamer. These components will be useful throughout this chapter. The core component of the program was a GStreamer pipeline that had instructions to play the given audio file. Additionally, we learned how to create a thread and then start a `gobject` event loop to ensure that the audio file is played until the end.

Have a go hero – play audios from a playlist

The simple audio player we developed can only play a single audio file, whose path is hardcoded in the constructed GStreamer pipeline. Modify this program so it can play audios in a "playlist". In this case, play list should define full paths of the audio files you would like to play, one after the other. For example, you can specify the file paths as arguments to this application or load the paths defined in a text file or load all audio files from a directory. Hint: In a later section, we will develop an audio file converter utility. See if you can use some of that code here.

Building a pipeline from elements

In the last section, a gst.Pipeline was automatically constructed for us by the gst.parse_launch method. All it required was an appropriate command string, similar to the one specified while running the command-line version of GStreamer. The creation and linking of elements was handled internally by this method. In this section, we will see how to construct a pipeline by adding and linking individual element objects. 'GStreamer Pipeline' construction is a fundamental technique that we will use throughout this chapter and also in other chapters related to audio and video processing.

Time for action – playing an audio: method 2

We have already developed code for playing an audio. Let's now tweak the method `AudioPlayer.constructPipeline` to build the `gst.Pipeline` using different element objects.

1. Rewrite the `constructPipeline` method as follows. You can also download the file `PlayingAudio.py` from the Packt website for reference. This file has all the code we discussed in this and previous sections.

```
1 def constructPipeline(self):
2   self.player = gst.Pipeline()
3   self.filesrc = gst.element_factory_make("filesrc")
4   self.filesrc.set_property("location",
5                 "C:/AudioFiles/my_music.mp3")
6
7   self.decodebin = gst.element_factory_make("decodebin",
8                         "decodebin")
9   # Connect decodebin signal with a method.
10  # You can move this call to self.connectSignals)
11  self.decodebin.connect("pad_added",
12              self.decodebin_pad_added)
13
14  self.audioconvert = \
15  gst.element_factory_make("audioconvert",
16              "audioconvert")
17
18  self.audiosink = \
19  gst.element_factory_make("autoaudiosink",
20              "a_a_sink")
21
22  # Construct the pipeline
23  self.player.add(self.filesrc, self.decodebin,
24          self.audioconvert, self.audiosink)
25  # Link elements in the pipeline.
26  gst.element_link_many(self.filesrc, self.decodebin)
27  gst.element_link_many(self.audioconvert, self.audiosink)
```

2. We begin by creating an instance of class `gst.Pipeline`.

3. Next, on line 2, we create the element for loading the audio file. Any new `gst` element can be created using the API method, `gst.element_factory_make`. The method takes the element name (string) as an argument. For example, on line 3, this argument is specified as `"filesrc"` in order to create an instance of element `GstFileSrc`. Each element will have a set of properties. The path of the input audio file is stored in a property `location` of `self.filesrc` element. This property is set on line 4. Replace the file path string with an appropriate audio file path.

 You can get a list of all properties by running the `'gst-inspect-0.10'` command from a console window. See the introductory section on **GSreamer** for more details.

4. The second optional argument serves as a custom name for the created object. For example, on line 20, the name for the `autoaudiosink` object is specified as `a_a_sink`. Like this, we create all the essential elements necessary to build the pipeline.

5. On line 23 in the code, all the elements are put in the pipeline by calling the `gst.Pipeline.add` method.

6. The method `gst.element_link_many` establishes connection between two or more elements for the audio data to flow between them. The elements are linked together by the code on lines 26 and 27. However, notice that we haven't linked together the elements `self.decodebin` and `self.audioconvert`. Why? That's up next.

7. We cannot link the `decodebin` element with the `audioconvert` element at the time the pipeline is created. This is because `decodebin` uses *dynamic pads*. These pads are not available for connection with the `audioconvert` element when the pipeline is created. Depending upon the input data , it will create a pad. Thus, we need to watch out for a signal that is emitted when the `decodebin` adds a pad! How do we do that? It is done by the code on line 11 in the code snippet above. The `"pad-added"` signal is connected with a method, `decodebin_pad_added`. Whenever `decodebin` adds a dynamic pad, this method will get called.

8. Thus, all we need to do is to manually establish a connection between decodebin and audioconvert elements in the method decodebin_pad_added. Write the following method.

```
1 def decodebin_pad_added(self, decodebin, pad ):
2   caps = pad.get_caps()
3   compatible_pad = \
4       self.audioconvert.get_compatible_pad(pad, caps)
5
6   pad.link(compatible_pad)
```

The method takes the element (in this case it is self.decodebin) and pad as arguments. The pad is the new pad for the decodebin element. We need to link this pad with the appropriate one on self.audioconvert.

9. On line 2 in this code snippet, we find out what type of media data the pad handles. Once the capabilities (caps) are known, we pass this information to the method get_compatible_pad of object self.audioconvert. This method returns a compatible pad which is then linked with pad on line 6.

10. The rest of the code is identical with the one illustrated in the earlier section. You can run this program the same way described earlier.

What just happened?

We learned some very crucial components of GStreamer framework. With the simple audio player as an example, we created a GStreamer pipeline 'from scratch' by creating various element objects and linking them together. We also learned how to connect two elements by 'manually' linking their pads and why that was required for the element self.decodebin.

Pop Quiz – element linking

In the earlier example, most of the elements in the pipeline linked using gst.element_link_many in method AudioPlayer.constructPipeline. However, we did not link the elements self.decodebin and self.audioconvert at the time when the pipeline was constructed. Why? Choose the correct answer from the following.

1. We were just trying out a different technique of manually linking these elements together.

2. Decodebin uses a dynamic pad that is created at the runtime. This pad is not available when the pipeline is created.

3. We don't need to link these elements in the pipeline. The media data will just find its way somehow.

4. What are you talking about? It is impossible to connect decodebin and audioconvert elements no matter what you try.

Playing an audio from a website

If there is an audio somewhere on a website that you would like to play, we can pretty much use the same AudioPlayer class developed earlier. In this section, we will illustrate the use of gst.Playbin2 to play an audio by specifying a URL. The code snippet below shows the revised AudioPlayer.constructPipeline method. The name of this method should be changed as it is playbin object that it creates.

```
1 def constructPipeline(self):
2   file_url = "http://path/to/audiofile.wav"
3   buf_size = 1024000
4   self.player = gst.element_factory_make("playbin2")
5   self.player.set_property("uri", file_url)
6   self.player.set_property("buffer-size", buf_size)
7   self.is_playing = False
8   self.connectSignals()
```

On line 4, the gst.Playbin2 element is created using `gst.element_factory_make` method. The argument to this method is a string that describes the element to be created. In this case it is "playbin2" . You can also define a custom name for this object by supplying an optional second argument to this method. Next, on line 5 and 6, we assign values to the properties uri and buffer-size. Set the uri property to an appropriate URL , the full path to the audio file you would like to play.

> Note: When you execute this program, Python application tries to access the Internet. The anti-virus installed on your computer may block the program execution. In this case, you will need to allow this program to access the Internet. Also, you need to be careful of hackers. If you get the `fil_url` from an untrusted source, perform a safety check such as `assert not re.match("file://", file_url)`.

Have a go hero – use 'playbin' to play local audios

In the last few sections, we learned different ways to play an audio file using Python and GStreamer. In the previous section, you must have noticed another simple way to achieve this, using a playbin or playbin2 object to play an audio. In the previous section, we learned how to play an audio file from a URL. Modify this code so that this program can now play audio files located in a drive on your computer. Hint: You will need to use the correct "uri" path. Convert the file path using Python's module `urllib.pathname2url` and then append it to the string: `"file://"`.

Converting audio file format

Suppose you have a big collection of songs in wav file format that you would like to load on a cell phone. But you find out that the cell phone memory card doesn't have enough space to hold all these. What will you do? You will probably try to reduce the size of the song files right? Converting the files into mp3 format will reduce the size. Of course you can do it using some media player. Let's learn how to perform this conversion operation using Python and GStreamer. Later we will develop a simple command-line utility that can be used to perform a batch conversion for all the files you need.

1. Like in the earlier examples, let's first list the important building blocks we need to accomplish file conversion. The first three elements remain the same.

2. As before, the first thing we need is to load an audio file for reading.

3. Next, we need a decoder to transform the encoded information.

4. Then, there needs to be an element to convert the raw audio buffers into an appropriate format.

5. An encoder is needed that takes the raw audio data and encodes it to an appropriate file format to be written.

6. An element where the encoded data will be streamed to is needed. In this case it is our output audio file.

Okay, what's next? Before jumping into the code, first check if you can achieve what you want using the command-line version of GStreamer.

```
$gstlaunch-0.10.exe filesrc location=/path/to/input.wav ! decodebin !
audioconvert ! lame ! Filesink location=/path/to/output.mp3
```

Specify the correct input and output file paths and run this command to convert a wave file to an mp3. If it works, we are all set to proceed. Otherwise check for missing plugins.

You should refer to the GStreamer API documentation to know more about the properties of various elements illustrated above. Trust me, the `gst-inspect-0.10` (or `gst-inspect-0.10.exe` for Windows users) command is a very handy tool that will help you understand the components of a GStreamer plugin. The instructions on running this tool are already discussed earlier in this chapter.

Time for action – audio file format converter

Let's write a simple audio file converter. This utility will batch process input audio files and save them in a user-specified file format. To get started, download the file AudioConverter.py from the Packt website. This file can be run from the command line as:

```
python AudioConverter.py [options]
```

Where, the [options] are as follows:

- --input_dir : The directory from which to read the input audio file(s) to be converted.

- --input_format: The audio format of the input files. The format should be in a supported list of formats. The supported formats are "mp3", "ogg", and "wav". If no format is specified, it will use the default format as ".wav".

- --output_dir : The output directory where the converted files will be saved. If no output directory is specified, it will create a folder OUTPUT_AUDIOS within the input directory.

- --output_format: The audio format of the output file. Supported output formats are "wav" and "mp3".

Let's write this code now.

1. Start by importing necessary modules.

```
import os, sys, time
import thread
import getopt, glob
import gobject
import pygst
pygst.require("0.10")
import gst
```

2. Now declare the following class and the utility function. As you will notice, several of the methods have the same names as before. The underlying functionality of these methods will be similar to what we already discussed. In this section we will review only the most important methods in this class. You can refer to file AudioConverter.py for other methods or develop those on your own.

```
def audioFileExists(fil):
    return os.path.isfile(fil)


class AudioConverter:
    def __init__(self):
      pass
    def constructPipeline(self):
      pass
    def connectSignals(self):
      pass
    def decodebin_pad_added(self, decodebin, pad):
      pass
    def processArgs(self):
      pass
```

```
def convert(self):
    pass
def convert_single_audio(self, inPath, outPath):
    pass
def message_handler(self, bus, message):
    pass
def printUsage(self):
    pass
def printFinalStatus(self, inputFileList,
              starttime, endtime):
    pass

# Run the converter
converter = AudioConverter()
thread.start_new_thread(converter.convert, ())
gobject.threads_init()
evt_loop = gobject.MainLoop()
evt_loop.run()
```

3. Look at the last few lines of code above. This is exactly the same code we used in the Playing Music section. The only difference is the name of the class and its method that is put on the thread in the call `thread.start_new_thread`. At the beginning, the function `audioFileExists()` is declared. It will be used to check if the specified path is a valid file path.

4. Now write the constructor of the class. Here we do initialization of various variables.

```
def __init__(self):
    # Initialize various attrs
    self.inputDir = os.getcwd()
    self.inputFormat = "wav"
    self.outputDir = ""
    self.outputFormat = ""
    self.error_message = ""

    self.encoders = {"mp3":"lame",
        "wav": "wavenc"}
    self.supportedOutputFormats = self.encoders.keys()
    self.supportedInputFormats = ("ogg", "mp3", "wav")
    self.pipeline = None
    self.is_playing = False

    self.processArgs()
    self.constructPipeline()
    self.connectSignals()
```

5. The self.supportedOutputFormats is a tuple that stores the supported output formats. self.supportedInputFormats is a list obtained from the *keys* of self.encoders and stores the supported input formats. These objects are used in self.processArguments to do necessary checks. The dictionary self.encoders provides the correct type of encoder string to be used to create an encoder element object for the GStreamer pipeline. As the name suggests, the call to self.constructPipeline() builds a gst.Pipeline instance and various signals are connected using self.connectSignals().

6. Next, prepare a GStreamer pipeline.

```python
def constructPipeline(self):
    self.pipeline = gst.Pipeline("pipeline")

    self.filesrc = gst.element_factory_make("filesrc")
    self.decodebin = gst.element_factory_make("decodebin")
    self.audioconvert = gst.element_factory_make(
                        "audioconvert")
    self.filesink = gst.element_factory_make("filesink")

    encoder_str = self.encoders[self.outputFormat]
    self.encoder= gst.element_factory_make(encoder_str)



    self.pipeline.add( self.filesrc, self.decodebin,
            self.audioconvert, self.encoder,
            self.filesink)

    gst.element_link_many(self.filesrc, self.decodebin)
    gst.element_link_many(self.audioconvert, self.encoder,
            self.filesink)
```

7. This code is similar to the one we developed in the *Playing Music* sub-section. However there are some noticeable differences. In the Audio Player example, we used the autoaudiosink plugin as the last element. In the Audio Converter, we have replaced it with elements self.encoder and self.filesink. The former encodes the audio data coming out of the self.audioconvert. The encoder will be linked to the sink element. In this case, it is a filesink. The self.filesink is where the audio data is written to a file given by the location property.

8. The encoder string, `encoder_str` determines the type of encoder element to create. For example, if the output format is specified as "mp3" the corresponding encoder to use is "`lame`" mp3 encoder. You can run the *gst-inspect-0.10* command to know more about the `lame` mp3 encoder. The following command can be run from shell on Linux.

```
$gst-inspect-0.10 lame
```

9. The elements are added to the pipeline and then linked together. As before, the `self.decodebin` and `self.audioconvert` are not linked in this method as the `decodebin` plugin uses dynamic pads. The pad_added signal from the `self.decodebin` is connected in the `self.connectSignals()` method.

10. Another noticeable change is that we have not set the `location` property for both, `self.filesrc` and `self.filesink`. These properties will be set at the runtime. The input and output file locations keep on changing as the tool is a batch processing utility.

11. Let's write the main method that controls the conversion process.

```
1 def convert(self):
2     pattern = "*." + self.inputFormat
3     filetype = os.path.join(self.inputDir, pattern)
4     fileList = glob.glob(filetype)
5     inputFileList = filter(audioFileExists, fileList)
6
7     if not inputFileList:
8       print "\n No audio files with extension %s "\
9           "located in dir %s"%(
10              self.outputFormat, self.inputDir)
11      return
12   else:
13     # Record time before beginning audio conversion
14     starttime = time.clock()
15     print "\n Converting Audio files.."
16
17   # Save the audio into specified file format.
18   # Do it in a for loop If the audio by that name already
19   # exists, do not overwrite it
20   for inPath in inputFileList:
21     dir, fil = os.path.split(inPath)
22     fil, ext = os.path.splitext(fil)
23     outPath = os.path.join(
24             self.outputDir,
```

```
25                    fil + "." + self.outputFormat)
26
27
28    print "\n Input File: %s%s, Conversion STARTED..."\
29      % (fil, ext)
30    self.convert_single_audio(inPath, outPath)
31    if self.error_message:
32      print "\n Input File: %s%s, ERROR OCCURED" \
33      % (fil, ext)
34      print self.error_message
35    else:
36      print "\nInput File: %s%s,Conversion COMPLETE"\
37      % (fil, ext)
38
39    endtime = time.clock()
40
41    self.printFinalStatus(inputFileList, starttime,
42              endtime)
43    evt_loop.quit()
```

12. The code between lines 2 to 26 is similar to the one developed in the Image File conversion utility in this book. Refer to the *Reading and Writing Images* section of *Chapter 2* to know what that code does. All the input audio files are collected in the list `inputFileList` by the code between lines 2 to 6 . Then, we loop over each of these files. First, the output file path is derived based on user inputs and then the input file path.

13. The highlighted line of code is the workhorse method, `AudioConverter.convert_single_audio`, that actually does the job of converting the input audio. We will discuss that method next. On line 43, the main event loop is terminated. The rest of the code in method convert is self-explanatory.

14. The code in method `convert_single_audio` is illustrated below.

```
1 def convert_single_audio(self, inPath, outPath):
2   inPth = repr(inPath)
3   outPth = repr(outPath)
4
5   # Set the location property for file source and sink
6   self.filesrc.set_property("location", inPth[1:-1])
7   self.filesink.set_property("location", outPth[1:-1])
8
9   self.is_playing = True
```

```
10    self.pipeline.set_state(gst.STATE_PLAYING)
11    while self.is_playing:
12      time.sleep(1)
```

15. As mentioned in the last step, `convert_single_audio` method is called within a for loop in the `self.convert()`. The for loop iterates over a list containing input audio file paths. The input and output file paths are given as arguments to this method. The code between lines 8-12 looks more or less similar to `AudioPlayer.play()` method illustrated in the *Play audio section*. The only difference is the main event loop is not terminated in this method. Earlier we did not set the location property for the file source and sink. These properties are set on lines 6 and 7 respectively.

16. Now what's up with the code on lines 2 and 3? The call `repr(inPath)` returns a printable representation of the string inPath. The `inPath` is obtained from the 'for loop'. The `os.path.normpath` doesn't work on this string. In Windows, if you directly use `inPath`, GStreamer will throw an error while processing such a path string. One way to handle this is to use `repr(string)`, which will return the whole string including the quotes . For example: if inPath be `"C:/AudioFiles/my_music.mp3"`, then `repr(inPath)` will return `"'C:\\\\AudioFiles\\\\my_music.mp3'"`. Notice that it has two single quotes. We need to get rid of the extra single quotes at the beginning and end by slicing the string as `inPth[1:-1]`. There could be some other better ways. You can come up with one and then just use that code as a path string!

17. Let's quickly skim through a few more methods. Write these down:

```
def connectSignals(self):

    # Connect the signals.
    # Catch the messages on the bus
    bus = self.pipeline.get_bus()
    bus.add_signal_watch()
    bus.connect("message", self.message_handler)
    # Connect the decodebin "pad_added" signal.
    self.decodebin.connect("pad_added",
                self.decodebin_pad_added)

def decodebin_pad_added(self, decodebin, pad):
    caps = pad.get_caps()
    compatible_pad=\
    self.audioconvert.get_compatible_pad(pad, caps)
    pad.link(compatible_pad)
```

18. The `connectSignal` method is identical to the one discussed in the *Playing music* section, except that we are also connecting the `decodebin` signal with a method `decodebin_pad_added`. Add a print statement to `decodebin_pad_added` to check when it gets called. It will help you understand how the dynamic pad works! The program starts by processing the first audio file. The method `convert_single_audio` gets called. Here, we set the necessary file paths. After that, it begins playing the audio file. At this time, the `pad_added` signal is generated. Thus based on the input file data, `decodebin` will create the pad.

19. The rest of the methods such as `processArgs`, `printUsage`, and `message_handler` are self-explanatory. You can review these methods from the file `AudioConverter.py`.

20. The audio converter should be ready for action now! Make sure that all methods are properly defined and then run the code by specifying appropriate input arguments. The following screenshot shows a sample run of audio conversion utility on Windows XP. Here, it will batch process all audio files in directory `C:\AudioFiles` with extension `.ogg` and convert them into **mp3** file format . The resultant mp3 files will be created in directory `C:\AudioFiles\OUTPUT_AUDIOS`.

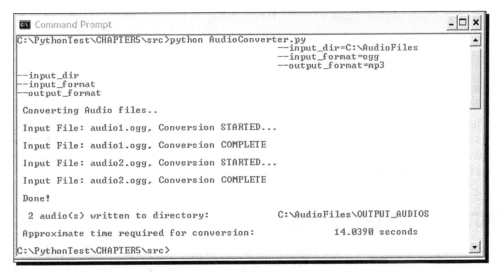

What just happened?

A basic audio conversion utility was developed in the previous section. This utility can batch-convert audio files with ogg or mp3 or wav format into user-specified output format (where supported formats are wav and mp3). We learned how to specify encoder and filesink elements and link them in the GStreamer pipeline. To accomplish this task, we also applied knowledge gained in earlier sections such as creation of GStreamer pipeline, capturing bus messages, running the main event loop, and so on.

Have a go hero – do more with audio converter

The audio converter we wrote is fairly simple. It deserves an upgrade.

Extend this application to support more audio output formats such as ogg, `flac`, and so on. The following pipeline illustrated one way of converting an input audio file into ogg file format.

```
filesrc location=input.mp3 ! decodebin ! audioconvert ! vorbisenc !
oggmux ! filesink location=output.ogg
```

Notice that we have an audio muxer, oggmux, that needs to be linked with encoder vorbisenc. Similarly, to create an MP4 audio file, it will need { faac ! mp4mux} as encoder and audio muxer. One of the simplest things to do is to define proper elements (such as encoder and muxer) and instead of constructing a pipeline from individual elements, use the `gst.parse_launch` method we studied earlier and let it automatically create and link elements using the command string. You can create a pipeline instance each time the audio conversion is called for. But in this case you would also need to connect signals each time the pipeline is created. Another better and simpler way is to link the audio muxer in the `AudioConverter.constructPipeline` method. You just need to check if it is needed based on the type of plugin you are using for encoding. In this case the code will be:

```
gst.element_link_many(self.audioconvert, self.encoder,
              self.audiomuxer, self.filesink)
```

The audio converter illustrated in this example takes input files of only a single audio file format. This can easily be extended to accept input audio files in all supported file formats (except for the type specified by the `--output_format` option). The decodebin should take care of decoding the given input data. Extend Audio Converter to support this feature. You will need to modify the code in the `AudioConverter.convert()` method where the input file list is determined.

Extracting part of an audio

Suppose you have recorded a live concert of your favorite musician or a singer. You have saved all this into a single file with MP3 format but you would like to break this file into small pieces. There is more than one way to achieve this using Python and GStreamer. We will use the simplest and perhaps the most efficient way of cutting a small piece from an audio track. It makes use of an excellent GStreamer plugin, called Gnonlin.

The Gnonlin plugin

The multimedia editing can be classified as linear or non-linear. Non-linear multimedia editing enables control over the media progress in an interactive way. For example, it allows you to control the order in which the sources should be executed. At the same time it allows modifications to the position in a media track. While doing all this, note that the original source (such as an audio file) remains unchanged. Thus the editing is non-destructive. The Gnonlin or (G-Non-Linear) provides essential elements for non-linear editing of a multimedia. It has five major elements, namely, `gnlfilesource`, `gnlurisource`, `gnlcomposition`, `gnloperation`, and `gnlsource`. To know more about their properties, run gst-inspect-0.10 command on each of these elements.

Here, we will only focus on the element gnlfilesource and a few of its properties. This is really a GStreamer bin element. Like decodebin, it determines which pads to use at the runtime. As the name suggests, it deals with the input media file. All you need to specify is the input media source it needs to handle. The media file format can be any of the supported media formats. The gnlfilesource defines a number of properties. To extract a chunk of an audio, we just need to consider three of them:

- `media-start`: The position in the input media file, which will become the start position of the extracted media. This is specified in nanoseconds.

- `media-duration`: Total duration of the extracted media file (beginning from `media-start`). This is specified in nanoseconds as well.

- `uri`: The full path of the input media file. For example, if it is a file on your local hard drive, the `uri` will be something like `file:///C:/AudioFiles/my_music.mp3`. If the file is located on a website, then the `uri` will something of this sort: `http://path/to/file.mp3`.

The gnlfilesource internally does operations like loading and decoding the file, seeking the track to the specified position, and so on. This makes our job easier. We just need to create basic elements that will process the information furnished by gnlfilesource, to create an output audio file. Now that we know the basics of gnlfilesource, let's try to come up with a GStreamer pipeline that will cut a portion of an input audio file.

- First the `gnlfilesource` element that does the crucial job of loading, decoding the file, seeking the correct start position, and finally presenting us with an audio data that represents the portion of track to be extracted.

- An `audioconvert` element that will convert this data into an appropriate audio format.

- An encoder that encodes this data further into the final audio format we want.

- A sink where the output data is dumped. This specifies the output audio file.

Try running the following from the command prompt by replacing the uri and location paths with appropriate file paths on your computer.

```
$gst-launch-0.10.exe gnlfilesource uri=file:///C:/my_music.mp3
        media-start=0 media-duration=15000000000 !
        audioconvert !
        lame !
        filesink location=C:/my_chunk.mp3
```

This should create an extracted audio file of duration 15 seconds, starting at the initial position on the original file. Note that the media-start and media-duration properties take the input in nanoseconds. This is really the essence of what we will do next.

Time for action – MP3 cutter!

In this section we will develop a utility that will cut out a portion of an MP3 formatted audio and save it as a separate file.

1. Keep the file `AudioCutter.py` handy. You can download it from the Packt website. Here we will only discuss important methods. The methods not discussed here are similar to the ones from earlier examples. Review the file `AudioCutter.py` which has all the necessary source code to run this application.

2. Start the usual way. Do the necessary imports and write the following skeleton code.

```
import os, sys, time
import thread
import gobject
import pygst
pygst.require("0.10")
import gst

class AudioCutter:
    def __init__(self):
        pass
    def constructPipeline(self):
        pass
    def gnonlin_pad_added(self, gnonlin_elem, pad):
        pass
    def connectSignals(self):
        pass
    def run(self):
        pass
```

```
    def printFinalStatus(self):
        pass
    def message_handler(self, bus, message):
        pass


#Run the program
audioCutter = AudioCutter()
thread.start_new_thread(audioCutter.run, ())
gobject.threads_init()
evt_loop = gobject.MainLoop()
evt_loop.run()
```

The overall code layout looks familiar doesn't it? The code is very similar
to the code we developed earlier in this chapter. The key here is the
appropriate choice of the file source element and linking it with the rest
of the pipeline! The last few lines of code create a thread with method
`AudioCutter.run` and run the main event loop as seen before.

3. Now fill in the constructor of the class. We will keep it simple this time. The things
we need will be hardcoded within the constructor of the `class AudioCutter`. It
is very easy to implement a `processArgs()` method as done on many occasions
before. Replace the input and output file locations in the code snippet with a proper
audio file path on your computer.

```
    def __init__(self):
        self.is_playing = False
        # Flag used for printing purpose only.
        self.error_msg = ''

        self.media_start_time = 100
        self.media_duration = 30
        self.inFileLocation = "C:\AudioFiles\my_music.mp3"
        self.outFileLocation = "C:\AudioFiles\my_music_chunk.mp3"

        self.constructPipeline()
        self.connectSignals()
```

4. the `self.media_start_time` is the new starting position of the mp3 file in
seconds. This is the new start position for the extracted output audio. The `self.`
`duration` variable stores the total duration extracted track. Thus, if you have an
audio file with a total duration of 5 minutes, the extracted audio will have a starting
position corresponding to 1 min, 40 seconds on the original track. The total duration
of this output file will be 30 seconds, that is, the end time will correspond to 2
minutes, 10 seconds on the original track. The last two lines of this method
build a pipeline and connect signals with class methods.

5. Next, build the GStreamer pipeline.

```
1 def constructPipeline(self):
2   self.pipeline = gst.Pipeline()
3   self.filesrc = gst.element_factory_make(
4                   "gnlfilesource")
5
6   # Set properties of filesrc element
7   # Note: the gnlfilesource signal will be connected
8   # in self.connectSignals()
9   self.filesrc.set_property("uri",
10                  "file:///" + self.inFileLocation)
11  self.filesrc.set_property("media-start",
12                  self.media_start_time*gst.SECOND)
13  self.filesrc.set_property("media-duration",
14                  self.media_duration*gst.SECOND)
15
16  self.audioconvert = \
17  gst.element_factory_make("audioconvert")
18
19  self.encoder = \
20  gst.element_factory_make("lame", "mp3_encoder")
21
22  self.filesink = \
23  gst.element_factory_make("filesink")
24
25  self.filesink.set_property("location",
26                  self.outFileLocation)
27
28  #Add elements to the pipeline
29  self.pipeline.add(self.filesrc, self.audioconvert,
30              self.encoder, self.filesink)
31  # Link elements
32  gst.element_link_many(self.audioconvert, self.encoder,
33              self.filesink)
```

The highlighted line of code (line 3) creates the `gnlfilesource`. We call this as `self.filesrc`. As discussed earlier, this is responsible for loading and decoding audio data and presenting only the required portion of audio data that we need. It enables a higher level of abstraction in the main pipeline.

6. The code between lines 9 to 13 sets three properties of `gnlfilesource`, `uri`, `media-start` and `media-duration`. The `media-start` and `media-duration` are specified in nanoseconds. Therefore, we multiply the parameter value (which is in seconds) by `gst.SECOND` which takes care of the units.

7. The rest of the code looks very much similar to the Audio Converter example. In this case, we only support saving the file in mp3 audio format. The encoder element is defined on line 19. `self.filesink` determines where the output file will be saved. Elements are added to the pipeline by self.pipeline.add call and are linked together on line 32. Note that the `gnlfilesource` element, `self.filesrc`, is not linked with `self.audioconvert` while constructing the pipeline. Like the `decodebin`, the `gnlfilesource` implements *dynamic pads*. Thus, the pad is not available when the pipeline is constructed. It is created at the runtime depending on the specified input audio format. The "pad_added" signal of `gnlfilesource` is connected with a method `self.gnonlin_pad_added`.

8. Now write the `connectSignals` and `gnonlin_pad_added` methods.

```
def connectSignals(self):
    # capture the messages put on the bus.
    bus = self.pipeline.get_bus()
    bus.add_signal_watch()
    bus.connect("message", self.message_handler)

    # gnlsource plugin uses dynamic pads.
    # Capture the pad_added signal.
    self.filesrc.connect("pad-added",self.gnonlin_pad_added)


def gnonlin_pad_added(self, gnonlin_elem, pad):
    pad.get_caps()
    compatible_pad = \
    self.audioconvert.get_compatible_pad(pad, caps)
    pad.link(compatible_pad)
```

The highlighted line of code in method `connectSignals` connects the pad_added signal of `gnlfilesource` with a method gnonlin_pad_added. The gnonlin_pad_added method is identical to the decodebin_pad_added method of `class AudioConverter` developed earlier. Whenever `gnlfilesource` creates a pad at the runtime, this method gets called and here, we manually link the pads of `gnlfilesource` with the compatible pad on `self.audioconvert`.

9. The rest of the code is very much similar to the code developed in the *Playing an audio* section. For example, `AudioCutter.run` method is equivalent to `AudioPlayer.play` and so on. You can review the code for remaining methods from the file `AudioCutter.py`.

10. Once everything is in place, run the program from the command line as:

```
$python AudioCutter.py
```

11. This should create a new MP3 file which is just a specific portion of the original audio file.

What just happened?

We accomplished creation of a utility that can cut a piece out of an MP3 audio file (yet keep the original file unchanged). This audio piece was saved as a separate MP3 file. We learned about a very useful plugin, called Gnonlin, intended for non-linear multimedia editing. A few fundamental properties of gnlfilesource element in this plugin to extract an audio file.

Have a go hero – extend MP3 cutter

- Modify this program so that the parameters such as `media_start_time` can be passed as an argument to the program. You will need a method like `processArguments()`. You can use either `getopt` or `OptionParser` module to parse the arguments.

- Add support for other file formats. For example, extend this code so that it can extract a piece from a **wav** formatted audio and save it as an **MP3** audio file. The input part will be handled by `gnlfilesource`. Depending upon the type of output file format, you will need a specific encoder and possibly an audio muxer element. Then add and link these elements in the main GStreamer pipeline.

Recording

After learning how to cut out a piece from our favorite music tracks, the next exciting thing we will have is a 'home grown' audio recorder. Then use it the way you like to record music, mimicry or just a simple speech!

Remember what pipeline we used to play an audio? The elements in the pipeline to play an audio were `filesrc ! decodebin ! audioconvert ! autoaudiosink`. The autoaudiosink did the job of automatically detecting the output audio device on your computer.

For recording purposes, the audio source is going to be from the microphone connected to your computer. Thus, there won't be any `filesrc` element. We will instead replace with a GStreamer plugin that automatically detects the input audio device. On similar lines, you probably want to save the recording to a file. So, the `autoaudiosink` element gets replaced with a `filesink` element.

autoaudiosrc is an element we can possibly use for detecting input audio source. However, while testing this program on Windows XP, the autoaudiosrc was unable to detect the audio source for unknown reasons. So, we will use the `Directshow` audio capture source plugin called dshowaudiosrc, to accomplish the recording task. Run the `gst-inspect-0.10 dshowaudiosrc` command to make sure it is installed and to learn various properties of this element. Putting this plugin in the pipeline worked fine on Windows XP. The dshowaudiosrc is linked to the audioconvert.

With this information, let's give it a try using the command-line version of GStreamer. Make sure you have a microphone connected or built into your computer. For a change, we will save the output file in `ogg` format.

```
gst-launch-0.10.exe dshowaudiosrc num-buffers=1000 !
          audioconvert ! audioresample !
          vorbisenc ! oggmux !
          filesink location=C:/my_voice.ogg
```

The audioresample re-samples the raw audio data with different sample rates. Then the encoder element encodes it. The multiplexer or mux, if present, takes the encoded data and puts it into a single channel. The recorded audio file is written to the location specified by the filesink element.

Time for action – recording

Okay, time to write some code that does audio recording for us.

1. Download the file `RecordingAudio.py` and review the code. You will notice that the only important task is to set up a proper pipeline for audio recording. Content-wise, the other code is very much similar to what we learned earlier in the chapter. It will have some minor differences such as method names and print statements. In this section we will discuss only the important methods in the class AudioRecorder.

2. Write the constructor.
```
def __init__(self):
    self.is_playing = False
    self.num_buffers = -1
    self.error_message = ""
```

```
self.processArgs()
self.constructPipeline()
self.connectSignals()
```

3. This is similar to the `AudioPlayer.__init__()` except that we have added a call to `processArgs()` and initialized the error reporting variable `self.error_message` and the variable that indicates the total duration of the recording.

4. Build the GStreamer pipeline by writing `constructPipeline` method.

```
1 def constructPipeline(self):
2    # Create the pipeline instance
3    self.recorder = gst.Pipeline()
4
5    # Define pipeline elements
6    self.audiosrc = \
7    gst.element_factory_make("dshowaudiosrc")
8
9    self.audiosrc.set_property("num-buffers",
10               self.num_buffers)
11
12   self.audioconvert = \
13   gst.element_factory_make("audioconvert")
14
15   self.audioresample = \
16   gst.element_factory_make("audioresample")
17
18   self.encoder = \
19   gst.element_factory_make("lame")
20
21   self.filesink = \
22   gst.element_factory_make("filesink")
23
24   self.filesink.set_property("location",
25               self.outFileLocation)
26
27   # Add elements to the pipeline
28   self.recorder.add(self.audiosrc, self.audioconvert,
29          self.audioresample,
30          self.encoder, self.filesink)
31
32   # Link elements in the pipeline.
33   gst.element_link_many(self.audiosrc, self.audioconvert,
34          self.audioresample,
35          self.encoder, self.filesink)
```

5. We use the `dshowaudiosrc` (Directshow audiosrc) plugin as an audio source element. It finds out the input audio source which will be, for instance, the audio input from a microphone.

6. On line 9, we set the number of buffers property to the one specified by `self. num_buffers`. This has a default value as `-1`, indicating that there is no limit on the number of buffers. If you specify this value as `500` for instance, it will output `500` buffers (5 second duration) before sending a **End of Stream** message to end the run of the program.

7. On line 15, an instance of element `'audioresample'` is created. This element is takes the raw audio buffer from the `self.audioconvert` and re-samples it to different sample rates. The encoder element then encodes the audio data into a suitable format and the recorder file is written to the location specified by `self.filesink`.

8. The code between lines 28 to 35 adds various elements to the pipeline and links them together.

9. Review the code in file `RecordingAudio.py` to add rest of the code. Then run the program to record your voice or anything that you want to record that makes an audible sound! Following are sample command-line arguments. This program will record an audio for 5 seconds.

```
$python RecordingAudio.py --num_buffers=500
              --out_file=C:/my_voice.mp3
```

What just happened?

We learned how to record an audio using Python and GStreamer. We developed a simple audio recording utility to accomplish this task. The GStreamer plugin, dshowaudiosrc, captured the audio input for us. We created the main GStreamer Pipeline by adding this and other elements and used it for the Audio Recorder program.

Summary

This chapter gave us deeper insight into the fundamentals of audio processing using Python and the GStreamer multimedia framework. We used several important components of GStreamer to develop some frequently needed audio processing utilities. The main learning points of the chapter can be summarized as follows:

- GStreamer installation: We learned how to install GStreamer and the dependent packages on various platforms. This set up a stage for learning audio processing techniques and will also be useful for the next chapters on audio/video processing.

- A primer on GStreamer: A quick primer on GStreamer helped us understand important elements required for media processing.

- Use of GStreamer API to develop audio tools: We learned how to use GStremer API for general audio processing. This helped us develop tools such as an Audio player, a file format converter, an MP3 cutter, and audio recorder.

Now that we've learned about basic audio processing using GStreamer, we're ready to add some 'spice' to the audio. In the next chapter we will learn techniques that will help us add special effects to an audio.

6

Audio Controls and Effects

In the previous chapter, the focus was on learning fundamentals of audio processing. It introduced us to the GStreamer multimedia framework. We applied this knowledge to develop some frequently needed audio processing tools. In this chapter, we will go one step further by developing tools for adding audio effects, mixing audio tracks, creating custom music tracks, and so on.

In this chapter, we shall:

- ◆ Learn how to control a streaming audio.
- ◆ Spice up the audio by adding effects such as fading, echo, and panorama.
- ◆ Work on a project where a custom music track will be created by combining different audio clips.
- ◆ Add visualization effect to a streaming audio.
- ◆ Mix two audio streams into a single track. For example, mix an audio containing only a *vocal track* with an audio containing only *background music track*.

So let's get on with it.

Controlling playback

In an audio player, various options such as Play, Pause, Stop, and so on, provide a way to control the streaming audio. Such playback controls also find use in other audio processing techniques. We have already used some of the playback controls in *Chapter 5, Working with Audios*. In this chapter, we will study some more controlling options.

Play

In the previous chapter, we developed a preliminary command-line audio player using GStreamer. The audio streaming can be started by instructing the GStreamer pipeline to begin the flow of audio data. This was achieved by the following code:

```
self.pipeline.set_state(gst.STATE_PLAYING)
```

With the above instruction, the audio will be streamed until the end of the stream is reached. Refer to the code in the *Playing Audio* section of *Chapter 5, Working with Audios* to see what the surrounding code looks like. If you develop a user interface for a simple audio player, the "Play" button can be connected to a method that will set the state of pipeline to `gst.STATE_PLAYING`.

Pause/resume

The streaming audio can be paused temporarily by setting the GStreamer pipeline state to `gst.STATE_PAUSED`. Pausing music in an audio player is another commonly performed operation. But this also finds use while doing some special audio processing.

Time for action – pause and resume a playing audio stream

We will now review a very simple example demonstrating various playback control techniques. The same example will be used in the next few sections. This exercise will be an ideal preparation while working on the project 'Extract Audio Using Playback Controls'. So let's get started!

1. Download the file `PlaybackControlExamples.py` from the Packt website. This file has all the necessary code that illustrates various playback controls. The overall class and its methods are illustrated below for reference. See the source file to know more about each of these methods.

```
class AudioPlayer:
    def __init__(self):
        pass
    def constructPipeline(self):
        pass
    def connectSignals(self):
        pass
    def decodebin_pad_added(self, decodebin, pad ):
        pass
    def play(self):
        pass
    def runExamples(self):
        pass
```

```
def runPauseExample(self):
    pass
def runStopExample(self):
    pass
def runSeekExample(self):
    pass
def okToRunExamples(self):
    pass
def message_handler(self, bus, message):
    pass
```

The overall code layout is very similar to the code developed in the *Playing audio* section of *Chapter 5, Working with Audios*. Thus, we will just review some of the newly added methods relevant to this section.

2. Here is the code for `self.play` method.

```
1   def play(self):
2       self.is_playing = True
3       self.player.set_state(gst.STATE_PLAYING)
4       self.position = None
5       while self.is_playing:
6           time.sleep(0.5)
7           try:
9               self.position = (
10              self.player.query_position(gst.FORMAT_TIME,
11                                          None) [0] )
16          except gst.QueryError:
17              # The pipeline has probably reached
18              # the end of the audio, (and thus has 'reset'
itself.
19              # So, it may be unable to query the current
position.
20              # In this case, do nothing except to reset
21              # self.position to None.
22              self.position = None
23
24          if not self.position is None:
25              #Convert the duration into seconds.
26              self.position = self.position/gst.SECOND
27              print "\n Current playing time: ",
28                                              self.position
29
30          self.runExamples()
31   evt_loop.quit()
```

Inside the `while` loop, on line 9, the current position of the streaming audio is queried using the `query_position` call. This is an API method of GStreamer Pipeline object. When the pipeline approaches the end of the stream, it may throw an error while querying the current position. Therefore, we catch the exception `gst.QueryError`, in the `try-except` block. The `time.sleep` call is important before entering the `try-except` block. It ensures that the position is queried every 0.5 seconds. If you remove this call, the next code will be executed for each incremental tiny step. From a performance standpoint this is unnecessary. The current position thus obtained is expressed in nanoseconds, Thus, if the time is say 0.1 seconds, it is obtained as 100 000 000 nanoseconds. To convert it into seconds, it is divided by a GStreamer constant `gst.SECOND`. On line 30, the main method that runs various audio control examples is called.

3. Let's see the code in `self.runExamples` method now.

```
1   def runExamples(self):
2
3       if not self.okToRunExamples():
4           return
5
6       # The example will be roughly be run when the streaming
7       # crosses 5 second mark.
8       if self.position >= 5 and self.position < 8:
9           if self.pause_example:
10              self.runPauseExample()
11          elif self.stop_example:
12              self.runStopExample()
13          elif self.seek_example:
14              self.runSeekExample()
15          # this flag ensures that an example is run
16          # only once.
17          self.ranExample = True
```

The method `self.okToRunExamples` does some preliminary error checking and ensures that the total streaming duration is greater than 20 seconds. This method will not be discussed here. When the current track position reaches 5 seconds, one of the examples is run. Which example to run is determined by the corresponding `boolean` flag. For instance, if `self.pause_example` flag is set to `True`, it will run the code that will 'pause' the audio stream. Likewise for the other examples. These three flags are initialized to `False` in the __init__ method.

4. The last method we will review is `self.runPauseExample`.

```
1 def runPauseExample(self):
2      print ("\n Pause example: Playback will be paused"
3            " for 5 seconds and will then be resumed...")
4      self.player.set_state(gst.STATE_PAUSED)
5      time.sleep(5)
6      print "\n .. OK now resuming the playback"
7      self.player.set_state(gst.STATE_PLAYING)
```

The streaming audio is paused by the call on line 4. The `time.sleep` call will keep the audio paused for 5 seconds and then the audio playback is resumed by the call on line 7.

5. Make sure to set the flag `self.pause_example` to True in the `__init__` method and specify the proper audio file path for the variable for `self.inFileLocation`. Then run this example from the command prompt as:

```
$python PlaybackControlExamples.py
```

The audio will be played for the first 5 seconds. It will be then paused for another 5 seconds and finally the playback will be resumed.

What just happened?

With the help of a simple example, we learned how to pause a streaming audio. We also saw how the current position of the streaming audio is queried. This knowledge will be used in a project later in this chapter.

Stop

Setting the state of the GStreamer pipeline to `gst.STATE_NULL` stops the audio streaming. Recall the `message_handler` method explained in the Playing Audio section of the previous chapter. We made use of this state when the end of stream message was put on the `bus`. In the file `PlaybackControlExamples.py`, the following code stops the streaming of the audio.

```
def runStopExample(self):
    print ("\n STOP example: Playback will be STOPPED"
    " and then the application will be terminated.")
    self.player.set_state(gst.STATE_NULL)
    self.is_playing = False
```

In this file, set the flag `self.stop_example` to `True` and then run the program from the command line to see this illustration.

Fast-forward/rewind

Fast-forwarding or rewinding a track simply means that the current position on the audio track being played is shifted to some other position. This is also called seeking a position on a track. The `pipeline` element of GStreamer defines an API method, `seek_simple`, that facilitates jumping to a specified position on the track in a streaming audio. In the file `PlabackControlExamples.py`, this is illustrated by the following method.

```
def runSeekExample(self):
    print ("\n SEEK example: Now jumping to position at 15 seconds"
    "the audio will continue to stream after this")

    self.player.seek_simple(gst.FORMAT_TIME,
                            gst.SEEK_FLAG_FLUSH,
                            15*gst.SECOND)
    self.player.set_state(gst.STATE_PAUSED)
    print "\n starting playback in 2 seconds.."
    time.sleep(2)
    self.player.set_state(gst.STATE_PLAYING)
```

When this method is called, the current audio position is shifted to a position corresponding to 15 seconds duration on the audio track. The highlighted lines of code are the key. The `seek_simple` method takes three arguments. The first argument, `gst.FORMAT_TIME`, represents the time on the track. The second argument,`gst.SEEK_GLAG_FLUSH`, is a 'seek flag'. It tells the pipeline to clear the currently playing audio data. In other words it instructs to flush the pipeline. This makes the seek operation faster according to the documentation. There are several other seek flags. Refer to the GStreamer documentation to know more about these flags. The third argument specifies the time on the track that will be the new 'current position' of the streaming audio. This time I specified in nanoseconds and so, it is multiplied by a constant `gst.SECOND`. Note that pipeline should be in playing state, before calling `seek_simple` method.

Project: extract audio using playback controls

In the last chapter, we learned how to use `gnonlin` plugin to extract a piece of audio. Gnonlin made our job very easy. In this project, we will see another way of extracting the audio files, by applying basic audio processing techniques using GStreamer. We will use some of the audio playback controls just learned. This project will serve as a refresher on various fundamental components of GStreamer API.

Time for action – MP3 cutter from basic principles

Let's create an MP3 cutter from 'basic principles'. That is we won't be using `gnonlin` to do this. In this project, we will apply knowledge about seeking a track playing, pausing the pipeline along with the basic audio processing operations.

This utility can be run from the command line as:

```
$python AudioCutter_Method2.py [options]
```

Where, the `[options]` are as follows:

- `--input_file`: The input audio file in MP3 format from which a piece of audio needs to be cut.
- `--output_file`: The output file path where the extracted audio will be saved. This needs to be in MP3 format.
- `--start_time`: The position in seconds on the original track. This will be the starting position of the audio to be extracted.
- `--end_time`: The position in seconds on the original track. This will be the end position of the extracted audio.
- `--verbose_mode`: Prints useful information such as current position of the track (in seconds) while extracting the audio. By default, this flag is set to `False`.

1. Download the file `AudioCutter_Method2.py` from the Packt website. We will discuss only the most important methods here. You can refer to the source code in this file for developing the rest of the code.

2. We will start as usual, by defining a class with empty methods.

```python
import os, sys, time
import thread
import gobject
from optparse import OptionParser

import pygst
pygst.require("0.10")
import gst

class AudioCutter:
    def __init__(self):
        pass
    def constructPipeline(self):
        pass
    def decodebin_pad_added(self, decodebin, pad):
```

```
            pass
        def connectSignals(self):
            pass
        def run(self):
            pass
        def extractAudio(self):
            pass
        def processArgs(self):
            pass
        def printUsage(self):
            pass
        def printFinalStatus(self):
            pass
        def message_handler(self, bus, message):
            pass

    audioCutter = AudioCutter()
    thread.start_new_thread(audioCutter.run, ())
    gobject.threads_init()
    evt_loop = gobject.MainLoop()
    evt_loop.run()
```

3. As you can see, the overall structure and the method names are very much consistent with the MP3 cutter example in earlier chapters. Instead of method `gnonlin_pad_added` we have `decodebin_pad_added` which indicates we are going to capture the `pad_added` signal for the `decodebin`. Also, there are new methods `run` and `extractAudio`. We will discuss these in detail.

4. Now let's review the constructor of the class.

```
1   def __init__(self):
2       self.start_time = None
3       self.end_time = None
4       self.is_playing = False
5       self.seek_done = False
6       self.position = 0
7       self.duration = None
8       #Flag used for printing purpose only.
9       self.error_msg = ''
10      self.verbose_mode = False
11
12      self.processArgs()
13      self.constructPipeline()
14      self.connectSignals()
```

5. The `__init__` method calls methods to process user input and then constructs the GStreamer pipeline by calling the `constructPipeline()` method. This is similar to what we have seen in several examples earlier.

6. Think about this. To extract an audio, what elements do you need? We need all the elements used in audio conversion utility developed in last chapter. Note that in this example we are saving the output in the same audio format as the input. Let's try to construct an initial pipeline.

```
1   def constructPipeline(self):
2       self.pipeline = gst.Pipeline()
3       self.fakesink = gst.element_factory_make("fakesink")
4       filesrc = gst.element_factory_make("filesrc")
5       filesrc.set_property("location", self.inFileLocation)
6
7       autoaudiosink = gst.element_factory_make(
8                                   "autoaudiosink")
9
10      self.decodebin = gst.element_factory_make("decodebin")
11
12      self.audioconvert = gst.element_factory_make(
13                                   "audioconvert")
14
15      self.encoder = gst.element_factory_make("lame",
16                                   "mp3_encoder")
17
18      self.filesink = gst.element_factory_make("filesink")
19      self.filesink.set_property("location",
20                              self.outFileLocation)
21
22      self.pipeline.add(filesrc, self.decodebin,
23                          self.audioconvert,
24                          self.encoder, self.fakesink)
25
26      gst.element_link_many(filesrc, self.decodebin)
27      gst.element_link_many(self.audioconvert,
28                          self.encoder, self.fakesink)
```

7. We are already familiar with most of the elements included in this pipeline. The pipeline looks identical to the one in audio conversion utility except for the sink element. Notice that the `filesink` element is created on line 18. But it is not added to the pipeline! Instead we have added a `fakesink` element. Can you guess why? This is an extraction utility. We just need to save a portion of an input audio file. The start position of the extracted portion may not be the start position of the original track. Thus, at this time, we will not add the `filesink` to the pipeline.

8. Next write the `AudioCutter.run` method.

```
1 def run(self):
2     self.is_playing = True
3     print "\n Converting audio. Please be patient.."
4     self.pipeline.set_state(gst.STATE_PLAYING)
5     time.sleep(1)
6     while self.is_playing:
7         self.extractAudio()
8     self.printFinalStatus()
9     evt_loop.quit()
```

9. On line 4, we apply one of the playback control commands to instruct the pipeline to 'begin'. The state of the input audio is set to `STATE_PLAYING`. As seen earlier, the flag `self.is_playing` is changed in the `message_handler` method. In the `while` loop, the workhorse method `self.extractAudio()` is called. The rest of the code is self-explanatory.

10. Now we will review the method that does the job of cutting the piece of input audio. Let us first see the important things considered in `extractAudio()` method. Then it will be very easy to understand the code. This following illustration lists these important things.

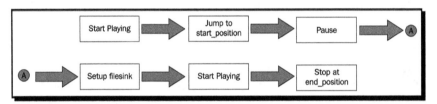

Important steps considered in `AudioCutter.extractAudio()` method appear in the preceding image.

11. To extract a piece of audio from the input, the flow of data through the pipeline needs to be 'started'. Then, we need to jump to a position in the input audio that corresponds to the start position of the audio file to be extracted. Once the start position is identified, the GStreamer pipeline needs to be tweaked so that there is a `filesink` element. The `filesink` will specify the output audio file. After setting the pipeline, we need to begin the flow of data. When the user-specified end position is reached, the program execution should stop. Now let's write the code.

```
1  def extractAudio(self):
2      if not self.seek_done:
3          time.sleep(0.1)
4          self.duration = \
5          self.pipeline.query_duration(gst.FORMAT_TIME,
6                                        None) [0]
7          self.duration = self.duration/gst.SECOND
```

```
8
9           if self.start_time > self.duration:
10              print "\n start time specified" \
11              " is more than the total audio duration"\
12              " resetting the start time to 0 sec"
13              self.start_time = 0.0
14
15          self.pipeline.seek_simple(gst.FORMAT_TIME,
16                                  gst.SEEK_FLAG_FLUSH,
17                                  self.start_time*gst.SECOND)
18
19          self.pipeline.set_state(gst.STATE_PAUSED)
20          self.seek_done = True
21          self.pipeline.remove(self.fakesink)
22
23          self.pipeline.add(self.filesink)
24          gst.element_link_many(self.encoder, self.filesink)
25          self.pipeline.set_state(gst.STATE_PLAYING)
26
27      time.sleep(0.1)
28      try:
29          self.position = self.pipeline.query_position(
30                              gst.FORMAT_TIME, None)[0]
31          self.position = self.position/gst.SECOND
32      except gst.QueryError:
33          # The pipeline has probably reached
34          # the end of the audio, (and thus has 'reset' itself)
35          if self.duration is None:
36              self.error_msg = "\n Error cutting the audio
37               file.Unable to determine the audio duration."
38              self.pipeline.set_state(gst.STATE_NULL)
39              self.is_playing = False
40          if ( self.position <= self.duration and
41                  self.position > (self.duration - 10) ):
42              # Position close to the end of file.
43              # Do nothing to avoid a possible traceback.
44              #The audio cutting should work
45              pass
46          else:
47              self.error_msg =" Error cutting the audio file"
48              self.pipeline.set_state(gst.STATE_NULL)
49              self.is_playing = False
50
51      if not self.end_time is None:
52          if self.position >= self.end_time:
53              self.pipeline.set_state(gst.STATE_NULL)
54              self.is_playing = False
55
56      if self.verbose_mode:
57          print "\n Current play time: =", self.position
```

12. The code block between lines 3 to 25 is executed only once, when the program enters this method for the first time. The flag `self.seek_done` ensures it is executed only once. This is an important piece of code that does the steps 2 to 5 represented by rectangular blocks in the above illustration. Let's review this code in detail now.

13. On line 3, we ask the program to wait for 0.1 seconds by `time.sleep` call. This is necessary for the next line of code that queries the total duration of the playback. The API method query duration returns the total duration of the playback. The argument `gst.FORMAT_TIME` ensures that the return value is in time format (nanoseconds). To get it in seconds, we divide it by `gst.SECOND`.

14. Next, on lines 15-17, we jump to the position on the input audio track pertaining to the user-supplied argument `self.start_time`. Note that the time argument in the method `seek_simple` needs to be in nanoseconds. So it is multiplied by `gst.SECOND`.

15. On line 19, the `gst.STATE_PAUSED` call pauses the flow of data in the pipeline. The `fakesink` element is removed from the pipeline with `self.pipline.remove` call. This also unlinks it from the pipeline. Then the `self.filesink` element is added and linked in the pipeline on lines 23 and 24. With this, we are all set to start playing the audio file again. Here onwards, the audio data will be saved to the audio file indicated by the `filesink` element.

16. On line 27, the current position being played is queried. Note that this is done in a try-except block to avoid any possible error while querying the position when the audio is very near to the end of the file. When `self.position` reaches the specified `self.end_time`, the data flow through the pipeline is stopped by the `gst.STATE_NULL` call.

17. Write other methods such as `decodebin_pad_added`, `connectSignals`. The source code can be found in the file `AudioCutter_Method2.py`.

18. We are now all set to run the program. Run it from the command line by specifying the appropriate arguments mentioned at the beginning of this section.

What just happened?

By applying fundamental audio processing techniques, we developed an MP3 cutter utility. This is just another way of extracting audio. We accomplished this task by making use of various playback controls learned in earlier sections.

Adjusting volume

One of the most common audio operations we perform is to adjust the volume level of a playing audio. Suppose you have a collection of your favourite songs on your computer. You have been adding songs to this collection from various sources over the years and have created a 'playlist' so that you can listen to them one after the other. But some of the songs start much louder than the others. Of course you can adjust the volume every time such songs start playing but that's not what you would like to do is it?? You want to fix this, but how? Let's learn how!

The `volume` element in GStreamer can be used to control the volume of the streaming audio. It is classified as a type of audio filter. Run `gst-inspect-0.10` command on `volume` to know more details about its properties.

How will you adjust volume using the command-line version of GStreamer? Here is the command on Windows XP that accomplishes this. You should use forward slashes as the backward slashes are not parsed properly by the 'location' property.

```
$gstlaunch-0.10  filesrc location=/path/to/audio.mp3 ! decodebin !
Audioconvert ! volume volume=0.8 ! autoaudiosink
```

This pipeline is very similar to the audio playing example. All we did was to add a `volume` element after `audioconvert`.

Time for action – adjusting volume

Now let's develop a Python example of modifying volume of an audio file. We will write a utility that can take an input audio file and write the output file with increased or decreased level of the default volume. The utility will support writing audio files with MP3 format. If you need some other formats, you can extend this application. Refer to the Audio Converter project we did in the previous chapter.

1. Download the file `AudioEffects.py` from Packt website. It has the source code for this example as well as for the *Fading effect*.

2. Write the constructor of the class `AudioEffects`.

```
1 def __init__(self):
2     self.is_playing = False
3     # Flag used for printing purpose only.
4     self.error_msg = ''
5     self.fade_example = False
6     self.inFileLocation = "C:/AudioFiles/audio1.mp3"
7     self.outFileLocation = (
8             "C:/AudioFiles/audio1_out.mp3" )
9
10     self.constructPipeline()
11     self.connectSignals()
```

3. The flag `self.fade_example` should be set to `False` in this example. You can ignore it for now. It will be used in the *Fading effects* section. Specify appropriate input and output audio file paths on lines 6 and 8.

4. We will review the `self.constructPipeline()` method next.

```
1   def constructPipeline(self):
2       self.pipeline = gst.Pipeline()
3
4       self.filesrc = gst.element_factory_make("filesrc")
5       self.filesrc.set_property("location",
6                                       self.inFileLocation)
7
8       self.decodebin = gst.element_factory_make("decodebin")
9       self.audioconvert = gst.element_factory_make(
10                                      "audioconvert")
11      self.encoder = gst.element_factory_make("lame")
12
13      self.filesink = gst.element_factory_make("filesink")
14      self.filesink.set_property("location",
15                                      self.outFileLocation)
16
17      self.volume = gst.element_factory_make("volume")
18      self.volumeLevel = 2.0
19
20      if self.fade_example:
21          self.setupVolumeControl()
22      else:
23          self.volume.set_property("volume",
24                                       self.volumeLevel)
25
26
27      self.pipeline.add(self.filesrc,
28                        self.decodebin,
29                        self.audioconvert,
30                        self.volume,
31                        self.encoder,
32                        self.filesink)
33
34      gst.element_link_many( self.filesrc, self.decodebin)
35      gst.element_link_many(self.audioconvert,
36                               self.volume,
37                               self.encoder,
38                               self.filesink)
```

5. Various GStreamer elements are created the usual way. On line 17, the volume element is created.

6. The `volume` element has a "volume" property. This determines the level of volume in the streaming audio. By default, this has a value of 1.0 which indicates 100% of the current default volume of the audio. A value of 0.0 indicates no volume. A value greater than 1.0 will make the audio louder than the original level. Let's set this level as 2.0, which means the resultant volume will be louder than the original. The rest of the code in this method adds and links elements in the GStreamer pipeline.

7. Review the rest of the code from the file mentioned earlier. It is self- explanatory.

8. Run the program on the command prompt as:

   `$python AudioEffects.py`

9. Play the resultant audio and compare its default sound level with the original audio.

What just happened?

With a very simple illustration, we learned how to change the default sound level of an audio file. What if you want to have varying sound levels at certain points in the audio? We will discuss that very soon, in the *Fading effects* section.

Audio effects

One adds spices for improved taste to food, similarly, to enhance the music or any sound we add audio effects. There is a wide range of audio effect plugins available in GStreamer. We will discuss some of the commonly used audio effects in the coming sections.

Fading effects

Fading is a gradual increase or decrease in the volume level of an audio. Fading-out means gradually decreasing the volume of the audio file as it approaches the end. Typically, at the end, the volume level is set as 0. On similar lines, fade-in effect gradually increases the volume level from the beginning of an audio. In this chapter, we will learn how to add fade-out effect to an audio. Once we learn that, it is trivial to implement fade-in effects.

Time for action – fading effects

Let's add fade-out effect to an input audio. We will use the same source file as used in the *Adjusting volume* section.

1. If you haven't already, download the file `AudioEffects.py` that has the source code for this example.

2. In the `__init__` method of this class, you will need to do one small change. Set the flag `self.fade_example` to `True` so that it now runs the code that adds fade-out effect.

3. We already reviewed the `self.constructPipeline()` method in *Adjusting volume* section. It calls the method `self.setupVolumeControl()`.

    ```
    1 def setupVolumeControl(self):
    2      self.volumeControl = gst.Controller(self.volume,
    3                                          "volume")
    4      self.volumeControl.set("volume", 0.0*gst.SECOND,
    5                              self.volumeLevel)
    6      self.volumeControl.set_interpolation_mode("volume",
    7                                  gst.INTERPOLATE_LINEAR)
    ```

4. The GStreamer `Controller` object is created on line 2. It is a light-weight object that provides a way to control various properties of GStreamer objects. In this case, it will be used to adjust the 'volume' property of `self.volume`. The set method of the `Controller` takes three arguments, namely, the property that needs to be controlled (`"volume"`), the time on the audio track at which it needs to be changed, and the new value of that property (`self.volumeLevel`). Here, the volume level at the beginning of the audio is set `self.volumeLevel`. Next, the interpolation mode is set for the `volume` property being adjusted by the `Controller` object. Here, we ask the `self.volumeControl` to linearly change the volume from its earlier value to the new value as the audio track progresses. For example, if the sound level at the beginning is set as 1.0 and at 30 seconds it is set as 0.5, the volume levels between 0 to 30 seconds on the track will be linearly interpolated. In this case it will linearly decrease from level 1.0 at 0 seconds to level 0.5 at 30 seconds.

The GStreamer documentation suggests that `Controller.set_interpolation_mode` is deprecated (but is still backward compatible in the version 0.10.5 which is used in this book). See a 'TODO' comment in file `AudioEffects.py`.

5. In order to add a fade-out effect towards the end, first we need to get the total duration of the audio being played. We can query the duration only after the audio has been set for playing (example, when it is in gst.STATE_PLAYING mode). This is done in self.play() method.

```
def play(self):
    self.is_playing = True
    self.pipeline.set_state(gst.STATE_PLAYING)

    if self.fade_example:
        self.addFadingEffect()

    while self.is_playing:
        time.sleep(1)
    self.printFinalStatus()
    evt_loop.quit()
```

6. Once the pipeline's state is set to gst.STATE_PLAYING, the self.addFadingEffects() method will be called as shown by the highlighted line of code.

7. We will review this method now.

```
1   def addFadingEffect(self):
2       # Fist make sure that we can add the fading effect!
3       if not self.is_playing:
4           print ("\n Error: unable to add fade effect"
5           "addFadingEffect() called erroniously")
6           return
7
8       time.sleep(0.1)
9       try:
10          duration = (
11          self.pipeline.query_duration(gst.FORMAT_TIME,
12                                      None) [0] )
13          #Convert the duration into seconds.
14          duration = duration/gst.SECOND
15      except gst.QueryError:
16          # The pipeline has probably reached
17          # the end of the audio, (and thus has 'reset' itself)
18          print ("\n Error: unable to determine duration."
19          "Fading effect not added." )
20          return
21
22      if duration < 4:
```

```
23              print ("ERROR: unable to add fading effect."
24              "\n duration too short.")
25              return
26
27      fade_start = duration - 4
28      fade_volume = self.volumeLevel
29      fade_end = duration
30
31      self.volumeControl.set("volume",
32                             fade_start * gst.SECOND,
33                             fade_volume)
34
35      self.volumeControl.set("volume",
36                             fade_end * gst.SECOND,
37                             fade_volume*0.01)
```

8. First we ensure that duration of the audio being played can be computed without any errors. This is done by the code block 2-24. Next, the `fade_start` time is defined. At this control point the fade-out effect will begin. The fade-out will start 4 seconds before the end of the audio. The volume will linearly decrease from `fade_start` time to `fade_end` time. The fade_volume is the reference volume level when the fade-out begins. On lines 30 and 34 we actually set these fade timing and volume parameters for `self.volumeController`, the `Controller` object that adjusts the volume. The gradual decrease in the volume level is achieved by the `gst.INTERPOLATE_LINEAR`, discussed in an earlier step.

9. Develop or review the remaining code using the reference file `AudioEffects.py`. Make sure to specify appropriate input and output audio paths for variables `self.inFileLocation` and `self.outFileLocation` respectively. Then run the program from the command line as:

`$python AudioEffects.py`

10. This should create the output audio file, with a fade-out effect that begins 4 seconds before the end of the file.

What just happened?

We learned how to add a fading effect to an audio file using GStreamer multimedia framework. We used the same GStreamer pipeline as the one used in the *Adjusting volume* section, but this time, the volume level was controlled using the `Controller` object in GStreamer. The technique we just learned will come handy while working on project 'Combining Audio Clips ' later in this chapter.

Have a go hero – add fade-in effect

This is going to be straightforward. We added a fade-out effect earlier. Now extend this utility by adding a fade-in effect to the input audio. Use a total fade duration of 4 seconds. The `fade_start` time in this case will be 0 seconds. Try the interpolation mode as `gst.INTERPOLATE_CUBIC`.

Echo echo echo...

Echo is a reflection of a sound heard a short time period after the original sound. In audio processing, to achieve this effect the input audio signal is recorded and then played back after the specified 'delay time' with a specified intensity. An echo effect can be added using the `audioecho` plugin in GStreamer. The audio echo plugin should be available by default in your GStreamer installation. Check this by running the following command:

```
$gst-inspect-0.10   audioecho
```

If it is not available, you will need to install it separately. Refer to the GStreamer website for installation instructions.

Time for action – adding echo effect

Let's write code to add an echo effect to an input audio. The code is very similar to the one in the `AudioEffects.py` file discussed in earlier section. Just to simplify the matter, we will use the code in file `EchoEffect.py` file for easier understanding. Later, you can easily integrate this with the code in `AudioEffects.py`.

1. Download the file `EchoEffect.py` that has the source code to add audio echo effect. The file contains class `AudioEffects` whose constructor has the following code.

```python
def __init__(self):
    self.is_playing = False
    # Flag used for printing purpose only.
    self.error_msg = ''

    #the flag that determines whether to use
    # a gst Controller object to adjust the
    # intensity of echo while playing the audio.
    self.use_echo_controller = False

    self.inFileLocation = "C:/AudioFiles/audio1.mp3"
    self.outFileLocation = "C:/AudioFiles/audio1_out.mp3"

    self.constructPipeline()
    self.connectSignals()
```

It is similar to the __init__ method discussed in the *Fading Effects* section. One difference here is the flag self.use_echo_controller. If it is set to True, the GStreamer Controller object will be used to adjust certain echo properties while the audio is being streamed. We will first see how a simple echo effect can be implemented and then discuss the echo control details. Specify the appropriate values for audio file path variables self.inFileLocation and self. outFileLocation.

2. Let's build the GStreamer pipeline.

```
1   def constructPipeline(self):
2       self.pipeline = gst.Pipeline()
3
4       self.filesrc = gst.element_factory_make("filesrc")
5       self.filesrc.set_property("location",
6                                      self.inFileLocation)
7
8       self.decodebin = gst.element_factory_make("decodebin")
9
10      self.audioconvert = gst.element_factory_make(
11                                     "audioconvert")
12      self.audioconvert2 = gst.element_factory_make(
13                                     "audioconvert")
14
15      self.encoder = gst.element_factory_make("lame")
16
17      self.filesink = gst.element_factory_make("filesink")
18      self.filesink.set_property("location",
19                                     self.outFileLocation)
20
21      self.echo = gst.element_factory_make("audioecho")
22      self.echo.set_property("delay", 1*gst.SECOND)
23      self.echo.set_property("feedback", 0.3)
24
25      if self.use_echo_controller:
26          self.setupEchoControl()
27      else:
28          self.echo.set_property("intensity", 0.5)
29
30      self.pipeline.add(self.filesrc,self.decodebin,
31                          self.audioconvert,
32                          self.echo,
33                          self.audioconvert2,
34                          self.encoder,
35                          self.filesink)
36
37      gst.element_link_many( self.filesrc, self.decodebin)
```

```
38        gst.element_link_many(self.audioconvert,
39                              self.echo,
40                              self.audioconvert2,
44                              self.encoder,
45                              self.filesink)
```

The audioecho element is created on line 21. The property delay specifies the duration after which the echo sound will be played. We specify it as 1 second, and you can increase or decrease this value further. The echo feedback value is set as 0.3. On line 28, the intensity property is set to 0.5. It can be set in a range 0.0 to 1.0 and determines the sound intensity of the echo. Thus, if you set it to 0.0, the echo won't be heard.

3. Notice that there are two audioconvert elements. The first audioconvert converts the decoded audio stream into a playable format input to the self.echo element. Similarly on the other end of the echo element, we need audioconvert element to process the audio format after the echo effect has been added. This audio is then encoded in MP3 format and saved to the location specified by self.filesink.

4. Run the program from the command line as:

   $python EchoEffect.py

   If you play the output file, the echo sound will be audible throughout the playback duration.

5. Now we will add a feature that will allow us to add echo effect only for a certain duration of the audio track. In the __init__ method, set the flag self.use_echo_controller to True.

6. We will now review the method self.setupEchoControl() which is called in self.constructPipeline().

   ```
   def setupEchoControl(self):
       self.echoControl = gst.Controller(self.echo, "intensity")
       self.echoControl.set("intensity", 0*gst.SECOND, 0.5)
       self.echoControl.set("intensity", 4*gst.SECOND, 0.0)
   ```

7. Setting up gst.Controller object is very similar to the one developed in the *Fading effects* section. Here, we ask the Controller object, self.echoControl, to control the property 'intensity' of the audioecho element, self.echo. At the beginning of the playback (0 seconds), we set the echo intensity as 0.5. We add another control point at 4 seconds during the playback and set the intensity level as 0.0. What this effectively means is that we don't want to hear any echo after the first 4 seconds of the audio playback! .

8. Run the program again from the command line as:

```
$python EchoEffect.py
```

Note that the only change done here is the value of flag `self.use_echo_controller` is set to True. Play the output file; the echo sound will be audible only for the first 4 seconds during the playback.

What just happened?

We learned how to add echo to an audio clip. To accomplish this, the `audioecho` element was added and linked in the GStreamer pipeline. We also learned how to selectively add echo effect to the audio using GStreamer `Controller` object.

Have a go hero – add Reverberation Effect

Suppose you are in a theater. When an actor at the center stage talks, the sound waves are reflected from the surfaces of the theater before reaching your ears. Thus what you hear is a bunch of these reflected sounds. This is known as reverberation effect. According to the `audioecho` plugin documentation, if you set the `delay` property to a value of less than 0.2 seconds in `audioecho` element, it produces a reverberation effect. Try setting different values for `delay`, less than 0.2 seconds and see how it affects the output audio. Note, this argument is taken as an integer. Therefore, specify this value in nanoseconds. For example specify 0.05 seconds as `50000000` instead of `0.05*gst.SECOND`. This is illustrated below.

```
self.echo.set_property("delay", 50000000)
```

Panning/panorama

The stereo panorama effect can be added to a sound by using `audiopanorama` plugin (part of `audiofx` plugin). This plugin should be available by default in your GStreamer installation. Use `gst-inspect-0.10` to verify it is there and also to know more about its properties. Download the file `PanoramaEffect.py` from the Packt website. This file is more or less identical to `AudioEffects.py` or `EchoEffect.py`. The following is a code snippet from the `self.contructPipeline` method in file `PanoramaEffect.py`

```
1    # Stereo panorama effect
2    self.panorama = gst.element_factory_make("audiopanorama")
3    self.panorama.set_property("panorama", 1.0)
4
5
6    self.pipeline.add(self.filesrc,
7                      self.decodebin,
8                      self.audioconvert,
9                      self.panorama,
```

```
10                        self.encoder,
11                        self.filesink)
12
13
14   gst.element_link_many( self.filesrc, self.decodebin)
15   gst.element_link_many(self.audioconvert,
16                        self.panorama,
17                        self.encoder,
18                        self.filesink)
```

We have discussed the following many times. Let's go over the code once again as a refresher... just in case you missed it earlier. The code block 6-11 adds all the elements to the GStreamer pipeline. Notice that we call `gst.element_link_many` twice. Do you recall why? The first call on line 14 makes a connection between `self.filesrc` and `self.decodebin`. There is one important point to note when we make a second call to `gst.element_link_many`. Notice that we have not linked `self.decodebin` with `self.audioconvert`. This is because `self.decodebin` implements dynamic pads. So we connect it at the runtime, using the callback method, `decodebin_pad_added`.

You can review the rest of the code from this file. The `audiopanorama` element is created on line 2 in the code snippet. The `panorama` property can have a value in the range `-1.0` to `1.0`. If you have stereo speakers connects, the sound will entirely come from the left speaker if a value of `-1.0` is specified. Likewise, a value of `1.0` will make the sound come from right speaker only. In the above code snippet, we instruct the program to exclusively use the right speaker for audio streaming. The audio will be streamed from both speakers if the value is in-between these two limits. Each speaker's contribution will be determined by actual value.

Have a go hero – control panorama effect and more...

'Move' the sound around! Add a GStreamer `Controller` object to adjust the `panorama` property of the `self.panorama` element. This is similar to what we did in `EchoEffect.py`. Add some control points in the audio stream as done earlier, and specify different values for the `panorama` property.

Integrate this feature with the code in `AudioEffects.py` discussed earlier in this chapter.

Project: combining audio clips

It is time for a project! In this project, we will create a single audio file, which has custom audio clips appended one after the other. Here, we will apply several of the things learned in earlier section, and also in the previous chapter on audio processing.

Creating a new audio file, which is a combination of several audio tracks of your choice involves the following steps:

- First thing we need are the audio files that need to be included. Depending upon our requirement, we may need only a small portion of an audio track. So we will develop a general application considering this possibility. This is illustrated in the time-line illustrated earlier.
- Next, we need to make sure that these audio pieces are played in a specified order.
- There should be a 'blank' or a 'silent' audio in-between the two audio pieces.
- Next, we will also implement audio fade-out effect for each of the pieces in the track. This will ensure that the audio doesn't end abruptly.

Media 'timeline' explained

Before we begin this project, it is important to understand the concept of a timeline. A timeline can be viewed as the overall representation of a path where you can control the time for which an individual audio clip is played.

In this project, since we are saving the resultant audio, it is the same as the total playback time of the resultant audio. In this timeline, we can specify 'when' an audio needs to be played and how long it needs to be played. This is better explained with the illustration below. Consider a timeline with a total duration of 250 seconds. This is represented by the central thick line with circles at the end. Suppose there are three audio clips, namely, Media #1, Media #2 and Media #3 as indicated in the illustration. We wish to include a portion of each of these audio clips in the main timeline (the audio file to be saved). In the main media timeline, the audio between 0 seconds to 80 second represents a portion from Media #1. It corresponds to the audio between 30 seconds to 110 seconds in Media #1. Likewise, audio between 90 to 200 seconds on main media timeline represents a chunk from Media #2 and so on. Thus, we can tweak the priority and position of the individual audio clips on the main media timeline to create the desired audio output.

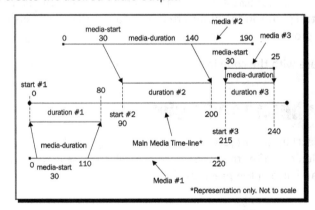

Main media timeline is represented with multiple media tracks in the preceding image.

Time for action – creating custom audio by combining clips

Let's develop an application where we will combine multiple audio clips into a single audio file.

1. Download the file `CombiningAudio.py`. This file contains all the code necessary to run this application. As done earlier, we will discuss only the most important methods in this class.

2. Write the following code.

```
1   import os, sys, time
2   import thread
3   import gobject
4   from optparse import OptionParser
5
6   import pygst
7   pygst.require("0.10")
8   import gst
9
10  class AudioMerger:
11      def __init__(self):
12          pass
13      def constructPipeline(self):
14          pass
15      def addFadingEffect(self):
16          pass
17      def setupFadeBin(self):
18          pass
19      def addGnlFileSources(self):
20          pass
21      def gnonlin_pad_added(self, gnonlin_elem, pad):
22          pass
23      def run(self):
24          pass
25      def connectSignals(self):
26          pass
27      def printUsage(self):
28          pass
29      def printFinalStatus(self):
30          pass
31      def message_handler(self, bus, message):
32          pass
33  #Run the program
34  audioMerger = AudioMerger()
35  thread.start_new_thread(audioMerger.run, ())
36  gobject.threads_init()
37  evt_loop = gobject.MainLoop()
38  evt_loop.run()
```

The overall structure of the code is identical to several other examples in this book. We will expand some of the class methods such as `addFadingEffect`, `setupFadeBin` in the next steps.

3. Now, let's review the `constructPipeline` method.

```
1  def constructPipeline(self):
2      self.pipeline = gst.Pipeline()
3      self.composition = (
4      gst.element_factory_make("gnlcomposition") )
5
6      # Add audio tracks to the gnl Composition
7      self.addGnlFileSources()
8
9      self.encoder = gst.element_factory_make("lame",
10                                         "mp3_encoder")
11     self.filesink = gst.element_factory_make("filesink")
12     self.filesink.set_property("location",
13                                 self.outFileLocation)
14
15     # Fade out the individual audio pieces
16     # when that audio piece is approaching end
17     self.addFadingEffect()
18
19     self.pipeline.add(self.composition,
20                         self.fadeBin,
21                         self.encoder,
22                         self.filesink)
23
24     gst.element_link_many(self.fadeBin,
25                             self.encoder,
26                             self.filesink)
```

We used functionality such as `gnlcomposition`, `gnlcontroller`, and so on while implementing audio fading effects in an earlier section. These modules will be used in this project as well. On line 7, all the audio clips we wish to include are added to the timeline or `gnlcomposition`. We will review this method later. Note that the `gnlcomposition` uses dynamic pads. The `pad-added` signal is connected in `self.connectSignals`. On line 17, a fading effect is set up for the audio clips. This ensures smooth termination of individual audio clips in the timeline. Finally, the code block between lines 19 to 26 constructs the pipeline and links various GStreamer elements in the pipeline. Let's review other important methods in this class one by one.

4. The method `self.addGnlFileSources` does multiple things. It adds the audio clips to the main timeline in a desired order. This method also ensures that there is some 'breathing space' or a blank audio of a short duration in between any two audio clips. Write the following method.

```
1   def addGnlFileSources(self):
2       #Parameters for gnlfilesources
3       start_time_1 = 0
4       duration_1 = 20
5       media_start_time_1 = 20
6       media_duration_1 = 20
7       inFileLocation_1 = "C:/AudioFiles/audio1.mp3"
8
9       start_time_2 = duration_1 + 3
10      duration_2 = 30
11      media_start_time_2 = 20
12      media_duration_2 = 30
13      inFileLocation_2 ="C:/AudioFiles/audio2.mp3"
14
15      #Parameters for blank audio between 2 tracks
16      blank_start_time = 0
17      blank_duration = start_time_2 + duration_2 + 3
18
19      # These timings will be used for adding fade effects
20      # See method self.addFadingEffect()
21      self.fade_start_1 = duration_1 - 3
22      self.fade_start_2 = start_time_2 + duration_2 - 3
23      self.fade_end_1 = start_time_1 + duration_1
24      self.fade_end_2 = start_time_2 + duration_2
25
26      filesrc1 = gst.element_factory_make("gnlfilesource")
27      filesrc1.set_property("uri",
28                          "file:///" + inFileLocation_1)
29      filesrc1.set_property("start", start_time_1*gst.SECOND)
30      filesrc1.set_property("duration",
31                          duration_1 * gst.SECOND )
32      filesrc1.set_property("media-start",
33                          media_start_time_1*gst.SECOND)
34      filesrc1.set_property("media-duration",
35                          media_duration_1*gst.SECOND)
36      filesrc1.set_property("priority", 1)
37
38      # Setup a gnl source that will act like a blank audio
39      # source.
```

```
40      gnlBlankAudio=  gst.element_factory_make("gnlsource")
41      gnlBlankAudio.set_property("priority", 4294967295)
42      gnlBlankAudio.set_property("start",blank_start_time)
43      gnlBlankAudio.set_property("duration",
44                                 blank_duration * gst.SECOND)
45
46      blankAudio = gst.element_factory_make("audiotestsrc")
47      blankAudio.set_property("wave", 4)
48      gnlBlankAudio.add(blankAudio)
49
50      filesrc2 = gst.element_factory_make("gnlfilesource")
51      filesrc2.set_property("uri",
52                            "file:///" + inFileLocation_2)
53      filesrc2.set_property("start",
54                            start_time_2 * gst.SECOND)
55      filesrc2.set_property("duration",
56                            duration_2 * gst.SECOND )
57      filesrc2.set_property("media-start",
58                            media_start_time_2*gst.SECOND)
59      filesrc2.set_property("media-duration",
60                            media_duration_2*gst.SECOND)
61      filesrc2.set_property("priority", 2)
63
63      self.composition.add(gnlBlankAudio)
64      self.composition.add(filesrc1)
65      self.composition.add(filesrc2)
```

First we declare various parameters needed to put the audio clips in the main timeline. Here, the audio clips are mostly the `gnlfilesource` elements whereas the timeline is the total length of the output audio track. This parameter setting is done by the code between lines 3 to 13. In this example, we are combining only two audio clips. Replace the audio file paths on lines 7 and 13 with the appropriate file paths on your machine.

Important note for Windows users: Make sure to specify the file path with forward slashes '/' as shown on line 13 of the code snippet. If the path is specified as, for instance, `C:\AudioFiles\audio2.mp3`, the '\a' is treated differently by GStreamer! A workaround could be to normalize the path or to always use forward slashes while specifying the path. In this case `C:/AudioFiles/audio2.mp3`.

The first media file will be placed for 20 seconds on the main timeline. The total duration of the audio is specified by the parameter media_duration_1. The parameter media_start_1 specifies the actual time of the first audio file which will be the start_time_1 on the main timeline. The basic concept behind timeline is explained earlier in this section. Try tweaking a few parameters to get a good grasp of how the timeline works. For the second audio, notice how the start_time_2 is specified. It is equal to duration_1 + 3. A time of 3 seconds is added so that there is a 'sound of silence' between two tracks. You can change this to a silent duration of your choice.

5. Next, the parameters necessary for the blank audio are defined. In general, the gnlcomposition will 'play' the blank audio when nothing else is being played (this is with the assumption that a proper priority is set). We define the total duration of this silent track sufficiently long enough, longer than the combined duration of all the audio clips, so that this track is 'available to play' when the time comes. Note that gnlcomposition won't play the silent track for its complete duration! It is just so that we have a long enough track that can be played at various points. In this project, we are only using two audio files. So, it is not really necessary to set blank duration parameter as greater than or equal to the total timeline duration. It is okay if we just have it for 3 seconds. But imagine that you have more than 2 audio clips. The silent audio will be played between tracks 1 and 2 but then it won't be available for tracks between 2 and 3! If we were to have 3 audio tracks, then the blank audio duration can be set as illustrated in the following code snippet and by adding another gnlfilesource to the self.composition. You can also test the resultant audio file by specifying blank_duration = 3. In that case, there won't be a silent track between audio clips 2 and 3!

```
start_time_3 = start_time_2 + duration_2 + 3
duration_3 = 30
media_start_time_3 = 0
media_duration_3 = 30
inFileLocation_3 ="C:\AudioFiles\audio3.mp3"
# Parameters for blank audio between 2 tracks
blank_start_time = 0
blank_duration = start_time_3 + duration_3 + 3
```

6. The code between lines 19 to 24 sets up some instance variables needed to add fade-out effect to the individual audio clips in the gnlcomposition. These will be used in the self.addFadingEffect method.

7. The code blocks 26-36 and 50-61 define the `gnlfilesource` elements to be added to the `self.composition` along with their properties. We have already learned about `gnlfilesource`, so these code blocks should be self-explanatory. However, see the code on lines 36 ad 61? Here we set the priority of the audio clips in the main timeline. It is important step. If you don't define the priority, by default, each `gnlsource` will have highest priority indicated by value '0'. This is a little bit tricky. It is best explained by tweaking certain values and actually playing the output audio! Let's keep it simple for now. See the next 'Have a go Hero' section that asks you to experiment a few things related to the `priority`.

8. Let's review the code block 40-44. Here, a `gnlsource` (and not `gnlfilesource`) is created on line 40. We call it `gnlBlankAudio`. Line 41 is very important. It tells the program to consider this element last. That is, `gnlBlankAudio` is set with the least possible priority among the elements added to the `gnlcomposition`. This ensures that the blank piece of audio is played only between the tracks and not as an audio clip of its own. Whenever the start point of the next audio in the `gnlcomposition` approaches, it will push the `gnlBlankAudio` to a backseat and start playing this new audio clip instead. This is because the other audio clips are set at a higher `priority` than the `gnlBlankAudio`. You might be wondering what the value `4294967295` for `priority` signifies. If you run `gst-inspect-0.10` command on `gnlsource` you will notice that the `priority` has a range from `0` to `4294967295`. Thus the least possible priority level is `4294967295`. In this example, we can get away with the priority level of `3` because we have specified the `blank_duration` parameter appropriately. But, suppose you don't know beforehand what `blank_duration` should be and you set it to a large number. In this case, if you have set the priority of `gnlBlankAudio` as `3`, at the end of the output audio it will play the remaining portion of the `gnlBlankAudio`. Thus, the total track duration will be unnecessarily increased. Instead, if you use priority as `4294967295`, it won't play the surplus portion of the blank audio. If you have multiple of audio tracks and if their number is not known to begin with, the least priority level we are using is the safest value for the blank audio clip. As mentioned earlier, the following priority for `gnlBlankAudio` should work as well.

    ```
    gnlBlankAudio.set_property("priority", 3)
    ```

9. On line 46, an `audiotestsrc` element is created. This plugin should be available in your installation of GStreamer. This plugin can be used to generate several elementary audio signals such as a sine waveform, a silent wave form, and so on. Run `gst-inspect-0.10` on `audiotestsrc` to see what types of audio signals it can generate. The type of audio signal we need can be specified by the 'wave' property of `audiotestsrc`. The value of 4 for `wave` property corresponds to a silence waveform. A value of 3 generates triangle wave forms and so on. On line 48, the `audiotestsrc` element is added to the `gnlsource` element (`gnlBlankAudio`). This simply means that when we start playing the `gnlcomposition`, the silent audio pertaining `gnlsource` element is generated using `audiotestsrc` element within it.

10. Finally, the code between lines 63-65 adds the `gnlfilesource` and `gnlsource` elements to the `self.composition`.

11. Now we will quickly review the method `self.addFadingEffect()`.

```
1   def addFadingEffect(self):
2       self.setupFadeBin()
3
4       #Volume control element
5       self.volumeControl = gst.Controller(self.volume,
6                                           "volume")
7       self.volumeControl.set_interpolation_mode("volume",
8                                   gst.INTERPOLATE_LINEAR)
9
10      fade_time = 20
11      fade_volume = 0.5
12      fade_end_time = 30
13
14      reset_time = self.fade_end_1 + 1
15
16      self.volumeControl.set("volume",
17                             self.fade_start_1 * gst.SECOND,
18                             1.0)
19      self.volumeControl.set("volume",
20                             self.fade_end_1 * gst.SECOND,
21                             fade_volume*0.2)
22      self.volumeControl.set("volume",
23                             reset_time * gst.SECOND,
24                             1.0)
25      self.volumeControl.set("volume",
26                             self.fade_start_2 * gst.SECOND,
27                             1.0)
28      self.volumeControl.set("volume",
29                             self.fade_end_2 * gst.SECOND,
30                             fade_volume*0.2)
```

12. In *Fading effects* section, we added fade-out effect to an audio file. In that section individual elements such as audio convert and volume were added and linked in the main pipeline. Here, we will follow a different way, so as to learn a few more things in GStreamer. We will create a GStreamer `bin` element to add the fade-out effect to the audio clips. You can choose to do it the old way, but creating a `bin` provides a certain level of abstraction. The `bin` element is created by the highlighted line of code. We will review that method next. The rest of the code in this method is very similar to the one developed earlier. The `self.volumeControl` is a GStreamer `Controller` element. We specify volume at appropriate time intervals in the timeline to implement fade-out effect for the individual audio clips. It is important to adjust the level of volume back to the original one after each `fade_end` time. This ensures that the next clip starts with an appropriate level of volume. This is achieved by code between lines 22-24.

13. Now let's see how to construct a GStreamer bin element for the fading effect.

```
1   def setupFadeBin(self):
2       self.audioconvert = gst.element_factory_make(
3                                       "audioconvert")
4       self.volume = gst.element_factory_make("volume")
5       self.audioconvert2 = gst.element_factory_make(
6                                       "audioconvert")
7
8       self.fadeBin = gst.element_factory_make("bin",
9                                       "fadeBin")
10      self.fadeBin.add(self.audioconvert,
11                       self.volume,
12                       self.audioconvert2)
13
14      gst.element_link_many(self.audioconvert,
15                       self.volume,
16                       self.audioconvert2)
17
18      # Create Ghost pads for fadeBin
19      sinkPad = self.audioconvert.get_pad("sink")
20      self.fadeBinSink = gst.GhostPad("sink", sinkPad)
21      self.fadeBinSrc = (
22       gst.GhostPad("src", self.audioconvert2.get_pad("src"))   )
23
24      self.fadeBin.add_pad(self.fadeBinSink)
25      self.fadeBin.add_pad(self.fadeBinSrc)
```

14. On lines 2-6, we define the elements necessary to change volume of an audio in a GStreamer pipeline. This is nothing new. On line 8, we create `self.fadeBin`, a GStreamer bin element. A `bin` is a container that manages the element objects added to it. The essential elements are added to this bin on line 10. The elements are then linked the same way we link elements in a GStreamer pipeline. The bin itself is pretty much set up. But there is one more important thing. We need to ensure that this bin can be linked with other elements in a GStreamer pipeline. For that we need to create ghost pads.

15. Recall what a `ghost pad` is from the last chapter. A `bin` element is an 'abstract element'. It doesn't have `pads` of its own. But in order to work like an element, it needs `pads` to connect to the other elements within the pipeline. So the `bin` uses a pad of an element within it as if it was its own pad. This is called a ghost pad. Thus the `ghost pads` are used to connect an appropriate element inside a `bin`. It enables using a `bin` object as an abstract element in a GStreamer pipeline. We create two `ghost pads`. One as `src` pad and one as `sink` pad. It is done by the code on lines 19-22. Note that we use `sink` pad of `self.audioconvert` as the `sink` ghost pad of the bin and `src` pad of `self.audioconvert2` as `src` ghost pad. Which pad to use as src or sink is decided by how we link elements within the bin. Looking at the code between lines 14 to 17 will make it clear. Finally, the `ghost pads` are added to the `self.fadeBin` on lines 24 and 25.

16. The method `self.gnonlin_pad_added()` gets called whenever the `pad-added` signal is emitted for `self.composition`. Notice that `compatible_pad` in this method is obtained from `self.fadeBin`.

```
def gnonlin_pad_added(self, gnonlin_elem, pad):
    caps = pad.get_caps()
    compatible_pad = \
        self.fadeBin.get_compatible_pad(pad, caps)
    pad.link(compatible_pad)
```

17. Develop the rest of the methods by reviewing the code in file CombiningAudio. py. Be sure to specify appropriate input and output audio file locations. Once all the pieces are in place, run the program as:

python CombiningAudio.py

This should create the output audio file containing audio clips combined together!

What just happened?

In this project we developed a cool application that can combine two or more audio clips into a single audio file. To accomplish this, we used many audio processing techniques learned in earlier sections and the previous chapter on audio processing. We made use of various elements from gnonlin plugin such as gnlcomposition, gnlfilesource, and gnlsource . We learned how to create and link a GStreamer bin container to represent the fade-out effect as an abstract element in the pipeline. Among other things, we learned how to insert a blank audio in-between audio clips.

Have a go hero – change various properties of 'gnlfilesource'

In the earlier *Time for action* section, we set priority property for the two gnlfilesource elements added to the gnlcomposition. Tweak the start and the priority properties of the two gnlfilesource elements to see what happens to the output audio. For example, swap the priority of two gnlfilesource elements and change the start_time_ 2 to duration_1, and see what happens. Notice how it affects the playback of the first audio clip!

Audio mixing

Imagine that you have some instrumental music files in your collection. You have a hidden desire to become a playback singer and you wish to sing these songs with the background music. What will you do? Well, the simplest thing to do is to put on headphones and play any instrumental music. Then sing along and record your vocal. OK, what's next? You need to mix the instrumental music and your own vocal together to get what you want!

Let's see how to mix two audio tracks together. The interleave is a GStreamer plugin that facilitates mixing of two audio tracks. It merges multiple mono channel input audios into a single audio stream in a non-contiguous fashion. This plugin should be available in your default GStreamer installation.

Time for action – mixing audio tracks

Let's write a utility that can mix two audio streams together.

1. Download the file AudioMixer.py which contains the source code for this utility.

2. Now we will review the constructPipeline method. The API method gst.parse_launch() explained in the previous chapter will be used here.

```
1   def constructPipeline(self):
2       audio1_str = (" filesrc location=%s ! "
3       "decodebin ! audioconvert ! "
```

```
4          % (self.inFileLocation_1) )
5

6          audio2_str = ( " filesrc location=%s "
7          "! decodebin ! audioconvert ! "
8          %(self.inFileLocation_2) )
9

10         interleave_str = ( "interleave name=mix ! "
11         " audioconvert ! lame ! "
12         " filesink location=%s"%self.outFileLocation )
13

14         queue_str = " ! queue ! mix."
15

16         myPipelineString = (
17             interleave_str + audio1_str + queue_str +
18             audio2_str + queue_str )
19

20         self.pipeline = gst.parse_launch(myPipelineString)
```

3. The `audio1_str` and `audio2_str` are the portions of the main pipeline strings. Each of these contain `filesrc`, `decodebin`, and `audioconvert` elements. The `filesrc` provides the location of respective input audio files. By now, we very well know what this portion of a GStreamer pipeline does.

4. On lines 10-12, the `interleave_str` defines another portion of the main pipeline string. The data output from the `interleave` element needs to be converted into a format expected by the encoder element. The encoder is then connected to the `filesink` element where the output audio will be stored.

5. As mentioned earlier, the `interleave` merges multiple audio channels into a single audio stream. In this case, the `interleave` element reads in data from two different audio streams via queue elements.

The `sink pad` of the `queue` element is linked with the `audioconvert` element. The `queue` element is a buffer to which the audio data from the `audioconvert` is written. Then this data is further read by the `interleave` element. This linkage within the GStreamer pipeline can be represented by the following string "audioconvert ! queue ! mix.". Note that the dot '.' after 'mix' is important. It is a part of the syntax when `gst.parse_launch` is used.

6. To summarize, the data streamed from the portions of the pipeline, `audio1_str` and `audio2_str`, will be ultimately read by the `interleave` via 'queue' elements and then it will follow the rest of the pipeline represented by `interleave_str`.

On line 20, the pipeline string is fed to `gst.parse_launch` to create a GStreamer pipeline instance.

7. Review the rest of the code from the source file `AudioMixer.py`. Change the input and output audio file path strings represented by `self.inFileLocation_1`, `self.inFileLocation_2`, and `self.outFileLocation`. Then run the code as:

```
$python AudioMixer.py
```

This should create the interleaved audio output. If you play this audio file, you will hear both the audio clips playing at once. Try selecting only a single audio channel, such as "Left" channel or "Right" channel. In this case, you will notice that each of these audio clips is sent stored on a separate channel. For example, if you play only the left channel, only one of these audio clips will be heard, so would be the case for the other channel.

What just happened?

Using `interleave` element, we merged two audio tracks to create an interleaved audio. This can be used as an audio mixing utility. We learned how to use `queue` element as an audio data buffer which is then read by the interleave element.

Visualizing an audio track

Most of the popular audio players provide a feature to 'visualize' the audio being played. This visualization effect is typically generated on the fly and is synchronized with the audio signal. Typically, the visualizer responds to changes in audio frequency and volume level among other properties. These changes are then shown by use of animated graphics. GStreamer provides certain plugins to visualize a track. The 'monoscope' visualization plugin is generally available in the default GStreamer installation. It displays a highly stabilized waveform of the streaming audio. Make sure that the GStreamer installation has the `monoscope` plugin by running the `gst-inspect-0.10` command. There are several other popular plugins such as `goom` and `libvisual`. But these are not available by default in the GStreamer binary installed on Windows XP. You can install these plugins and try using these to add visualization effects.

Time for action – audio visualizer

The visualization effect can be added to the streaming audio using different techniques. We will use the simplest approach of all to develop a Music Visualizer utility.

Here, we will be using the `playbin` plugin of GStreamer. Recall that the `playbin` was first used in the *Playing an audio from a Website* section of the Working with Audios chapter. This plugin provides a higher level audio /video player and it should be available in the default GStreamer installation.

1. Download the file `MusicVisualizer.py` from the Packt website. This is a small program. The class methods are represented below. Look at the code from this file for more details.

    ```
    class AudioPlayer:
        def __init__(self):
            pass
        def connectSignals(self):
            pass
        def play(self):
            pass
        def message_handler(self, bus, message):
            pass
    ```

    Most of the code is identical to the one illustrated in the *Playing audio from a website* section of the previous chapter. The only difference here is the constructor of the class where various properties of the `playbin` element are defined.

    Now let's review the constructor of the class `AudioPlayer`.

    ```
     1 def __init__(self):
     2      self.is_playing = False
     3      inFileLocation = "C:/AudioFiles/audio1.mp3"
     4
     5      #Create a playbin element
     6      self.player = gst.element_factory_make("playbin")
     7
     8      # Create the audio visualization element.
     9      self.monoscope = gst.element_factory_make("monoscope")
    10      self.player.set_property("uri",
    11                              "file:///" + inFileLocation)
    12      self.player.set_property("vis-plugin", self.monoscope)
    13      self.connectSignals()
    ```

2. Modify the `inFileLocation` on line 3 to match an audio file path on your computer. On line 6 and 8, the `playbin` and `monoscope` elements are created. The latter is a plugin that enables audio visualization. On line 12, we set the value for property `vis-plugin` as the `monoscope` element created earlier. The `vis-plugin` stands for 'visualization plugin' that the `playbin` element should use to visualize the music.

3. That's all! You can review the rest of the code from the file `MusicVisualizer.py`. Now run the program from the command line as:

    ```
    $python MusicVisualizer.py
    ```

This should start playing the input audio file and at the same time, it should also pop up a small window where you can 'visualize' the streaming audio.

 Note: The overall performance of this application may depend on the number of processes running at the time this program is run. It may also depend on the specifications of your computer such as processor speed.

Here, the stable audio waveform will be shown as the music plays. The following shows a snapshot of this visualization window at two different timeframes.

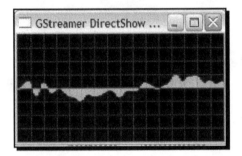 

Snapshots at some random timeframes using Music Visualizer using 'monoscope' are depicted here.

What just happened?

We used the GStreamer plugins `playbin` and `monoscope` to develop an audio visualization utility for a streaming audio. The `monoscope` element provided a way to visualize highly stable audio waveforms.

Have a go hero – use other visualization plugins

To illustrate visualization effects for an audio, the `monoscope` plugin was used. If you have some other visualization plugins available in the GStreamer installation, use those to create different visualization effects. The following are some of the plugins that can be used for this purpose: `goom`, `goom2k1`, `libvisual`, and `synaesthesia`. The audio visualization accomplished by `synaesthesia` plugin is shown in the next illustration.

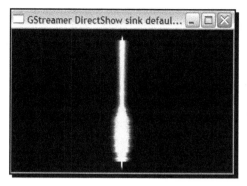 

Music Visualizer using 'synaesthesia': Snapshots at some random timeframes is depicted here.

Summary

We learned a lot in this chapter about various audio enhancement and control techniques. The GStreamer multimedia framework was used to accomplish this. We specifically covered:

- Audio controls: How to control the streaming of an audio data. With the help of coding illustrations, we learned about playback controls such as play, pause, seek, and stop. These controls were then used in a project where a portion of an audio was extracted.

- Adding effects: Enhancing the audio by adding audio effects such as fade-in, echo/reverberation, and so on.

- Non-linear audio editing: How to combine two or more audio streams into a single track. This was done in one of the projects we undertook.

- Audio mixing technique to merge multiple mono channel audio streams into a single interleaved audio.

Additionally, we also learned techniques such as visualizing an audio. This concludes our discussion on audio processing in Python using GStreamer framework.

In the next chapter, we will learn how to process videos using Python.

7
Working with Videos

Photographs capture the moment, but it is the video that helps us relive that moment! Video has become a major part of our lives. We preserve our memories by capturing the family vacation on a camcorder. When it comes to digitally preserving those recorded memories, the digital video processing plays an important role. In the previous chapter, to learn various audio processing techniques, the GStreamer multimedia framework was used. We will continue to use GStreamer for learning the fundamentals of video processing.

In this chapter, we shall:

- Develop a simple command-line video player
- Perform basic video manipulations such as cropping, resizing, and tweaking the parameters such as brightness, contrast, and saturation levels of a streaming video
- Add text string on top of a video stream
- Learn how to convert video between different video formats
- Write a utility that separates audio and video tracks from an input video file
- Mix audio and video tracks to create a single video file
- Save one or more video frames as still images

So let's get on with it.

Installation prerequisites

We will use Python bindings of GStreamer multimedia framework to process video data. See the installation instructions in *Chapter 5, Working with Audios* to install GStreamer and other dependencies.

For video processing, we will be using several GStreamer plugins not introduced earlier. Make sure that these plugins are available in your GStreamer installation by running the `gst-inspect-0.10` command from the console (`gst-inspect-0.10.exe` for Windows XP users). Otherwise, you will need to install these plugins or use an alternative if available.

Following is a list of additional plugins we will use in this chapter:

- `autoconvert`: Determines an appropriate converter based on the capabilities. It will be used extensively used throughout this chapter.
- `autovideosink`: Automatically selects a video sink to display a streaming video.
- `ffmpegcolorspace`: Transforms the color space into a color space format that can be displayed by the video sink.
- `capsfilter`: It's the capabilities filter—used to restrict the type of media data passing down stream, discussed extensively in this chapter.
- `textoverlay`: Overlays a text string on the streaming video. Used in the *Adding text and time on a video stream* section.
- `timeoverlay`: Adds a timestamp on top of the video buffer.
- `clockoverlay`: Puts current clock time on the streaming video.
- `videobalance`: Used to adjust brightness, contrast, and saturation of the images. It is used in the *Video manipulations and effects* section.
- `videobox`: Crops the video frames by specified number of pixels—used in the *Cropping* section.
- `ffmux_mp4`: Provides `muxer` element for MP4 video muxing.
- `ffenc_mpeg4`: Encodes data into MPEG4 format.
- `ffenc_png`: Encodes data in PNG format—used in the *Saving video frames as images* section.

Playing a video

Earlier, we saw how to play an audio. Like audio, there are different ways in which a video can be streamed. The simplest of these methods is to use the `playbin` plugin. Another method is to go by the basics, where we create a conventional pipeline and create and link the required pipeline elements. If we only want to play the 'video' track of a video file, then the latter technique is very similar to the one illustrated for audio playback. However, almost always, one would like to hear the audio track for the video being streamed. There is additional work involved to accomplish this. The following diagram is a representative GStreamer pipeline that shows how the data flows in case of a video playback.

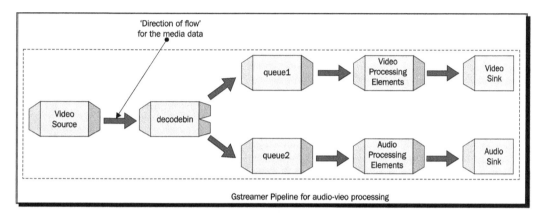

In this illustration, the `decodebin` uses an appropriate decoder to decode the media data from the source element. Depending on the type of data (audio or video), it is then further streamed to the audio or video processing elements through the `queue` elements. The two `queue` elements, `queue1` and `queue2`, act as media data buffer for audio and video data respectively. When the queue elements are added and linked in the pipeline, the thread creation within the pipeline is handled internally by the GStreamer.

Time for action – video player!

Let's write a simple video player utility. Here we will not use the `playbin` plugin. The use of `playbin` will be illustrated in a later sub-section. We will develop this utility by constructing a GStreamer pipeline. The key here is to use the queue as a data buffer. The audio and video data needs to be directed so that this 'flows' through audio or video processing sections of the pipeline respectively.

1. Download the file `PlayingVidio.py` from the Packt website. The file has the source code for this video player utility.

2. The following code gives an overview of the Video player class and its methods.

```python
import time
import thread
import gobject
import pygst
pygst.require("0.10")
import gst
import os


class VideoPlayer:
    def __init__(self):
        pass
    def constructPipeline(self):
        pass
    def connectSignals(self):
        pass
    def decodebin_pad_added(self, decodebin, pad):
        pass
    def play(self):
        pass
    def message_handler(self, bus, message):
        pass


# Run the program
player = VideoPlayer()
thread.start_new_thread(player.play, ())
gobject.threads_init()
evt_loop = gobject.MainLoop()
evt_loop.run()
```

As you can see, the overall structure of the code and the main program execution code remains the same as in the audio processing examples. The `thread` module is used to create a new thread for playing the video. The method `VideoPlayer.play` is sent on this thread. The `gobject.threads_init()` is an initialization function for facilitating the use of Python threading within the `gobject` modules. The main event loop for executing this program is created using `gobject` and this loop is started by the call `evt_loop.run()`.

> Instead of using `thread` module you can make use of `threading` module as well. The code to use it will be something like:
>
> 1. `import threading`
>
> 2. `threading.Thread(target=player.play).start()`

You will need to replace the line `thread.start_new_thread(player.` `play, ())` in earlier code snippet with line 2 illustrated in the code snippet within this note. Try it yourself!

3. Now let's discuss a few of the important methods, starting with `self.contructPipeline`:

```
1   def constructPipeline(self):
2       # Create the pipeline instance
3       self.player = gst.Pipeline()
4
5       # Define pipeline elements
6       self.filesrc = gst.element_factory_make("filesrc")
7       self.filesrc.set_property("location",
8                                   self.inFileLocation)
9       self.decodebin = gst.element_factory_make("decodebin")
10
11      # audioconvert for audio processing pipeline
12      self.audioconvert = gst.element_factory_make(
13                                  "audioconvert")
14      # Autoconvert element for video processing
15      self.autoconvert = gst.element_factory_make(
16                                  "autoconvert")
17      self.audiosink = gst.element_factory_make(
18                                  "autoaudiosink")
19
20      self.videosink = gst.element_factory_make(
21                                  "autovideosink")
22
23      # As a precaution add videio capability filter
24      # in the video processing pipeline.
25      videocap = gst.Caps("video/x-raw-yuv")
26      self.filter = gst.element_factory_make("capsfilter")
27      self.filter.set_property("caps", videocap)
28      # Converts the video from one colorspace to another
29      self.colorSpace = gst.element_factory_make(
30                                  "ffmpegcolorspace")
31
32      self.videoQueue = gst.element_factory_make("queue")
33      self.audioQueue = gst.element_factory_make("queue")
34
35      # Add elements to the pipeline
36      self.player.add(self.filesrc,
37                      self.decodebin,
38                      self.autoconvert,
```

```
39                         self.audioconvert,
40                         self.videoQueue,
41                         self.audioQueue,
42                         self.filter,
43                         self.colorSpace,
44                         self.audiosink,
45                         self.videosink)
46
47      # Link elements in the pipeline.
48      gst.element_link_many(self.filesrc, self.decodebin)
49
50      gst.element_link_many(self.videoQueue, self.autoconvert,
51                            self.filter, self.colorSpace,
52                            self.videosink)
53
54      gst.element_link_many(self.audioQueue, self.audioconvert,
55                            self.audiosink)
```

4. In various audio processing applications, we have used several of the elements defined in this method. First, the pipeline object, `self.player`, is created. The `self.filesrc` element specifies the input video file. This element is connected to a `decodebin`.

5. On line 15, `autoconvert` element is created. It is a GStreamer `bin` that automatically selects a converter based on the capabilities (`caps`). It translates the decoded data coming out of the `decodebin` in a format playable by the video device. Note that before reaching the video sink, this data travels through a `capsfilter` and `ffmpegcolorspace` converter. The `capsfilter` element is defined on line 26. It is a filter that restricts the allowed capabilities, that is, the type of media data that will pass through it. In this case, the `videoCap` object defined on line 25 instructs the filter to only allow `video-xraw-yuv` capabilities .

6. The `ffmpegcolorspace` is a plugin that has the ability to convert video frames to a different color space format. At this time, it is necessary to explain what a color space is. A variety of colors can be created by use of basic colors. Such colors form, what we call, a **color space**. A common example is an rgb color space where a range of colors can be created using a combination of red, green, and blue colors. The color space conversion is a representation of a video frame or an image from one color space into the other. The conversion is done in such a way that the converted video frame or image is a closer representation of the original one.

The video can be streamed even without using the combination of `capsfilter` and the `ffmpegcolorspace`. However, the video may appear distorted. So it is recommended to use `capsfilter` and `ffmpegcolorspace` converter. Try linking the `autoconvert` element directly to the `autovideosink` to see if it makes any difference.

7. Notice that we have created two sinks, one for audio output and the other for the video. The two `queue` elements are created on lines 32 and 33. As mentioned earlier, these act as media data buffers and are used to send the data to audio and video processing portions of the GStreamer pipeline. The code block 35-45 adds all the required elements to the pipeline.

8. Next, the various elements in the pipeline are linked. As we already know, the `decodebin` is a plugin that determines the right type of decoder to use. This element uses dynamic pads. While developing audio processing utilities, we connected the `pad-added` signal from `decodebin` to a method `decodebin_pad_added`. We will do the same thing here; however, the contents of this method will be different. We will discuss that later.

9. On lines 50-52, the video processing portion of the pipeline is linked. The `self.videoQueue` receives the video data from the `decodebin`. It is linked to an `autoconvert` element discussed earlier. The `capsfilter` allows only `video-xraw-yuv` data to stream further. The `capsfilter` is linked to a `ffmpegcolorspace` element, which converts the data into a different color space. Finally, the data is streamed to the `videosink`, which, in this case, is an `autovideosink` element. This enables the 'viewing' of the input video. The audio processing portion of the pipeline is very similar to the one used in earlier chapter.

10. Now we will review the `decodebin_pad_added` method.

```
1   def decodebin_pad_added(self, decodebin, pad):
2       compatible_pad = None
3       caps = pad.get_caps()
4       name = caps[0].get_name()
5       print "\n cap name is =%s"%name
6       if name[:5] == 'video':
7           compatible_pad = (
8               self.videoQueue.get_compatible_pad(pad, caps) )
9       elif name[:5] == 'audio':
10          compatible_pad = (
11              self.audioQueue.get_compatible_pad(pad, caps) )
12
13      if compatible_pad:
14          pad.link(compatible_pad)
```

11. This method captures the `pad-added` signal, emitted when the `decodebin` creates a dynamic pad. In an earlier chapter, we simply linked the `decodebin` pad with a compatible pad on the `autoaudioconvert` element. We could do this because the `caps` or the type media data being streamed was always the audio data. However, here the media data can either represent an audio or video data. Thus, when a dynamic pad is created on the `decodebin`, we must check what `caps` this pad has. The name of the `get_name` method of `caps` object returns the type of media data handled. For example, the name can be of the form `video/x-raw-rgb` when it is a video data or `audio/x-raw-int` for audio data. We just check the first five characters to see if it is video or audio media type. This is done by the code block 4-11 in the code snippet. The `decodebin` pad with video media type is linked with the compatible pad on `self.videoQueue` element. Similarly, the `pad` with audio `caps` is linked with the one on `self.audioQueue`.

12. Review the rest of the code from the `PlayingVideo.py`. Make sure you specify an appropriate video file path for the variable `self.inFileLocation` and then run this program from the command prompt as:

```
$python PlayingVideo.py
```

This should open a GUI window where the video will be streamed. The audio output will be synchronized with the playing video.

What just happened?

We created a command-line video player utility. We learned how to create a GStreamer pipeline that can play synchronized audio and video streams. It explained how the `queue` element can be used to process the audio and video data in a pipeline. In this example, the use of GStreamer plugins such as `capsfilter` and `ffmpegcolorspace` was illustrated. The knowledge gained in this section will be applied in the upcoming sections in this chapter.

Have a go hero – add playback controls

In *Chapter 6, Audio Controls and Effects* we learned different techniques to control the playback of an audio. Develop command-line utilities that will allow you to pause the video or directly jump to a specified position on the video track.

Playing video using 'playbin'

The goal of the previous section was to introduce you to the fundamental method of processing input video streams. We will use that method one way or another in the future discussions. If just video playback is all that you want, then the simplest way to accomplish this is by means of `playbin` plugin. The video can be played just by replacing the `VideoPlayer.constructPipeline` method in file `PlayingVideo.py` with the following code. Here, `self.player` is a `playbin` element. The `uri` property of `playbin` is set as the input video file path.

```
def constructPipeline(self):
    self.player = gst.element_factory_make("playbin")
    self.player.set_property("uri",
                            "file:///" + self.inFileLocation)
```

Video format conversion

Saving the video in a different file format is one of the frequently performed tasks—for example, the task of converting a recorded footage on to your camcorder to a format playable on a DVD player. So let's list out the elements we need in a pipeline to carry out the video format conversion.

- ◆ A `filesrc` element to stream the video file and a `decodebin` to decode the encoded input media data.

- ◆ Next, the audio processing elements of the pipeline, such as `audioconvert`, an encoder to encode the raw audio data into an appropriate audio format to be written.

- ◆ The video processing elements of the pipeline, such as a video encoder element to encode the video data.

- ◆ A multiplexer or a **muxer** that takes the encoded audio and video data streams and puts them into a single channel.

- ◆ There needs to be an element that, depending on the media type, can send the media data to an appropriate processing unit. This is accomplished by `queue` elements that act as data buffers. Depending on whether it is an audio or video data, it is streamed to the audio or video processing elements. The queue is also needed to stream the encoded data from audio pipeline to the multiplexer.

- ◆ Finally, a `filesink` element to save the converted video file (containing both audio and video tracks).

Time for action – video format converter

We will create a video conversion utility that will convert an input video file into a format specified by the user. The file you need to download from the Packt website is `VideoConverter.py`. This file can be run from the command line as:

`python VideoConverter.py [options]`

Where, the options are as follows:

- --input_path: The full path of the video file we wish to convert. The video format of the input files. The format should be in a supported list of formats. The supported input formats are MP4, OGG, AVI, and MOV.

- --output_path: The full path of the output video file. If not specified, it will create a folder OUTPUT_VIDEOS within the input directory and save the file there with same name.

- --output_format: The audio format of the output file. The supported output formats are OGG and MP4.

> As we will be using a decodebin element for decoding the input media data; there is actually a wider range of input formats this utility can handle. Modify the code in VideoPlayer.processArguments or add more formats to dictionary VideoPlayer.supportedInputFormats.

1. If not done already, download the file VideoConverter.py from the Packt website.

2. The overall structure of the code is:

```
import os, sys, time
import thread
import getopt, glob
import gobject
import pygst
pygst.require("0.10")
import gst

class VideoConverter:
    def __init__(self):
        pass
    def constructPipeline(self):
        pass
    def connectSignals(self):
        pass
    def decodebin_pad_added(self, decodebin, pad):
        pass
    def processArgs(self):
        pass
    def printUsage(self):
        pass
    def printFinalStatus(self, starttime, endtime):
        pass
```

```
      def convert(self):
          pass
      def message_handler(self, bus, message):
          pass


  # Run the converter
  converter = VideoConverter()
  thread.start_new_thread(converter.convert, ())
  gobject.threads_init()
  evt_loop = gobject.MainLoop()
evt_loop.run()
```

 A new thread is created by calling `thread.start_new_thread`, to run the application. The method `VideoConverter.convert` is sent on this thread. It is similar to the `VideoPlayer.play` method discussed earlier. Let's review some key methods of the class `VideoConverter`.

3. The __init__ method contains the initialization code. It also calls methods to process command-line arguments and then build the pipeline. The code is illustrated as follows:

```
1   def __init__(self):
2       # Initialize various attrs
3       self.inFileLocation = ""
4       self.outFileLocation = ""
5       self.inputFormat = "ogg"
6       self.outputFormat = ""
7       self.error_message = ""
8       # Create dictionary objects for
9       # Audio / Video encoders for supported
10      # file format
11      self.audioEncoders = {"mp4":"lame",
12                 "ogg": "vorbisenc"}
13
14      self.videoEncoders={"mp4":"ffenc_mpeg4",
15                 "ogg": "theoraenc"}
16
17      self.muxers = {"mp4":"ffmux_mp4",
18                     "ogg":"oggmux" }
19
20      self.supportedOutputFormats = self.audioEncoders.keys()
21
22      self.supportedInputFormats = ("ogg", "mp4",
23                          "avi", "mov")
```

```
24
25        self.pipeline = None
26        self.is_playing = False
27
28        self.processArgs()
29        self.constructPipeline()
30        self.connectSignals()
```

To process the video file, we need audio and video encoders. This utility will support the conversion to only MP4 and OGG file formats. This can be easily extended to include more formats by adding appropriate encoders and muxer plugins. The values of the `self.audioEncoders` and `self.videoEncoders` dictionary objects specify the encoders to use for the streaming audio and video data respectively. Therefore, to store the video data in MP4 format, we use the `ffenc_mp4` encoder. The encoders illustrated in the code snippet should be a part of the GStreamer installation on your computer. If not, visit the GStreamer website to find out how to install these plugins. The values of dictionary `self.muxers` represent the multiplexer to use in a specific output format.

4. The `constructPipeline` method does the main conversion job. It builds the required pipeline, which is then set to playing state in the `convert` method.

```
1    def constructPipeline(self):
2        self.pipeline = gst.Pipeline("pipeline")
3
4        self.filesrc = gst.element_factory_make("filesrc")
5        self.filesrc.set_property("location",
6                                              self.inFileLocation)
7
8        self.filesink = gst.element_factory_make("filesink")
9        self.filesink.set_property("location",
10                                             self.outFileLocation)
11
12       self.decodebin = gst.element_factory_make("decodebin")
13       self.audioconvert = gst.element_factory_make(
14                                         "audioconvert")
15
16       audio_encoder =  self.audioEncoders[self.outputFormat]
17       muxer_str =  self.muxers[self.outputFormat]
18       video_encoder =  self.videoEncoders[self.outputFormat]
19
20       self.audio_encoder= gst.element_factory_make(
21                                         audio_encoder)
22       self.muxer = gst.element_factory_make(muxer_str)
23       self.video_encoder = gst.element_factory_make(
24                                         video_encoder)
```

```
25
26        self.videoQueue = gst.element_factory_make("queue")
27        self.audioQueue = gst.element_factory_make("queue")
28        self.queue3 = gst.element_factory_make("queue")
29
30        self.pipeline.add( self.filesrc,
31                           self.decodebin,
32                           self.video_encoder,
33                           self.muxer,
34                           self.videoQueue,
35                           self.audioQueue,
36                           self.queue3,
37                           self.audioconvert,
38                           self.audio_encoder,
39                           self.filesink)
40
41        gst.element_link_many(self.filesrc, self.decodebin)
42
43        gst.element_link_many(self.videoQueue,
44              self.video_encoder, self.muxer, self.filesink)
45
46        gst.element_link_many(self.audioQueue, self.audioconvert,
47                              self.audio_encoder, self.queue3,
48                              self.muxer)
```

In an earlier section, we covered several of the elements used in the previous pipeline. The code on lines 43 to 48 establishes linkage for the audio and video processing elements. On line 44, the multiplexer, self.muxer is linked with the video
encoder element. It puts the separate parts of the stream—in this case, the video
and audio data, into a single file. The data output from audio encoder, self.au-
dio_encoder, is streamed to the muxer via a queue element, self.queue3. The
muxed data coming out of self.muxer is then streamed to the self.filesink.

5. Let's quickly review the VideoConverter.convert method.

```
1    def convert(self):
2        # Record time before beginning Video conversion
3        starttime = time.clock()
4
5        print "\n Converting Video file.."
6        print "\n Input File: %s, Conversion STARTED..." %
7                                        self.inFileLocation
8
9        self.is_playing = True
10       self.pipeline.set_state(gst.STATE_PLAYING)
11       while self.is_playing:
12           time.sleep(1)
```

```
13
14     if self.error_message:
15         print "\n Input File: %s, ERROR OCCURED." %
16                                     self.inFileLocation
17         print self.error_message
18     else:
19         print "\n Input File: %s, Conversion COMPLETE " %
20                                     self.inFileLocation
21
22     endtime = time.clock()
23     self.printFinalStatus(starttime, endtime)
24     evt_loop.quit()
```

On line 10, the GStreamer pipeline built earlier is set to playing. When the conversion is complete, it will generate the `End Of Stream` (EOS) message. The `self.is_playing` flag is modified in the method `self.message_handler`. The `while` loop on line 11 is executed until the EOS message is posted on the bus or some error occurs. Finally, on line 24, the main execution loop is terminated.

 On line 3, we make a call to `time.clock()`. This actually gives the CPU time spent on the process.

6. The other methods such as `VideoConverter.decodebin_pad_added` are identical to the one developed in the *Playing a video* section. Review the remaining methods from the file `VideoConverter.py` and then run this utility by specifying appropriate command-line arguments. The following screenshot shows sample output messages when the program is run from the console window.

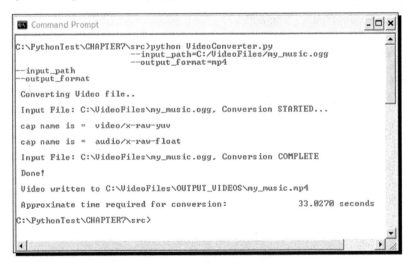

This is a sample run of the video conversion utility from the console.

What just happened?

We created another useful utility that can convert video files from one format to the other. We learned how to encode the audio and video data into a desired output format and then use a multiplexer to put these two data streams into a single file.

Have a go hero – batch-convert the video files

The video converter developed in previous sections can convert a single video file at a time. Can you make it a batch-processing utility? Refer to the code for the audio conversion utility developed in the *Working with Audios* chapter. The overall structure will be very similar. However, there could be challenges in converting multiple video files because of the use of queue elements. For example, when it is done converting the first file, the data in the queue may not be flushed when we start conversion of the other file. One crude way to address this would be to reconstruct the whole pipeline and connect signals for each audio file. However, there will be a more efficient way to do this. Think about it!

Video manipulations and effects

Suppose you have a video file that needs to be saved with an adjusted default brightness level. Alternatively, you may want to save another video with a different aspect ratio. In this section, we will learn some of the basic and most frequently performed operations on a video. We will develop code using Python and GStreamer for tasks such as resizing a video or adjusting its contrast level.

Resizing

The data that can flow through an element is described by the capabilities (caps) of a pad on that element. If a decodebin element is decoding video data, the capabilities of its dynamic pad will be described as, for instance, `video/x-raw-yuv`. Resizing a video with GStreamer multimedia framework can be accomplished by using a `capsfilter` element, that has `width` and `height` parameters specified. As discussed earlier, the `capsfilter` element limits the media data type that can be transferred between two elements. For example, a `cap` object described by the string, `video/x-raw-yuv, width=800, height=600` will set the width of the video to 800 pixels and the height to 600 pixels.

Time for action – resize a video

We will now see how to resize a streaming video using the width and height parameters described by a GStreamer cap object.

1.   Download the file VideoManipulations.py from the Packt website. The overall class design is identical to the one studied in the *Playing a video* section.

2.   The methods self.constructAudioPipeline() and self.constructVideoPipeline(), respectively, define and link elements related to audio and video portions of the main pipeline object self.player. As we have already discussed most of the audio/video processing elements in earlier sections, we will only review the constructVideoPipeline method here.

```
1    def constructVideoPipeline(self):
2        # Autoconvert element for video processing
3        self.autoconvert = gst.element_factory_make(
4                                        "autoconvert")
5        self.videosink = gst.element_factory_make(
6                                        "autovideosink")
7
8        # Set the capsfilter
9        if self.video_width and self.video_height:
10           videocap = gst.Caps(
11           "video/x-raw-yuv," "width=%d, height=%d"%
12                (self.video_width,self.video_height))
13       else:
14           videocap = gst.Caps("video/x-raw-yuv")
15
16       self.capsFilter = gst.element_factory_make(
17                                        "capsfilter")
18       self.capsFilter.set_property("caps", videocap)
19
20       # Converts the video from one colorspace to another
21       self.colorSpace = gst.element_factory_make(
22                                        "ffmpegcolorspace")
23
24       self.videoQueue = gst.element_factory_make("queue")
25
26       self.player.add(self.videoQueue,
27                       self.autoconvert,
28                       self.capsFilter,
29                       self.colorSpace,
30                       self.videosink)
31
```

```
32          gst.element_link_many(self.videoQueue,
33                                 self.autoconvert,
34                                 self.capsFilter,
35                                 self.colorSpace,
36                                 self.videosink)
```

The `capsfilter` element is defined on line 16. It is a filter that restricts the type of media data that will pass through it. The `videocap` is a GStreamer `cap` object created on line 10. This `cap` specifies the `width` and `height` parameters of the streaming video. It is set as a property of the `capsfilter`, `self.capsFilter`. It instructs the filter to only stream `video-xraw-yuv` data with `width` and `height` specified by the `videocap` object.

 In the source file, you will see an additional element `self.videobox` linked in the pipeline. It is omitted in the above code snippet. We will see what this element is used for in the next section.

3. The rest of the code is straightforward. We already covered similar methods in earlier discussions. Develop the rest of the code by reviewing the file `VideoManipulations.py`. Make sure to specify an appropriate video file path for the variable `self.inFileLocation` .Then run this program from the command prompt as:

```
$python VideoManipulations.py
```

This should open a GUI window where the video will be streamed. The default size of this window will be controlled by the parameters `self.video_width` and `self.video_height` specified in the code.

What just happened?

The command-line video player developed earlier was extended in the example we just developed. We used `capsfilter` plugin to specify the `width` and `height` parameters of the streaming video and thus resize the video.

Cropping

Suppose you have a video that has a large 'gutter space' at the bottom or some unwanted portion on a side that you would like to trim off. The `videobox` GStreamer plugin facilitates cropping the video from left, right, top, or bottom.

Time for action – crop a video

Let's add another video manipulation feature to the command-line video player developed earlier.

1. The file we need here is the one used in the earlier section, `VideoManipulations.py`.

2. Once again, we will focus our attention on the `constructVideoPipeline` method of the class `VideoPlayer`. The following code snippet is from this method. The rest of the code in this method is identical to the one reviewed in the earlier section.

```
1   self.videobox = gst.element_factory_make("videobox")
2   self.videobox.set_property("bottom", self.crop_bottom )
3   self.videobox.set_property("top", self.crop_top )
4   self.videobox.set_property("left", self.crop_left )
5   self.videobox.set_property("right", self.crop_right )
6
7   self.player.add(self.videoQueue,
8                   self.autoconvert,
9                   self.videobox,
10                  self.capsFilter,
11                  self.colorSpace,
12                  self.videosink)
13
14  gst.element_link_many(self.videoQueue,
15                        self.autoconvert,
16                        self.videobox,
17                        self.capsFilter,
18                        self.colorSpace,
19                        self.videosink)
```

3. The code is self-explanatory. The `videobox` element is created on line 1. The properties of `videobox` that crop the streaming video are set on lines 2-5. It receives the media data from the `autoconvert` element. The source pad of `videobox` is connected to the sink of either `capsfilter` or directly the `ffmpegcolorspace` element.

4. Develop the rest of the code by reviewing the file `VideoManipulations.py`. Make sure to specify an appropriate video file path for the variable `self.inFileLocation`. Then run this program from the command prompt as:

    `$python VideoManipulations.py`

This should open a GUI window where the video will be streamed. The video will be cropped from left, right, bottom, and top sides by the parameters `self.crop_left`, `self.crop_right`, `self.crop_bottom`, and `self.crop_top` respectively.

What just happened?

We extended the video player application further to add a GStreamer element that can crop the video frames from sides. The `videobox` plugin was used to accomplish this task.

Have a go hero – add borders to a video

1. In the previous section, we used `videobox` element to trim the video from sides. The same plugin can be used to add a border around the video. If you set negative values for `videobox` properties, such as, bottom, top, left and right, instead of cropping the video, it will add black border around the video. Set negative values of parameters such as `self.crop_left` to see this effect.

2. The video cropping can be accomplished by using `videocrop` plugin. It is similar to the `videobox` plugin, but it doesn't support adding a border to the video frames. Modify the code and use this plugin to crop the video.

Adjusting brightness and contrast

We saw how to adjust the brightness and contrast level in *Chapter 3, Enhancing Images*. If you have a homemade video recorded in poor lighting conditions, you would probably adjust its brightness level. The contrast-level highlights the difference between the color and brightness level of each video frame. The `videobalance` plugin can be used to adjust the brightness, contrast, hue, and saturation. The next code snippet creates this element and sets the brightness and contrast properties. The brightness property can accept values in the range -1 to 1, the default (original) brightness level is 0. The contrast can have values in the range 0 to 2 with the default value as 1.

```
self.videobalance = gst.element_factory_make("videobalance")
self.videobalance.set_property("brightness", 0.5)
self.videobalance.set_property("contrast", 0.5)
```

The `videobalance` is then linked in the GStreamer pipeline as:

```
gst.element_link_many(self.videoQueue,
                      self.autoconvert,
                      self.videobalance,
                      self.capsFilter,
                      self.colorSpace,
                      self.videosink)
```

Review the rest of the code from file `VideoEffects.py`.

Creating a gray scale video

The video can be rendered as gray scale by adjusting the saturation property of the `videobalance` plugin. The saturation can have a value in the range 0 to 2. The default value is 1. Setting this value to 0.0 converts the images to gray scale. The code is illustrated as follows:

```
self.videobalance.set_property("saturation", 0.0)
```

You can refer to the file `VideoEffects.py`, which illustrates how to use the `videobalance` plugin to adjust saturation and other parameters discussed in earlier sections.

Adding text and time on a video stream

Ability to add a text string or a subtitles track to a video is yet another desirable feature one needs when processing videos. The GStreamer plugin `textoverlay` enables overlaying informative text string, such as the name of the file, on top of a video stream. The other useful plugins such as `timeoverlay` and `clockoverlay` provide a way to put the video buffer timestamp and the CPU clock time on top of the streaming video.

Time for action – overlay text on a video track

Let's see how to add a text string on a video track. We will write a simple utility, which essentially has the same code structure as the one we developed in the *Playing a video* section. This tool will also add the buffer timestamp and the current CPU clock time on the top of the video. For this section, it is important that you have `textoverlay`, `timeoverlay`, and `clockoverlay` plugins available in your GStreamer installation. Otherwise, you need to install these plugins or use some other plugins, such as `cairotextoverlay`, if available.

1. Download the file `VideoTextOverlay.py` from the Packt website.

2. The `constructVideoPipeline` method of the class `VideoPlayer` is illustrated in the following code snippet:

```
1   def constructVideoPipeline(self):
2       # Autoconvert element for video processing
3       self.autoconvert = gst.element_factory_make(
4               "autoconvert")
5       self.videosink = gst.element_factory_make(
6               "autovideosink")
7
8       # Set the capsfilter
9       videocap = gst.Caps("video/x-raw-yuv")
```

```
10    self.capsFilter = gst.element_factory_make(
11                                        "capsfilter")
12    self.capsFilter.set_property("caps", videocap)
13
14    # Converts the video from one colorspace to another
15    self.colorSpace = gst.element_factory_make(
16                                        "ffmpegcolorspace")
17
18    self.videoQueue = gst.element_factory_make("queue")
19
20    self.textOverlay = gst.element_factory_make(
21                                        "textoverlay")
22    self.textOverlay.set_property("text", "hello")
23    self.textOverlay.set_property("shaded-background",
24                                                    True)
25
26    self.timeOverlay = gst.element_factory_make(
27                                        "timeoverlay")
28    self.timeOverlay.set_property("valign", "top")
29    self.timeOverlay.set_property("shaded-background",
30                                                    True)
31
32    self.clockOverlay = gst.element_factory_make(
33                                        "clockoverlay")
34    self.clockOverlay.set_property("valign", "bottom")
35    self.clockOverlay.set_property("halign", "right")
36    self.clockOverlay.set_property("shaded-background",
37                                                    True)
38
39    self.player.add(self.videoQueue,
40                    self.autoconvert,
41                    self.textOverlay,
42                    self.timeOverlay,
43                    self.clockOverlay,
44                    self.capsFilter,
45                    self.colorSpace,
46                    self.videosink)
47
48    gst.element_link_many(self.videoQueue,
49                    self.autoconvert,
50                    self.capsFilter,
51                    self.textOverlay,
52                    self.timeOverlay,
53                    self.clockOverlay,
54                    self.colorSpace,
55                    self.videosink)
```

As you can see, the elements for overlaying text, time, or clock can be simply added and linked in a GStreamer pipeline like other elements. Let's discuss various properties of these elements now. On lines 20-23, the `textoverlay` element is defined. The `text` property sets the text string that appears on the streaming video. To ensure that the text string is clearly visible in the video, we add a background contrast to this text. This is done on line 23 by setting the `shaded-background` property to `True`. The other properties of this plugin help fix the text position on the video. Run `gst-inspect-0.10` on `textoverlay` plugin to see what these properties are.

3. Next, on lines 25-36, the time and clock overlay elements are defined. The properties are similar to the ones available in `textoverlay` plugin. The clock time will appear on the bottom-left corner of the streaming video. This is accomplished by setting the `valign` and `halign` properties. These three elements are then linked in the GStreamer pipeline. The internal order in which they are linked doesn't matter.

4. Develop the rest of the code by reviewing the file `VideoTextOverlay.py`. Make sure you specify an appropriate video file path for the variable `self.inFileLocation`. Then run this program from the command prompt as:

```
$python VideoTextOverlay.py
```

This should open a GUI window where the video will be streamed. The video will show a text string "hello" along with the running time and the clock time. This is illustrated by the following snapshot of a video frame.

The screenshot depicts a video frame showing text, time, and clock overlay.

What just happened?

We learned how to use elements such as `textoverlay`, `timeoverlay`, and `clockoverlay` in a GStreamer pipeline to add text string, timestamp, and clock respectively, on top of a video buffer. The `textoverlay` element can be used further to add a subtitle track to the video file.

Have a go hero – add subtitles to a video track!

Extend the code we just developed to add a subtitles track to the video file. To add a subtitle track, you will need the `subparse` plugin. Note that this plugin is not available by default in the windows installation of GStreamer using the GStreamer-WinBuilds binary. Thus, Windows users may need to install this plugin separately. Review the `subparse` plugin reference to see how to accomplish this task. The following code snippet shows how to create the `subparse` element.

```
self.subtitlesrc = gst.element_factory_make("filesrc")
self.subtitlesrc.set_property("location",
                              "/path/to/subtitles/file")
self.subparse = gst.element_factory_make("subparse")
```

Separating audio and video tracks

There are times when you would like to separate an audio and a video track. Imagine that you have a collection of your favorite video songs. You are going on a long drive and the old CD player in your car can only play audio files in a specific file format. Let's write a utility that can separate out the audio from a video file!

Time for action – audio and video tracks

We will develop code that takes a video file as an input and then creates two output files, one with only the audio track of the original file and the other with the video portion.

1. Download the file `SeparatingAudio.py` from the Packt website. The structure of the class `AudioSeparator` is similar to the one seen in the *Playing a Video* section. We will review two methods of this class, `constructPipeline` and `decodebin_pad_added`.

2. Let's start with the code in the `constructPipeline` method.

```
1   def constructPipeline(self):
2       # Create the pipeline instance
3       self.player = gst.Pipeline()
4
```

```
5        # Define pipeline elements
6        self.filesrc = gst.element_factory_make("filesrc")
7
8        self.filesrc.set_property("location",
9                                      self.inFileLocation)
10
11       self.decodebin = gst.element_factory_make("decodebin")
12
13       self.autoconvert = gst.element_factory_make(
14                                      "autoconvert")
15
16       self.audioconvert = gst.element_factory_make(
17                                      "audioconvert")
18
19       self.audio_encoder = gst.element_factory_make("lame")
20
21       self.audiosink = gst.element_factory_make("filesink")
22       self.audiosink.set_property("location",
23                                      self.audioOutLocation)
24
25       self.video_encoder = gst.element_factory_make("
26                  ffenc_mpeg4")
27       self.muxer = gst.element_factory_make("ffmux_mp4")
28
29       self.videosink = gst.element_factory_make("filesink")
30       self.videosink.set_property("location",
31                                      self.videoOutLocation)
32
33       self.videoQueue = gst.element_factory_make("queue")
34       self.audioQueue = gst.element_factory_make("queue")
35       # Add elements to the pipeline
36       self.player.add(self.filesrc,
37                       self.decodebin,
38                       self.videoQueue,
39                       self.autoconvert,
40                       self.video_encoder,
41                       self.muxer,
42                       self.videosink,
43                       self.audioQueue,
44                       self.audioconvert,
45                       self.audio_encoder,
46                       self.audiosink)
47
49       # Link elements in the pipeline.
```

```
50      gst.element_link_many(self.filesrc, self.decodebin)
51
52      gst.element_link_many(self. videoQueue,
53                              self.autoconvert,
54                              self.video_encoder,
55                              self.muxer,
56                              self.videosink)
57
58      gst.element_link_many(self.audioQueue,
59                              self.audioconvert,
60                              self.audio_encoder,
61                              self.audiosink)
```

We have already used all the necessary elements in various examples. The key here is to link them properly. The `self.audiosink` and `self.videoSink` elements are `filesink` elements that define audio and video output file locations respectively. Note that, in this example, we will save the output audio in MP3 format and video in MP4 format. Thus, the `lame` encoder is used for the audio file whereas we use encoder `ffenc_mpeg4` and multiplexer `ffmux_mp4` for the video output. Note that we have not used `ffmpegcolorspace` element. It just helps to get an appropriate color space format for the video sink (in this case, the output video file). In this case, it is not needed. You can always link it in the pipeline if the output file doesn't appropriately display the video frames. The media data decoded by `self.decodebin` needs to be streamed to the audio and video portions of the pipeline, using the `queue` elements as data buffers.

3. The `decodebin` creates dynamic pads to decode the input audio and video data. The `decodebin_pad_added` method needs to check the capabilities (`caps`) on the dynamic pad of the `decodebin`.

```
1   def decodebin_pad_added(self, decodebin, pad):
2       compatible_pad = None
3       caps = pad.get_caps()
4       name = caps[0].get_name()
5       print "\n cap name is = ", name
6       if name[:5] == 'video':
7           compatible_pad = (
8               self.videoQueue.get_compatible_pad(pad, caps) )
9       elif name[:5] == 'audio':
10          compatible_pad = (
11              self. audioQueue.get_compatible_pad(pad,caps) )
12
13      if compatible_pad:
14          pad.link(compatible_pad)
```

4. This check is done by the code block 6-12. If capabilities indicate it's an audio data, the `decodebin` pad is linked to the compatible pad on `self.audioQueue`. Similarly, a link between to `self.videoQueue` and `self.decodebin` is created when `caps` indicate it is the video data.

5. You can work through the remaining code in the file `SeparatingAudio.py`. Replace the paths represented by `self.inFileLocation`, `self.audioOutLocation`, and `self.videoOutLocation` with appropriate paths on your computer and then run this utility as:

```
$python SeparatingAudio.py
```

This should create two output files—a file in MP3 format that contains only the audio track from the input file and a file in MP4 format containing the video track.

What just happened?

We build a GStreamer pipeline that separates audio and video tracks from an input video file. Several of the GStreamer elements that we learned about in a number of examples earlier were used to develop this utility. We also learned how to use the capabilities (`caps`) on the dynamic pads of `decodebin` to make proper linkage between the `decodebin` and the `queue` elements.

Mixing audio and video tracks

Suppose you have recorded your friend's wedding on your camcorder. For some specific moments, you would like to mute all other sounds and replace those with background music. To accomplish this, first you need to save the video track without the audio as a separate file. We just learned that technique. Then you need to combine this video track with audio track containing the background music you wish to play. Let's now learn how to mix audio and video tracks into a single video file.

Time for action – audio/video track mixer

We will develop a program that generates a video output file, by mixing an audio and a video track. Think about what change we will need to incorporate when compared to the audio/ video track separation utility developed earlier. In that application, two `filesink` elements were required as two output files were created. Here, we need the opposite. We require two `filesrc` elements containing the audio and video data and a single `filesink` element that will contain both the audio and the video track.

1. Download the file `AudioVideoMixing.py` from the Packt website. We will review some of the important methods of class `AudioVideoMixer`.

2. The `constructPipeline` method, as usual, builds the GStreamer pipeline with all necessary elements.

```
1   def constructPipeline(self):
2       self.pipeline = gst.Pipeline("pipeline")
3
4       self.audiosrc = gst.element_factory_make("filesrc")
5       self.audiosrc.set_property("location",
6                                       self.audioInLocation)
7
8       self.videosrc = gst.element_factory_make("filesrc")
9       self.videosrc.set_property("location",
10                                      self.videoInLocation)
11
12      self.filesink = gst.element_factory_make("filesink")
13      self.filesink.set_property("location",
14                                      self.outFileLocation)
15
16      self.audio_decodebin = gst.element_factory_make(
17                                      "decodebin")
18      self.video_decodebin= gst.element_factory_make(
19                                      "decodebin")
20
21      self.audioconvert = gst.element_factory_make(
22                                      "audioconvert")
23      self.audio_encoder= gst.element_factory_make("lame")
24
25      self.video_encoder = (
26              gst.element_factory_make("ffenc_mpeg4") )
27      self.muxer = gst.element_factory_make("ffmux_mp4")
28      self.queue = gst.element_factory_make("queue")
29
30
31      videocap = gst.Caps("video/x-raw-yuv")
32      self.capsFilter = gst.element_factory_make(
33                                      "capsfilter")
34      self.capsFilter.set_property("caps", videocap)
35      # Converts the video from one colorspace to another
36      self.colorSpace = gst.element_factory_make(
37                                      "ffmpegcolorspace")
38
39      self.pipeline.add( self.videosrc,
40                          self. video_decodebin,
41                          self.capsFilter,
```

```
42                              self.colorSpace,
43                              self.video_encoder,
44                              self.muxer,
45                              self.filesink)
46
47      self.pipeline.add(self.audiosrc,
48                          self.audio_decodebin,
49                          self.audioconvert,
50                          self.audio_encoder,
51                          self.queue)
52
53      # Link audio elements
54      gst.element_link_many(self.audiosrc,
55                              self.audio_decodebin)
56      gst.element_link_many( self.audioconvert,
57                              self.audio_encoder,
58                              self.queue, self.muxer)
59      #Link video elements
60      gst.element_link_many(self.videosrc,
61              self.video_decodebin)
62      gst.element_link_many(self.capsFilter,
63                              self.colorSpace,
64                              self.video_encoder,
65                              self.muxer,
66                              self.filesink)
```

3. The audio and video file sources are defined by the elements self.audiosrc and self.videosrc respectively. These are connected to two separate decodebins (see lines 54 and 59). The pad-added signals of self.audio_decodebin and self.video_decodebin are connected in the connectSignals method.

The audio and video data then travels through a chain of audio and video processing elements respectively. The data is encoded by their respective encoders. The encoded data streams are combined so that the output video file contains both audio and video tracks. This job is done by the multiplexer, self.muxer. It is linked with the video encoder element. The audio data is streamed to the muxer through a queue element (line 57). The data is 'muxed' and fed to the filesink element, self.filesink. Note that the ffmpegcolorspace element and the capsfilter, self.capsfiter is not really required. In this case, the output video should have proper display format. You can try running this application by removing those two elements to see if it makes any difference.

4. In the `decodebin_pad_added` method, we will check a few extra things before linking the dynamic pads.

```
1   def decodebin_pad_added(self, decodebin, pad):
2       compatible_pad = None
3       caps = pad.get_caps()
4       name = caps[0].get_name()
5       print "\n cap name is =%s"%name
6       if ( name[:5] == 'video' and
7                   (decodebin is  self.video_decodebin) ):
8           compatible_pad = (
9               self.capsFilter.get_compatible_pad(pad, caps) )
10      elif ( name[:5] == 'audio' and
11                  (decodebin is self.audio_decodebin) ):
12          compatible_pad = (
13            self.audioconvert.get_compatible_pad(pad, caps) )
14
15      if compatible_pad:
16          pad.link(compatible_pad)
```

It could happen that each of the input files contains audio as well as video data. For example, both `self.audiosrc` and `self.videosrc` represent different video files with both audio and video data. The file `self.audiosrc` is linked to `self.audio_decodebin`. Thus, we should make sure that when the `self.audio_de-codebin` generates a `pad-added` signal, the dynamic pad is linked only when its caps have audio data. On similar lines, the pad on `self.video_decodebin` is linked only when caps represent video data. This is ensured by the code block 6 – 13.

5. Develop the rest of the code by reviewing file `AudioVideoMixer.py`. Replace the paths represented by, `self.audioInLocation`, `self.videoInLocation`, and `self.outFileLocation` with appropriate paths on your computer and then run this utility as:

`$python AudioVideoMixer.py`

This should create an output video file in MP4 format that contains the audio and video tracks from the specified input files!

What just happened?

We developed a tool that mixes input audio and video tracks and stores them into a single output file. To accomplish this task we used most of the audio/video processing elements that were used in video conversion utility. We learned how to link the dynamic pads on decodebin based on the streaming data represented by its 'caps'. The multiplexer plugin `ffmux_mp4` element was used to put the audio and video data together.

Saving video frames as images

Imagine that you have a wildlife video and it has recorded a very special moment. You would like to save this image. Let's learn how this can be achieved using the GStreamer framework.

Time for action – saving video frames as images

This file can be run from the command line as:

```
python ImagesFromVideo.py [options]
```

Here the [options] are:

- --input_file: The full path to input video file from which one or more frames need to be captured and saved as images.

- --start_time: The position in seconds on the video track. This will be the starting position from which one or more video frames will be captured as still image(s). The first snapshot will always be at start_time.

- --duration: The duration (in seconds) of the video track starting from the start_time. 'N' number of frames will be captured starting from the start_time.

- --num_of_captures: Total number of frames that need to be captured from start_time (including it) up to, end_time= start_time + duration (but not including the still image at end_time).

1. If not already done, download the file ImagesFromVideo.py from the Packt website. Following is an outline of the code for saving video frames.

```python
import os, sys, time
import thread
import gobject
import pygst
pygst.require("0.10")
import gst
from optparse import OptionParser

class ImageCapture:
    def __init__(self):
        pass
    def connectSignals(self):
        pass
    def constructPipeline(self):
        pass
    def gnonlin_pad_added(self, gnonlin_elem, pad):
        pass
```

```
        def captureImage(self):
            pass
        def capture_single_image(self, media_start_time):
            pass
        def message_handler(self, bus, message):
            pass
        def printUsage(self):
            pass
        def printFinalStatus(self, starttime, endtime):
            pass


# Run the program
imgCapture = ImageCapture()
thread.start_new_thread(imgCapture.captureImage, ())
gobject.threads_init()
evt_loop = gobject.MainLoop()
evt_loop.run()
```

The program execution starts by calling the captureImage method. The gnlfilesource element discussed in audio processing chapters will be used here to seek a particular frame on the streaming video. The capture_single_image does the main job of saving a single frame as an image. We will discuss some of these methods next.

2. Let's start with the constructPipeline method which defines and links various elements needed to capture the video frames.

```
1   def constructPipeline(self):
2       self.pipeline = gst.Pipeline()
3       self.gnlfilesrc = (
4       gst.element_factory_make("gnlfilesource") )
5
6       self.gnlfilesrc.set_property("uri",
7                           "file:///" + self.inFileLocation)
8       self.colorSpace = gst.element_factory_make(
9                                       "ffmpegcolorspace")
10
11      self.encoder= gst.element_factory_make("ffenc_png")
12
13      self.filesink = gst.element_factory_make("filesink")
14
15      self.pipeline.add(self.gnlfilesrc,
16                          self.colorSpace,
17                          self.encoder,
18                          self.filesink)
```

```
19
20        gst.element_link_many(self.colorSpace,
21                              self.encoder,
22                              self.filesink)
```

We already know how to create and connect the `gnlfilesource` element (called `self.gnlfilesrc`). In the examples we have seen so far, the encoder element used in a GStreamer pipeline encoded the streaming media data either in an audio or a video format. On line 11, we define a new encoder element that enables saving a particular frame in the streaming video as an image. In this example, we use the encoder `ffenc_png` to save the video frame as an image file with PNG file format. This plugin should be available by default in your GStreamer installation. If not, you will need to install it. There are similar plugins available to save the image in different file formats. For example, use `jpegenc` plugin to save it as a JPEG image and so on.

The `self.gnlfilesrc` uses dynamic pad, which is connected to an appropriate pad on `ffmpegcolorspace` discussed earlier. The `self.colorspace` element converts the color space and this video data is then encoded by the `ffenc_png` element. The `self.filesink` defines the location to save a particular video frame as an image.

3. The `captureImage` is the main controlling method. The overall structure is very similar to the audio conversion utility developer in *Chapter 5, Working with Audios*. This method runs the top-level controlling loop to capture the frames specified as an argument to the program.

```
1   def captureImage(self):
2         # Record start time
3         starttime = time.clock()
4
5         # Note: all times are in nano-seconds
6         media_end = self.media_start_time + self.media_duration
7         start = self.media_start_time
8         while start < media_end:
9             self.capture_single_image(start)
10            start += self.deltaTime
11
12        endtime = time.clock()
13        self.printFinalStatus(starttime, endtime)
14        evt_loop.quit()
```

The method `capture_single_image` does the main job of saving each of these frames. The `self.media_start_time` defines the position on the streaming video from which this utility should start saving the video frames as images. This is specified as a command-line argument to this utility. The `media_end` variable defines the position on the video track at which the program should 'stop' capturing the still images (the video frames). The `self.media_start_time` is when the first video frame will be saved as an image. This is the initial value assigned to the local variable `start`, which is then incremented in the loop.

The while loop (lines 8-10) calls the `capture_single_image` method for each of the video frames we wish to save as an image. The `self.deltaTime` variable defines the incremental time steps for capturing video frames. Its value is determined in the constructor as follows:

```
self.deltaTime = int(self.media_duration /
                     self.numberOfCaptures)
```

Here, `self.numberOfCaptures` is specified as an argument. If this argument is not specified, it will save only a single frame as an image. It is used to increment the variable `start`.

4. Now, let's see what `ImageCapture.capture_single_image` does. As the name suggests, its job is to save a single image corresponding to the video frame at `media_start_time` in the streaming video.

```
1   def capture_single_image(self, media_start_time):
2       # Set media_duration as int as
3       # gnlfilesrc takes it as integer argument
4       media_duration = int(0.01*gst.SECOND)
5
6       self.gnlfilesrc.set_property("media-start",
7                                     media_start_time)
8       self.gnlfilesrc.set_property("media-duration",
9                                     media_duration)
10
11      # time stamp in seconds, added to the name of the
12      # image to be saved.
13      time_stamp = float(media_start_time)/gst.SECOND
14      outFile = os.path.join(self.outputDirPath,
15                              "still_%.4f.png"%time_stamp )
16      print "\n outfile = ", outFile
17      self.filesink.set_property("location", outFile)
18      self.is_playing = True
19      self.pipeline.set_state(gst.STATE_PLAYING)
20      while self.is_playing:
21          time.sleep(1)
```

The media_duration is set to a very small value (0.01 seconds), just enough to play the video frame at media_start_time. The media_start_time and media_duration used to set the properties of the gnlfilesource represented by self.gnlfilesrc. On line 14, the location of the output image file is specified. Note that the filename is appended with a timestamp that represents the time on the timeline of the streaming video, at which this snapshot was taken. After setting up the necessary parameter, the pipeline is 'started' on line 20 and will be played until the EOS message is posted on the bus, that is, when it finishes writing the output PNG file.

Review the remaining methods from the file ImagesFromVideo.py and then run this utility by specifying appropriate command-line arguments. The following screenshot shows sample output messages when the program is run from the console window.

```
Command Prompt                                                    _ □ ×

C:\PythonTest\CHAPTER7\src>python ImagesFromVideo.py
                    --input_file=C:/VideoFiles/foo.mp4
                    --start_time=30
                    --duration=2
                    --num_of_captures=4

outfile =  C:\VideoFiles\STILL_IMAGES\still_30.0000.png

outfile =  C:\VideoFiles\STILL_IMAGES\still_30.5000.png

outfile =  C:\VideoFiles\STILL_IMAGES\still_31.0000.png

outfile =  C:\VideoFiles\STILL_IMAGES\still_31.5000.png

Done!

Still images saved to C:\VideoFiles\STILL_IMAGES

Approximate time required :              4.0223 seconds

C:\PythonTest\CHAPTER7\src>
```

What just happened?

We developed a very useful application that can save specified frames in a streaming video as image files. To accomplish this, we re-used several of the GStreamer elements/plugins studied earlier. For example, elements such as gnlfilesource, ffmpegcolorspace, and so on were used to construct the GStreamer pipeline. Additionally, we used an image encoder to save the video data in an image format.

Summary

We learned fundamentals of GStreamer API in previous chapters on audio processing.

In this chapter we moved one step further to develop some useful video processing utilities using Python and GStreamer. To accomplish this task, we learned about several new GStreamer plugins required for processing videos.

Specifically, we covered:

- ◆ Pipeline that handles audio and video: We learned how to build a GStreamer pipeline that can handle both audio and video tracks from the input video file. This was used to 'play' a video file and it was also the basic pipeline used in several video-processing tools developed in this chapter.

- ◆ Separating audio/video: With the help of example, we learned how to save an audio/video track of a video file into two different files.

- ◆ Mixing audio/video: We wrote a program that can mix an audio and video stream into a single video file.

- ◆ Video effects: How to adjust the properties such as brightness, contrast, and saturation for a streaming video.

- ◆ Text overlay: We developed a utility that can add text, timestamp, and clock strings on the streaming video.

- ◆ Still images from video: We learned how to save a video frame of a streaming video as an image.

This concludes our discussion on video processing using Python and GStreamer. For the audio as well as video processing, we mostly developed various command-line tools. It gave us a good understanding of the use of the underlying components of a multimedia framework. There was no user interface component involved in our discussion. The default GUI appeared only while playing a video.

The focus of the next chapter will be on GUI-based audio and video applications.

8

GUI-based Media Players Using QT Phonon

*The earlier chapters had focused on developing audio and video processing tools. The involvement of **Graphical User Interface (GUI)** was intentionally kept aside so that we could learn 'pure' multimedia-processing techniques using the GStreamer framework. However, to just 'play' an audio or a video, we would always prefer a media player with a user interface that provides an easy way to control the playback, adjust the volume, and so on.*

In this chapter, we shall:

- Develop a GUI for audio and video players using QT

- Learn fundamental components of the Phonon framework, such as `MediaObject`, `MediaSource`, `AudioOutput`, and so on to build a media graph

- Learn how to use QT Phonon framework to create media players with graphical user interface

So let's get on with it.

Installation prerequisites

We will cover the prerequisites for the installation of QT Python in this section.

PyQt4

This package provides Python bindings for QT libraries. We will use PyQt4 to generate GUI for the image processing application to be developed later in this chapter. The GPL version is available at:

```
http://www.riverbankcomputing.co.uk/software/pyqt/download
```

Note that you should install PyQt4 binary for Python version 2.6. The PyQt4 for Python version 2.5 or earlier may not support the Phonon module. Check the PyQt4 documentation to know more. The installation instructions for PyQt4 were already discussed in *Chapter 2, Working with Images*. Refer to that chapter for further details. The following table summarizes the installation prerequisites.

Summary of installation prerequisites

Package	Download location	Version	Windows platform	Linux/Unix/OS X platforms
Python	`http://python.org/download/releases/`	2.6.4 (or any 2.6.x)	Install using binary distribution	◆ Install from binary. Also install additional developer packages (for example, with python-devel in the package name for rpm-based linux distributions). ◆ Build and install from the source tarball.
PyQt4	`http://www.riverbankcomputing.co.uk/software/pyqt/download`	4.6.2 or later	Install using binary pertaining to Python2.6	◆ First install SIP 4.9 or later. ◆ Then install PyQt4.

Introduction to QT Phonon

In earlier chapters on audio and video processing, we extensively used GStreamer multimedia framework. **Phonon** is a multimedia framework used by QT to provide audio/video playback. With the GStreamer API knowledge under our belt, it should be very easy to grasp the fundamental concepts behind the Phonon multimedia framework.

Main components

Let's briefly discuss some of the fundamental components and concepts behind the Phonon architecture.

Media graph

This is analogous to a GStreamer `pipeline`. The media graph specifies various *nodes* (analogous to GStreamer elements) for processing the media stream. For example, the *sink* node gives the media data as output. To begin streaming the media data within the `Graph`, we call the `play()` method of the `MediaObject` module.

Media object

This object is used for the media playback. It is analogous to the portion of a GStreamer pipeline that handles the input media data. The instance of `MediaObject` class is used for this purpose. It provides methods to control the playback, such as playing, pausing, and stopping the streaming media.

Sink

Just like in GStreamer, Phonon has a media `Sink`. For example, an audio sink is used to output the audio through an audio output device.

Path

The `Path` object is used to connect nodes within a media graph in Phonon. For example, a `MediaObject` node is linked to an `AudioOutput` node to stream an audio.

Effects

To manipulate the streaming media, we need to insert `Effects` nodes within the `Graph`, between the source (`MediaObject`) and the `Sink` nodes. These nodes are also called processors. The `Effect` class of the Phonon framework facilitates adding various effects to the streaming media.

Backends

It is a `backend` that does the heavy lifting, which is, processing a media stream in Phonon. On Windows platform the backend framework is *DirectShow*. If you are using Linux, the backend framework for Phonon is GStreamer and, it is *QuickTime* in case you use Mac OS X. The supported functionality (for example, the media formats supported) may vary depending on the platform.

The namespace, `Phonon.BackendCapabilities`, includes functions that provide information about what the Phonon backend is capable of doing. For example, the function `BackendCapabilities.availableMimeTypes()` returns a list of all the mime types that the backend is capable of decoding. Additionally, it provides information about the available audio output devices and available effects.

Modules

Qt Phonon includes several modules that help to quickly develop applications for audio and video playback. We will briefly discuss a few of the important modules.

MediaNode

This is the superclass for all the nodes within a Phonon media graph. Therefore, it is inherited by modules such as `MediaObject`, `Effect`, and `AudioOutput`, which will be discussed next.

MediaSource

As the name indicates, this is used to the input the media source. The `MediaObject` uses the media data it provides. The following line of code shows how this is accomplished.

```
self.mediaObj.setCurrentSource(self.mediaSource)
```

The API method, `setCurrentSouce` of class `MediaObject`, is used to specify the `MediaSource` object from which to obtain the media data.

MediaObject

As mentioned earlier, the `MediaObject` module defines an API to manage the playback. The methods such as `play()`, `pause()`, and `stop()` provide playback controls.

Path

The `Path` class links the nodes within a graph. It can be created using an API method, `Phonon.createPath`. The following code snippet shows an example usage:

```
self.audioPath = Phonon.createPath(self.mediaObj, self.audioSink)
```

Here, `self.audioPath` is an instance of `Path` class. It links the instance of class `MediaObject` with `self.audioSink`, which is an instance of class `AudioOutPut`. More nodes can be added to the graph by using `Path.insertEffect`.

AudioOutput

The instance of this class provides an audio output node in the Phonon media graph. The output device is typically the sound card. `AudioOutput` is connected to the `MediaObject` (and `Effect` instances) using the `Path` object we just discussed. The property `AudioOutput.outputDevice()` contains information about the output device.

Effect

The instance of class `Effect` can be inserted as a node into the media graph. The `Path.insertEffect` can bring about this effect whereas `Path.removeEffect` facilitates removal of that node from the graph. This object modifies the streaming media data. For example, an echo effect will add an echo to the audio. Use `BackendCapabilities.availableAudioEffects` to find out which effects are supported by the Phonon backend.

VideoPlayer

This class provides an important functionality. It has several built-in features that eliminate the need of explicitly creating nodes such as `MediaObject`. We will discuss this in detail while developing the video player application.

SeekSlider

`SeekSlider` is a GUI widget. This class provides a slider to seek a specific position in the streaming media. It handles all the necessary updates and signal connections internally. All it needs is the media object instance.

volumeSlider

This class provides a widget for controlling the volume. It makes a programmer's job easy by internally connecting signals. The following line of code sets the audio output device for a volume slider.

```
volumeSlider.setAudioOutput(self.audioSink)
```

Here, the `volumeSlider` will control the volume for the audio output device of `self.audioSink`.

Project: GUI-based music player

Let's get straight to the business. We will develop a simple GUI-based music player using QT Phonon. The goal of this project is to learn how to put together important components of the Phonon framework discussed earlier. It will help us get familiar with the overall Phonon framework. In the second project, we will learn an even simpler way to accomplish the same task.

The application to be developed here will play an opened audio file. It will have GUI widgets to control the playback and add various effects to the streaming audio. The screenshot of the music player application is shown in the following illustration of its graphical user interface:

GUI elements in the music player

The illustrated music player application uses the following QT widgets.

- ♦ QMainWindow: This class provides the main application window. In this window, other elements such as buttons and menus are added in a layout.

- ♦ QToolButton: The play, pause, and stop buttons are created using the QToolButton class. The appearance of these QToolButtons can be tweaked using a number of properties; for example, calling QToolButtoon. setAutoRaise(True): Removes the raised button effect. On mouse hover, the button will be highlighted and appear raised above the surface.

- ♦ VolumeSlider: As discussed earlier, the volume slider widget is used for controlling the volume of the output audio device.

- ♦ SeekSlider: Used to seek a position within the streaming media. While the music is being played, its position is automatically updated. You can drag the slider using mouse to jump to a different position on the track.

- ♦ QLineEdit: This widget is used to display the full path of the media file currently being played.

- ♦ QMenubar: This is the menu bar above the QLineEdit. Here, we add different menus such as **File** and **Effects**.

- ♦ QAction: Various audio effect options are added to the **Effects** menu as QAction instances.

Some of these QT elements just discussed are pointed out in the following illustration of a music player application displaying various QT widgets used:

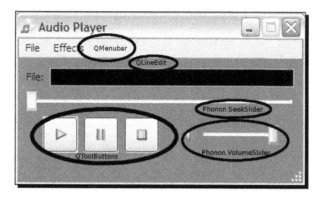

Generating the UI code

The required GUI is built using the QT Designer application. This should be included in the binary installer of PyQT4. QT Designer provides a quick way to design and develop the user interface code. It supports a number of commonly used QT widgets. One can interactively add these widgets to a layout. This tool is also very useful to enhance the aesthetic appeal of the application. For example, the widget colors and other properties can easily be changed using various features available in QT Designer.

Time for action – generating the UI code

The UI file necessary for this application is already created for you. The purpose of this section is not to show you how to generate the UI from scratch. It will just illustrate some of the important aspects of developing GUI using QT Designer for this application. You can then experiment with it further to add new widgets to the music player application. We used QT Designer while developing the 'Thumbnail Maker' application in *Chapter 2, Working with Images*. We will cover some of those things here as well.

1. Download the file `Ui_AudioPlayerDialog.ui` from the Packt website.

2. Start the QT Designer application that comes with the PyQt4 installation.

3. Open this file in QT Designer. Click on each widget element within this audio player dialog. The QT class associated with the selected widget will be displayed in the **Property Editor** panel of the QT Designer.

4. Notice the red-colored borders around various UI widgets within the dialog. These borders indicate a 'layout' in which the widgets are arranged. The layouts are created using the QLayout class and its various subclasses. It is a critical component of the user interface design using QT. Without a layout in place, the UI elements may appear distorted when you run the application and, for instance, resize the dialog.

The following illustration shows how the dialog appears when opened in QT Designer—the music player dialog (.ui file) in QT Designer.

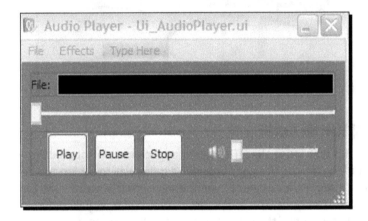

Closely observe the borders around the widgets that indicate the presence of a layout. You will notice that there are multiple borders. This implies that we have placed the widgets in multiple layouts. For example, the buttons **Play**, **Pause**, and **Stop** are arranged in a horizontal layout, QHBoxLayout. These are further arranged in another horizontal layout with the volumeSlider element. Refer to QT4 and QT Designer documentation to know how to arrange widgets in a layout.

5. If you click on the **Type Here** placeholder in the menu bar, it becomes editable. With this, you can add a new menu to the menu bar. Similarly, you can add menu items to the **File** and **Effects** menus by opening those menus and clicking on **Type Here** menu item. The **File** menu has two menu items: **Open** and **Exit**. Note that the **Effects** menu is empty. We will add menu items to this menu later. In the following few steps, we will make minor changes to this dialog just to get a feel of QT Designer.

6. We will now add a widget that can display digits. This widget can be used to update the playtime information of the streaming media. The left panel shows a bunch of widgets that can be mouse dragged and dropped inside the Audio Player dialog window. This is illustrated by the following screenshot:

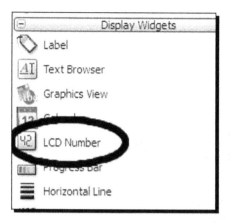
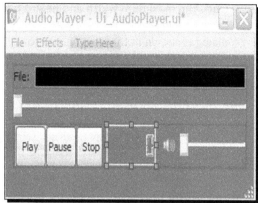

You can see the Display widget panel of QT Designer and the LCD number widget inserted into the dialog.

The inserted LCD number widget is shown selected in the screenshot on the right-hand side. It is inserted in a layout that arranges `QToolButtons` and the `volumeSlider` widgets in a horizontal fashion. Also, notice that the inserted LCD number widget has a default size. This size needs to be adjusted so that other widgets get their share of the space. Various parameters can be adjusted using the property editor panel within QT Designer for this widget. Here, we adjust the maximum size values as illustrated in the following screenshot.

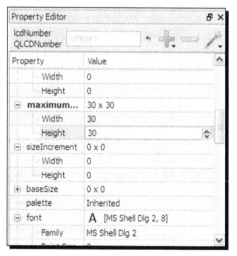

The **Property Editor** for LCD number widget—the screenshot on the right-hand side shows the edited size parameters.

Once the maximum width and height parameters are adjusted, the LCD number widget fits in nicely within the horizontal layout. The resultant dialog is shown in the next illustration.

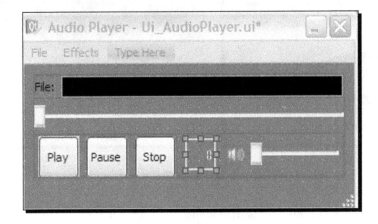

That's it! You can keep this LCD number widget in the dialog for now. After completion of this project, you can use it to add a feature that displays the time information for the streaming media. Note that LCD Number widget is not the only option to display the play time. You can even use a QTextLabel and update the label string with the time.

7. As mentioned in the chapter, *Chapter 2, Working with Images*, the QT Designer saves the user interface file with an extension .ui. To convert this into Python source code, PyQt4 provides a conversion utility called pyuic4. On Windows XP, for standard Python installation, the path for this utility is C:\Python26\Lib\ site-packages\PyQt4\pyuic4.bat. Add the path to the environment variable. Alternatively, specify the whole path each time you want to convert .ui file to Python source file. The conversion utility can be run from the command prompt as:

```
pyuic4 UI_AudioPlayerDialog.ui -o Ui_AudioPlayerDialog.py
```

This script will create a Python source file, Ui_AudioPlayerDialog.py from the input .ui file. You can further review this file to understand how the UI code is set up. We will use this file 'as-is' for the further discussion.

It is *not* a good idea to modify the autogenerated Python source file, Ui_ AudioPlayerDialog.py; if you make any changes to the corresponding .ui file of the QT Designer and run the pyuic4 script again, it will *overwrite* the previous Python source file, Ui_AudioPlayerDialog.py, provided we use the same filename. Instead, you can use the autogenerated file as a base class and create a subclass to add custom UI elements programmatically.

What just happened?

This section gave us a working knowledge of tweaking a user interface using QT Designer. Just to get the feel of user interface editing, we added a LCD number widget to the Audio Player dialog. We learned how to autogenerate the Python source code from a `.ui` file created with the help of QT Designer.

Connecting the widgets

The command-line utility `pyuic4` (`pyuic4.bat` for Windows users) enabled conversion of the user interface created by the QT-Designer into a Python source file. However, various widgets in this UI need to respond to the user actions. For example, when the **Play** button is clicked, it must start streaming the media file. Thus, we need to add necessary code that will instruct these widgets what they should do when a certain event occurs. This is accomplished using the slots and signals. A `signal` is emitted when a particular GUI event occurs. For example, when a user clicks on the **Pause** button, a `"clicked()"` signal is emitted. A `slot` is a method that is called for this `signal`. This is very similar to the how we connected `pad-added` signal by a `decodebin` element to a method `decodebin_pad_added` in earlier chapter. Refer to the PyQt4/ QT4 documentation that has a comprehensive list of available `signals` for various widgets.

Time for action – connecting the widgets

Let's learn how to make widgets respond to a particular user action, such as a button click.

1. Download the file `AudioPlayerDialog.py` from the Packt website. It defines the class `AudioPlayerDialog`.

2. We will now review the method that connects class methods to the emitted signals. These signals are generated whenever a particular 'event' occurs.

```
1   def _connect(self):
2       """
3       Connect slots with signals.
4       """
5       self.connect(self._dialog.fileOpenAction,
6                   SIGNAL("triggered()"),
7                   self._openFileDialog)
8
9       self.connect(self._dialog.fileExitAction,
10                  SIGNAL("triggered()"),
11                  self.close)
12
```

```
13    self.connect(self._dialog.menuAudioEffects,
14            SIGNAL("triggered(QAction*)"),
15            self._changeAudioEffects)
16
17    self.connect(self._dialog.playToolButton,
18            SIGNAL("clicked()"),
19            self._playMedia)
20
21    self.connect(self._dialog.stopToolButton,
22            SIGNAL("clicked()"),
23            self._stopMedia)
24
25    self.connect(self._dialog.pauseToolButton,
26            SIGNAL("clicked()"),
27              self._pauseMedia)
```

Here, the `self._dialog` is an instance of class `Ui_AudioPlayerDialog`. Note that, the `self.connect` is an inherited method of the QT class `QMainWindow`. It takes the following arguments (`QObject`, `SIGNAL`, `callable`). The `QObject` is any widget type; `SIGNAL` is generated when a specific event occurs. The `callable` is a method that handles this event. The `AudioPlayer._connect` method connects all the necessary signals with class methods.

3. The File menu in the Audio Player dialog contains two `QActions`, namely, `fileOpenAction` and `fileExitAction`. When File->Open is selected, a signal "triggered" is generated for the `QAction`. We need to watch out for this signal and then call a method that will do the job of opening a file. This signal is connected by the code between lines 5-7. Thus, when "`triggered()`" signal is emitted, for `fileopenAction`, a method `AudioPlayer._openFileDialog` is called that has necessary code to open an audio file.

4. Let's review the code on line 9-12. This code connects all the `QActions` within a `QMenu` to a method of class `AudioPlayer`. The first argument, `self._dialog.menuAudioEffects`, is the Effects menu in the menu bar. This is a `QMenu`. The second argument `SIGNAL("triggered(QAction*)")` tells QT that we want to capture the triggered signal for any of the `QActions` within the **Effects** menu. This is best explained with an example. Imagine that the audio **Effects** menu has menu items (`QActions`) such as Echo and Distortion. When a user selects **Effects | Echo** or **Effects | Distortion**, the `triggered(QAction*)` signal is emitted. The argument `QAction*` is just a pointer to that `QAction`. The third argument is the receiver method, `self._changeAudioEffects` that is called when this signal is emitted.

The `clicked()` signal emitted when a `QToolButton`, such as, **Play**, **Pause**, or **Stop** is clicked. This signal is connected to appropriate methods of class `AudioPlayer` by the code block 13-23.

5. Notice that we didn't connect the `SeekSlider` and `VolumeSlider`. The signals for these widgets are connected internally. All you need to do is set `MediaObject` and `AudioOutput` for these widgets respectively. We will learn how that's done in the next section.

What just happened?

We reviewed `AudioPlayerDialog._connect()` method to learn how various widgets within the Audio Player dialog are connected to internal methods. This helped us learn some preliminary concepts of GUI programming using QT.

Developing the audio player code

The discussion so far has been focused on the graphical user interface. We learned how to use QT Designer to create user interface and then generate a Python source file representing this UI. We also reviewed the code that connects the frontend of our application with the backend (the class methods). Now, it is time to review the workhorse audio processing code responsible for playing the audio, controlling the playback, and operations like adding audio effects.

Time for action – developing the audio player code

The source file, `AudioPlayerDialog.py`, used in the earlier section will be used here as well. The class `AudioPlayerDialog` inherits `QMainWindow`.

1. If you have not done so already, download the Python source file `AudioPlayerDialog.py`.

2. Let's start with the constructor of the class, `AudioPlayerDialog`.

```
1  def __init__(self):
2      QMainWindow.__init__(self)
3      self.mediaSource = None
4      self.audioPath = ''
5      self.addedEffects = {}
6      self.effectsDict = {}
7
8      # Initialize some other variables.
9      self._filePath = ''
10     self._dirPath = ''
11     self._dialog = None
12     # Create media object , audio sink and path
13     self.mediaObj = phonon.Phonon.MediaObject(self)
14     self.audioSink = Phonon.AudioOutput(
15                             Phonon.MusicCategory,
16                             self)
17     self.audioPath = Phonon.createPath(self.mediaObj,
18                             self.audioSink)
19
20     # Create self._dialog instance and call
21     # necessary methods to create a user interface
22     self._createUI()
23
24     # Connect slots with signals.
25     self._connect()
26
27     # Show the Audio player.
28     self.show()
```

The code block from lines 2 to 6 initializes some instance variables to be used later. The dictionary object `self.effectsDict` will be used to store information about the available audio effects. Whereas, `self.addedEffects` is used to check if an audio effect is already added to the streaming media.

On line 13, the instance of `Phonon.MediaObject` is created. It will be used for controlling the playback of a `MediaSource`.

An audio output node in the Phonon media graph is created by the code on lines 14-16. We will call it as `self.audioSink`, the terminology used in earlier chapter. The first argument for `AudioOutput` is used to specify the category. It is an object of class `Phonon.Category`. Since this is a music player application, we define the category as `Phonon.MusicCategory`. Review QT documentation to know more about the categories. The second argument is used as a parent for this audio sink.

The `Phonon.Path` class links the nodes within a media graph. This object is created using an API method, `Phonon.createPath`. On line 17, the `Path` `self.audioPath` links the media object `self.mediaObject` with the audio output `self.audioSink`.

The call to the `_createUI` method handles the defining of the user interface. We already learned how the frontend communicates with the backend using the connections set up in the `_connect` method.

Finally, on line 28, the API method `QMainWindow.show()` displays the audio player.

3. The method `_createUI` delegates most of the GUI creation to the class `UI_AudioPlayerDialog`. The method also has the code that further modifies the GUI.

```
1   def _createUI(self):
2       # Define the instance to access the the UI elements
3        defined in class Ui_AudioPlayerDialog.
4       self._dialog = Ui_AudioPlayerDialog()
5       self._dialog.setupUi(self)
6       self._dialog.retranslateUi(self)
7       playIcon= QIcon("play.png")
8       pauseIcon= QIcon("pause.png")
9       stopIcon= QIcon("stop.png")
10      musicIcon= QIcon("music.png")
11
12      self._dialog.playToolButton.setIcon(playIcon)
13      self._dialog.pauseToolButton.setIcon(pauseIcon)
14      self._dialog.stopToolButton.setIcon(stopIcon)
15      self.setWindowIcon(musicIcon)
16      self._setupEffectsMenu()
17      self._dialog.seekSlider.setMediaObject(self.mediaObj)
18      self._dialog.volumeSlider.setAudioOutput(
19                                      self.audioSink)
```

The instance of class `UI_AudioPlayerDialog` is created on line 4. `setupUI` and `retranslateUI` are the automatically generated methods. These are generated when the QT Designer file with the UI is converted into a Python source file. The `AudioPlayerDialog` instance is passed as an argument to these two methods.

The code block 7 to 14 sets up the icons for the three `QToolButton` instances. The `setIcon` API method takes `QIcon` instance as an argument. The music player icon in the caption (on top-left corner of the dialog) is created by the code on line 15. As mentioned earlier, the `Phonon.SeekSlider` signals are internally connected. We only need to tell which `MediaObject` it will handle. This is done on line 17. Similarly, on line 18, the `setAudioOutput` method of `volumeSlider` sets up the `self.audiosink` as the audio output for this `volumeSlider`. While setting up the UI design, we did not add any menu items to the **Effects** menu. This is done now, by calling the `_setupEffectsMenu` method on line 16.

4. Let's review the method `_setupEffectsMenu`. It adds various available audio effects in the Phonon framework as menu items to the **Effects** menu.

```
1   def _setupEffectsMenu(self):
2       availableEffects = (
3       Phonon.BackendCapabilities.availableAudioEffects())
4       for e in availableEffects:
5           effectName = e.name()
6           self.effectsDict[effectName] = e
7           action = QAction(effectName,
8                               self._dialog.menuAudioEffects)
9           action.setCheckable(True)
10          self._dialog.menuAudioEffects.addAction(action)
```

The namespace, `Phonon.BackendCapabilities` includes functions that provide information about the capability of the Phonon backend. `BackendCapabilities.availableAudioeffects()` returns a list of all audio effects supported by Phonon on a given platform. The list, `availableEffects`, contains objects of the class `Phonon.EffectDescription`. `self.effectsDict` stores the name of the effect and the `EffectDescription` object as `key-value` pairs. This `dictionary` will be used later. The **Effects** menu, `menuAudioEffects`, is populated with the `QAction` instances corresponding to each of the available audio effects. `QAction` is created on line 6. The `setCheckable` property of `QAction` toggles the checked state of the action on mouse click. The following screenshot shows the **Effects** menu items on Windows XP.

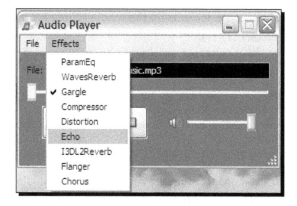

5. The method _openFileDialog is called when **File | Open** is clicked from the music player.

```
1   def _openFileDialog(self):
2
3       self._filePath = ''
4
5       self._filePath = (
6           str(QFileDialog.getOpenFileName(
7               self,
8               "Open Audio File",
9               "",
10              "MP3 file (*.mp3);;wav(*.wav);;All Files
11                                    (*.*);;")) )
12      if self._filePath:
13          self._filePath = os.path.normpath(self._filePath)
14          self._dialog.fileLineEdit.setText(self._filePath)
15          self._loadNewMedia()
```

This pops up a QFileDialog with the file type filters as specified on line 10. To know about the supported media formats, you can use the Phonon.BackEndCapabilities as illustrated by the following line of code.

```
types = Phonon.BackendCapabilities.availableMimeTypes()
```

Where, types is a list of available mime types.

The path of the file specified by the user is then stored in the variable self._filePath. This path is displayed in the fileLineEdit field of the dialog. On line 15, the method _loadNewMedia is called. We will review that next.

6. The method `_loadNewMedia` sets up the media source for the `MediaObject`.

```
1   def _loadNewMedia(self):
2           # This is required so that the player can play another
3           # file, if loaded while first one is still playing.
4           if self.mediaSource:
5               self._stopMedia()
6               del self.mediaSource
7           self.mediaSource = phonon.Phonon.MediaSource(
8                                         self._filePath)
9           self.mediaObj.setCurrentSource(self.mediaSource)
```

The `if` block on line 4 ensures that the current streaming audio (if any) is stopped by the media object before setting the new media source to a playing state. Although it is not necessary, the memory occupied by the `MediaSource` object is cleared up by the code on line 6. Line 8 creates a new instance of class `MediaSource`. The API method, `setCurrentSouce` of the class `MediaObject` is used to specify the `MediaSource` that provides the media data. With this, our media player is all set to stream the audio file.

7. When you click on the **Play** button in the music player, the `AudioPlayerDialog._playMedia` method is called.

```
1 def _playMedia(self):
2       if not self._okToPlayPauseStop():
3           return
4
5       if self.mediaObj is None:
6           print "Error playing Audio"
7           return
8
9       self.mediaObj.play()
```

First the program carries out some primary checks to ensure that the media is playable and then calls the `play()` method of `Phonon.MediaObject`, which begins streaming the audio. The methods `_pauseMedia` and `_stopMedia` of class `AudioPlayerDialog` contain similar code.

We just learned how to set up the media graph, stream the media, and control its playback. Now let's see how to add audio effects to this streaming media. If any of the items in the Effects menu are clicked, the `AudioPlayerDialog._changeAudioEffects` method is called:

```
1   def _changeAudioEffects(self, action):
2           effectName = action.text()
3
4           if action.isChecked():
5               effectDescription = self.effectsDict[effectName]
6               effect = Phonon.Effect(effectDescription)
```

```
7              self.addedEffects[effectName] = effect
8              self.audioPath.insertEffect(effect)
9        else:
10             effect = self.addedEffects[effectName]
11             self.audioPath.removeEffect(effect)
12             del self.addedEffects[effectName]
```

The `if` and `else` blocks in the preceding code snippet add and remove
effects nodes from the media graph respectively. The `if` block is
executed when an action in the **Effects** menu is checked. When an
already checked action is toggled, the program executes the `else` block.
In the `if` block, an instance of `Phonon.Effect` is created on line 6.
This takes an `EffectDescription` object as an argument. As seen in
the `_setupEffectsMenu` method, `self.effectsDict` stores the
`EffectDescription` objects as the `dictionary` values. On line 8, this
effect is inserted as a node in the media graph. The `self.audioPath` links
all the nodes within the media graph.

The `dictionary`, `self.addedEffects` keeps track of all the audio
effects inserted within the media graph. The `else` block removes an already
added effect.

On line 11, an added effect is removed by calling the `removeEffect` API
method of `Phonon.Path`. The corresponding key-value pair of `self.`
`addedEffects` is also deleted on line 12. This also ensures that there is no
memory leak.

> QT Phonon allows adding the same audio effect multiple times. For
> example, you can create multiple 'Chorus' effect nodes within the
> media graph using `Path.insertEffect`. Each of the added
> effects will have its own contribution. However, in our application,
> we support adding an effect only once. You can extend this to
> support adding the same effect multiple times. For this, you will
> need to tweak the **Effects** menu UI and make some other changes
> in the code to keep track of the added effects.

8. The application will not terminate properly if you close the GUI window while an
audio file is being played. To safely terminate the application without any memory
leaks, `AudioPlayerDialog` overrides the `QMainWindow.closeEvent`. Before
closing the window, we do the necessary cleanup to avoid memory leaks. The code
is illustrated below.

```
1 def closeEvent(self, evt):
2     print "\n in close event"
3     if self.mediaObj:
4         self.mediaObj.stop()
5
```

```
6    self.mediaObj = None
7    self._clearEffectsObjects()
8    QMainWindow.closeEvent(self, evt)
```

The streaming media, if any, is first stopped. The call to
_clearEffectsObject deletes all the Phonon.Effect and
Phonon.EffectDescription objects (if present). The method
_clearEffectsObject is self-explanatory.

9. The following code creates an instance of QApplication and executes
this program.

```
1    app = QApplication(sys.argv)
2    musicPlayer = AudioPlayerDialog()
3    app.exec_()
```

10. Review the rest of the code from the file AudioPlayerDialog.py and then run
the music player as:

$python AudioPlayerDialog.py

This should display the music player GUI window. Use **File | Open** to specify
a music file and then click on the **Play** button to enjoy the music!

What just happened?

We just created our own music player! We developed a frontend for this music player using
QT Phonon multimedia framework. Use of various modules in QT Phonon was thoroughly
discussed. We learned how to set up audio controls and effects in a media graph by using
modules such as MediaObject, AudioOutput, Path, and so on. We also gained some
higher-level understanding of GUI programming aspects using QT.

Have a go hero – add more features to the audio player

In the *Generating the UI code* section, we added a widget to the music player GUI window.
This is an LCD number widget that can display the frame numbers. Connect this widget to
the Audio Player backend, so that it can display the current media time. The next illustration
shows this LCD number widget in action for a streaming audio file.

- Extend this music player application so that it can play all the songs from a directory
  or CD one after the other. There are a number of ways to create a user interface to
  display the files. For example, you can try using widgets such as QDirectoryView,
  QTreeView, or QTableWidget.

Music player displaying the frame number (time) in the LCD number widget:

Project: GUI-based video player

In the first project, we learned the fundamentals of the QT Phonon framework. In this project, we will extend that knowledge further by developing a video player. The Audio player was developed by building a media graph. Various nodes such as MediaObject, AudioOutput, and Effects were linked together by creating a Phonon.Path. If the goal is just to develop a simple audio or video player, the job is even simpler. Phonon has a module VideoPlayer that provides an abstract way to play an audio or a video without the need to explicitly create MediaObject, AudioOutput, and some other objects. All it needs is a MediaSource. It is also possible to create a custom media graph by adding various audio-effect nodes. We will see how to do it later. For now, let's write a simple video player application using QT Phonon. The following illustration shows the video player in action.

Generating the UI code

QT Designer is an excellent resource for generating user interface interactively. As we have seen, most of the user interface for this project is built using QT Designer. In addition, some important points about the user interface design using QT were covered. This section will just walk you through the user interface generation for this application using QT Designer and `pyuic4`.

Time for action – generating the UI code

The `.ui` file is already created. In the following discussion, we will simply use this file and go through some of the GUI elements needed for this application.

1. Download the file `Ui_VideoPlayerDialog.ui` from the Packt website.

2. Open this file in QT Designer. Click on each widget element. The QT class associated with the selected widget will be displayed in the **Property Editor** panel on the right-hand side. Most of the widgets used here are same as the ones used in the earlier project. The only widget that is different is the `Phonon.VideoPlayer`. The following illustration shows how the dialog appears when opened in QT Designer. It also points out various Phonon widgets used in the dialog.

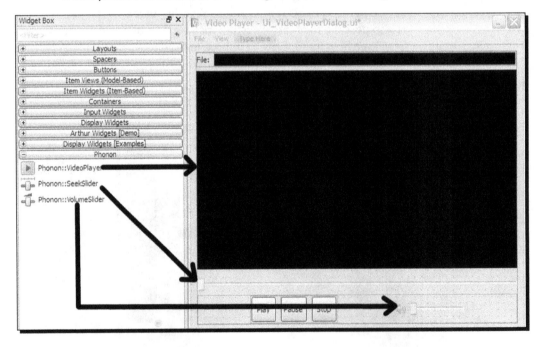

The video player widget in QT Designer appears as shown in the preceding screenshot.

3. Click on the `VideoPlayer` widget shown in the preceding illustration. The **Property Editor** will display its properties. Pay attention to how the size of this widget is defined. This Video Player will support an option to view the video in 'Full Screen' mode. Therefore, the maximum size parameters for the `VideoPlayer` widget are set to high values as shown in the next screenshot. In fact, we are using the QT default values for the maximum size property. The only property modified is the minimum size of the widget. This minimum size will be the default size of the video player widget.

The **Property editor** for Video Player widget:

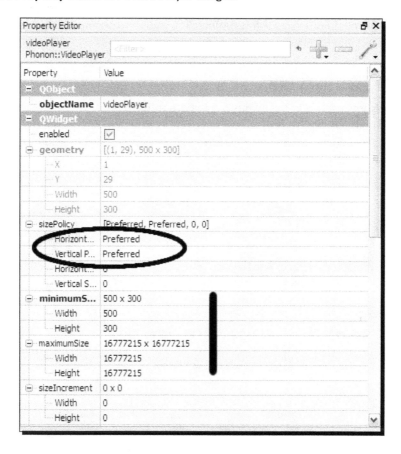

4. The rest of the widgets are the same as the one used in an earlier project. You can add the LCD **N**umber widget or a simple text label that displays the current time for the streaming media. Refer to the last project for instructions on adding such widgets.

5. Next, convert the `.ui` file into `.py` using the `pyuic4` conversion utility. The conversion utility can be run from the command prompt as:

```
pyuic4 UI_VideoPlayerDialog.ui -o Ui_VideoPlayerDialog.py
```

This script will create a Python source file, `Ui_VideoPlayerDialog.py`, from the input `.ui` file. We will use this file 'as-is' for the further discussion.

What just happened?

The previous discussion served as a refresher on use of QT Designer to generate most of the user interface elements needed for this project. The `pyuic4` conversion utility was used to convert the `.ui` file to a Python source file.

Connecting the widgets

Most of the widgets used in the previous project are re-used here. Therefore, this is going to be a short discussion. In this project, we have not included an **Effects** menu. Thus, the `VideoPlayerDialog._connect` method has minor changes. This method is illustrated as follows:

```python
def _connect(self):
    self.connect(self._dialog.fileOpenAction,
                SIGNAL("triggered()"),
                self._openFileDialog)

    self.connect(self._dialog.fileExitAction,
                SIGNAL("triggered()"),
                self.close)

    self.connect(self._dialog.fullScreenAction,
                SIGNAL("toggled(bool)"),
                self._toggleFullScreen)

    self.connect(self._dialog.playToolButton,
                SIGNAL("clicked()"),
                self._playMedia)

    self.connect(self._dialog.stopToolButton,
                SIGNAL("clicked()"),
                self._stopMedia)

    self.connect(self._dialog.pauseToolButton,
                SIGNAL("clicked()"),
                self._pauseMedia)
```

The highlighted lines of code are a new widget connection. The rest of the connections are the same as the ones discussed in the previous project. When **View | Full Screen** is selected, the toggled(bool) signal of fullScreenAction is emitted. When this happens the slot method self._toggleFullScreen is called. The next section will have more details about this method.

Developing the video player code

The generated frontend is connected to the backend for processing the media. In this section, we will review the video player backend that actually streams the media and controls the playback and volume. Our job is easier here. Most of the good work we did in the earlier project will be re-used here. There will be some minor modifications because we will be using Phonon.VideoPlayer for video processing instead of explicitly creating the objects such as MediaObject.

Time for action – developing the video player code

Let's develop the rest of the video player backend. We will re-use several methods from the AudioPlayerDialog class with a few minor changes. Only the important methods will be covered in this section.

1. Download the file VideoPlayerDialog.py from the Packt website.

2. The constructor of the class is shown below.

```
1  def __init__(self):
2      QMainWindow.__init__(self)
3      self.mediaSource = None
4      self.audioPath = ''
5
6      # Initialize some other variables.
7      self._filePath = ''
8      self._dialog = None
9
10     # Create self._dialog instance and call
11     # necessary methods to create a user interface
12     self._createUI()
13
14     self.mediaObj = self._dialog.videoPlayer.mediaObject()
15     self.audioSink = self._dialog.videoPlayer.audioOutput()
16
17     self._dialog.seekSlider.setMediaObject(self.mediaObj)
18     self._dialog.volumeSlider.setAudioOutput(
19                                  self.audioSink)
20
```

```
21      # Connect slots with signals.
22      self._connect()
23
24      # Show the Audio player.
25      self.show()
```

The `self._dialog` creates an instance of class `Phonon.VideoPlayer`. Once a media source is specified, `self._dialog.videoPlayer` is able to stream the media. Thus, for the media streaming itself, we don't need to create the nodes `MediaObject` and `AudioOutput` explicitly; the `Phonon.VideoPlayer` internally builds the media graph. However, `MediaObject` and `AudioOutput` are required for `seekSlider` and `volumeControl` widgets respectively. On lines 14 and 15, these objects are obtained from `self._dialog.videoPlayer`.

3. The `_createUI` method is almost identical to the corresponding method in `AudioPlayerDialog`, except that it doesn't have the **Effects** menu-related code.

4. Following that, the method to review is `_playMedia`:

```
1 def _playMedia(self):
2       if not self._okToPlayPauseStop():
3           return
4       self._dialog.videoPlayer.play(self.mediaSource)
```

The code is self-explanatory. The `self.mediaSource` is set in `VideoPlayerDialog._loadNewMedia`. This `MediaSource` instance is passed as an argument to the API method `VideoPlayer.play`. The `videoPlayer` then builds the media graph internally and plays the given media file.

5. This simple video player supports an option to view the streaming video in full screen mode. `QMainWindow` class provides an easy way to change the view between full screen and normal viewing mode. This is done by the method `_toggleFullScreen`.

```
def _toggleFullScreen(self, val):
    """
    Change between normal and full screen mode.
    """

    # Note: The program starts in Normal viewing mode
    # by default.

    if val:
        self.showFullScreen()
    else:
        self.showNormal()
```

The method, `self.showFullScreen()` is inherited from class `QMainWindow`. If the `QAction` in the **View** menu (**View | Full Screen**) is checked, the video player window is set to full screen. `QMainWindow.showNormal()` changes the video player back to the normal viewing mode. The following screenshot shows the video player in the full screen mode. Notice that the window caption bar is hidden in the full screen mode.

Video player in full screen mode is illustrated as shown in the next image:

6. Review the rest of the code from file `VideoPlayerDialog.py`. Keep this file in the same directory as `Ui_VideoPlayerDialog.py` and then run the program from the command line as:

   ```
   $python VideoPlayerDialog.py
   ```

7. The video player GUI window will appear. Open any supported audio or video file and click on the **Play** button to begin the playback.

What just happened?

We wrote our own video player. This video player is capable of playing video as well as audio files of supported formats. The module `Phonon.VideoPlayer` that enables media playback and control was used here. We also learned how to toggle view between full screen and normal viewing mode using the API methods of class `QMainWindow`.

Have a go hero – do more with the video player

1. Here is a simple enhancement. The full screen mode shows widgets such as playback control buttons, seek, and volume sliders. Hide these widgets when the **View | Full Screen** action is checked. Also, add a keyboard shortcut to toggle between normal and full screen view mode.

2. Add audio effects to the video player GUI. We already learned how to add audio effects to the media graph in the first project. You can re-use that code here. However, you will need an appropriate `Phonon.Path` object to which the `effects` node needs to be added. In the last project, we used `Phonon.createPath`—we can't create a new path as it is created internally by the VideoPlayer. Instead, the path can be obtained using API method `MediaObject.outputPaths()`. This method returns a list containing output (audio and video) paths. The line of code is shown as an example.

    ```
    self.audioPath = self.mediaObj.outputPaths()[0]
    ```

    However, be careful with the memory leaks. If you add audio effects, and then exit the application, the program may freeze. This could be because the effect nodes are not deleted from the original audio path. Alternatively, you can build the video player from basic principles. That is, don't use `Phonon.VideoPlayer`. Instead, build a custom media graph just like how we did for the audio player project. In this case, you will need to use modules such as `Phonon.VideoWidget`.

Summary

This chapter taught us several things about GUI multimedia application development using QT. We worked on two exciting projects where audio and video players using QT Phonon framework were developed. To accomplish these tasks, we:

◆ Used QT Designer to generate the UI source code

◆ Handled the QT generated events by connecting slots (class methods) with signals

◆ Used Phonon framework to set up media graphs for streaming of audio and video

Index

cropping, video manipulations
  about 217
  borders, adding 219
  video, cropping 218, 219
Cygwin 125

D

darwinports 125
decodebin_pad_added method 207
decodebin plugin 128
def convertImage method 26
def processArgs method 26
digital multimedia 8
Display module, PyAudiere 14
Draw module, PyAudiere 14
drive on a rainy day project 117-122
dshowaudiosrc plugin 157
dynamic pad 130

E

echo effect
  about 179
  adding 179-182
EDGE_ENHANCE filter 87
edge detection and enhancement filters 85
edges, image
  detecting 85, 86
  enhancing 85, 86
editing, audio and video compression 11
Effect module, QT Phonon 241
effects, QT Phonon components 239
Effects node 239
egg file 93
element linking 140
embossing 87
event module, PyAudiere 15

F

fade-out effect
  adding 175-178
fakesrc element 130
fast-forward control 166
ffenc_mpeg4 plugin 202
ffenc_png plugin 202

ffmpegcolorspace converter 206
ffmpegcolorspace plugin 202
ffmux_mp4 plugin 202
filesink element 209
filesrc element 134, 157
flipping, image manipulations 35
for loop 105
freetype2
  about 23
  URL 23

G

get_name method 208
getbands() method 59
getOutImagePath method 50
ghost pad 131, 193
glClearColor call 98
gnlcomposition element 151, 186, 189, 194
gnlcontroller element 186
gnlfilesource element 151, 188, 189, 194, 231
  properties 151
gnloperation element 151
gnlsource element 151
gnlurisource element 151
gnonlin_pad_added method 155
Gnonlin plugin
  about 151, 166
  elements 151
  features 151
  gnlcomposition element 151
  gnlfilesource element 151
  gnloperation element 151
  gnlsource element 151
  gnlurisource element 151
GObject 125
gobject modules 204
goom2k1 visualization plugin 198
goom visualization plugin 196-198
grayscale video
  creating 220
gst-inspect-0.10 command 173, 196
gst-inspect command, GStreamer 128
gst-launch command, GStreamer 128
gst.Bin class 129
gst.Bus.gst_bus_post() method 131

Thank you for buying
Python Multimedia Beginner's Guide

About Packt Publishing

Packt, pronounced 'packed', published its first book "*Mastering phpMyAdmin for Effective MySQL Management*" in April 2004 and subsequently continued to specialize in publishing highly focused books on specific technologies and solutions.

Our books and publications share the experiences of your fellow IT professionals in adapting and customizing today's systems, applications, and frameworks. Our solution based books give you the knowledge and power to customize the software and technologies you're using to get the job done. Packt books are more specific and less general than the IT books you have seen in the past. Our unique business model allows us to bring you more focused information, giving you more of what you need to know, and less of what you don't.

Packt is a modern, yet unique publishing company, which focuses on producing quality, cutting-edge books for communities of developers, administrators, and newbies alike. For more information, please visit our website: www.packtpub.com.

About Packt Open Source

In 2010, Packt launched two new brands, Packt Open Source and Packt Enterprise, in order to continue its focus on specialization. This book is part of the Packt Open Source brand, home to books published on software built around Open Source licences, and offering information to anybody from advanced developers to budding web designers. The Open Source brand also runs Packt's Open Source Royalty Scheme, by which Packt gives a royalty to each Open Source project about whose software a book is sold.

Writing for Packt

We welcome all inquiries from people who are interested in authoring. Book proposals should be sent to author@packtpub.com. If your book idea is still at an early stage and you would like to discuss it first before writing a formal book proposal, contact us; one of our commissioning editors will get in touch with you.

We're not just looking for published authors; if you have strong technical skills but no writing experience, our experienced editors can help you develop a writing career, or simply get some additional reward for your expertise.

Matplotlib for Python Developers

ISBN: 978-1-847197-90-0   Paperback: 308 pages

Build remarkable publication-quality plots the
easy way

1. Create high quality 2D plots by using Matplotlib
   productively

2. Incremental introduction to Matplotlib, from the
   ground up to advanced levels

3. Embed Matplotlib in GTK+, Qt, and wxWidgets
   applications as well as web sites to utilize them in
   Python applications

4. Deploy Matplotlib in web applications and expose it
   on the Web using popular web frameworks such as
   Pylons and Django

Expert Python Programming

ISBN: 978-1-847194-94-7   Paperback: 372 pages

Best practices for designing, coding, and distributing your
Python software

1. Learn Python development best practices from
   an expert, with detailed coverage of naming and
   coding convention

2. Apply object-oriented principles, design patterns,
   and advanced syntax tricks

3. Manage your code with distributed
   version control

4. Profile and optimize your code

Please check **www.PacktPub.com** for information on our titles

www.ingramcontent.com/pod-product-compliance
Lightning Source LLC
Chambersburg PA
CBHW060520060326
40690CB00017B/3337